Growing Up
Hockey

The Life and Times of Everyone
Who Ever Loved the Game

Brian Kennedy

Foreword by Kelly Hrudey

FOLK
LORE
PUBLISHING

The Publisher: Folklore Publishing
Website: www.folklorepublishing.com

Library and Archives Canada Cataloguing in Publication

Kennedy, Brian, 1962–
Growing up hockey : the life and times of everyone who ever
loved the game / Brian Kennedy.

ISBN 13: 1-894864-65-4
ISBN 10: 978-1-894864-65-7

1. Kennedy, Brian, 1962–. 2. Hockey—Biography. 3. Hockey.
I. Title.

GV848.5.K45A3 2007   796.962092   C2007-903970-7

Project Director: Faye Boer
Project Editor: Kathy van Denderen
Book Design: Marc Hamm
Cover Design: Joy Dirto
Photographs by Gabriela Moya
Cover image: Courtesy Getty Images, photography by Dave Reede.

We acknowledge the financial support of the Alberta Foundation for the
Arts for our publishing program.

We acknowledge the financial support of the Government of Canada
through the Book Publishing Industry Development Program for our
publishing activities.

Alberta Foundation for the Arts

 Canadian Heritage   Patrimoine canadien

For Gabriela
Who Never for a Second Stopped Believing

CONTENTS

Foreword

I've been broadcasting hockey on *Hockey Night in Canada* since 1998, and to me, the game in all its aspects is as relevant and moving a force in the lives of its fans now as it has ever been. Sometimes, though, it's easy to forget that hockey is not just the NHL, but the neighborhood rinks and local arenas where both kids and adults live out their passions and their hopes of glory. It is in these places that the real hockey is played. Real because there's often nothing more at stake than pride, but that is enough to inspire both heroic sacrifice and dreams.

In my case, the dream actually came to culmination with the chance to play in the NHL, and as you would expect, those days remain vivid in my mind. I remember, for instance, standing in the Montréal Forum the night I was to take to the ice with the Kings for the first game of the Stanley Cup finals in 1993. As the anthems played and the crowd roared, I looked around me. What I saw was a group of people in many ways different from me, a kid who had grown up out West, in Edmonton. But they were like me in the way that mattered most—we loved hockey above all, and at that moment, we were living it to the fullest. I was just a little luckier in that I was behind the mask, while they were in the stands.

Even though I took to the ice over 750 times in the uniforms of the Islanders, Kings and Sharks, the thrill never diminished, and the memories of being a kid and wanting this so badly it hurt never went away.

Maybe that's why, as time passes, the hockey memories that matter to me tend to encompass a wider scope than just those from my years in the NHL. They go back to my Junior days in Medicine Hat with the Tigers, and back further still to playing minor hockey in Edmonton in the community of Elmwood. My last year in midget hockey with the Canadiens organization (Inland Cement), we ended the season on an amazing high, having won the midget provincial championship in 1978 in Calgary.

That's one reason I enjoyed reading *Growing Up Hockey*. As I read, the stories took me back to a time when hockey was for me what it was then and is today for many Canadian and American kids—pure fun. Just as Brian describes strapping on the goalie pads for the first time, playing in net on the street and getting in the crease for the All Saints team, I remember when I first took up the challenge to play the position. I was 12, and looking back, the simple things are what I remember the most. The smell of the arena, the dressing rooms, and most importantly, the smell of my equipment.

However, what mattered, at least at the start, was less how I played and more that I was getting the chance to get out there and emulate my goaltending hero, Bernie Parent. That experience, like Brian's worship of Ken Dryden, motivated me to do more than play. It shaped my life.

I, too, was a hockey card collector and avid watcher of games on TV. Just as the stories in this book illustrate, my life was a combination of my own hockey dreams and my ups and downs on the ice and on the streets near my house. I'll bet that while you're reading these chapters, you'll find yourself saying the same thing, because our experiences, wherever and whenever they took place, are shared, each of us in our own way having been shaped by the love of hockey.

And even though our lives—yours, mine, the ones described in these stories—took different paths, in some ways, they ended up in the same place, with hockey experiences past and present as a core element.

Growing Up Hockey gave me a chance to reconnect with some of the moments and memories that mean the most to me. I think it will do the same for you, no matter who you are and regardless of whether you played pickup, house league or in the NHL.

KELLY HRUDEY
Calgary, Alberta, Canada

Preface

When you were a kid, you probably read the life story of your favorite hockey player and imagined that one day, your feats of Stanley Cup glory would be told to the world. Me too, but neither of us ended up in the NHL.

So what about our stories? Instead of letting mine die, I decided to write them down. But this book isn't just about me; it's about everyone who has ever laced up skates or shot a tennis ball around on a driveway in a quest to emulate the heroes of the NHL. It's about the memories we share as kids who grew up with what our dads called "hockey on the brain." These stories are about growing up—childhood boasting and jostling for playground supremacy, the loss of innocence that comes with aging and finally regaining what you love—all of which somehow crossed through hockey.

This book, "the life and times of everyone who ever loved the game," will help remind you of how the game shaped you and will reawaken you to the joy of loving something the way kids love hockey, whether you are still a fan or not.

I never played hockey professionally, and I was never all that good an amateur player. I put in my years like most Canadian kids. I even had my stint as a goalie, the glamour position then as now, and I impressed the coach of a rival team enough that my squad, the All Saints Pee Wees, loaned me to St. James United. But then my eligibility ran out, and I had to choose to stay with St. James as a goalie or return to All Saints and put on the regular equipment. I resumed my duties as a right-winger and played out my career on the third line of most of the teams whose sweaters I wore.

But it's not just playing that I remember. I've watched hockey for over 30 years, and I have witnessed many great moments of the modern era on TV. Every one of the NHL games I've been to live in my mind as if it happened yesterday. I've met Frank Mahovlich and spoken with him. But none of that makes me an expert nor gives you a reason to listen to me. What makes these stories interesting is that my stories are also your stories, tales that have been tucked away in your memory for as long as your hockey cards have been packed away in the attic. This book is a chance to unpack those mental boxes and enjoy the memories they hold.

What follows is a wander, a leisurely skate down the Rideau Canal at the height of the season. Of course, since time has passed, this collection represents what my memory tells me happened—things as I want to remember them, or things as I wish they had been. Though based in fact, in other words, these stories aren't to be taken strictly as history. You might think of *Growing Up Hockey* as an argument. What I seek to prove is that no matter how good or bad a player you may have been, a good portion of the person you are today was created by the game. Maybe you'll realize as you read, like I did as I wrote, that just maybe somewhere in your deepest hopes and dreams you still believe that you'll make it to the NHL.

Maybe you'll be convinced, as I am, that your life at some mythical level is a pursuit of the Stanley Cup, that the visions that formed you when you were eight, invading your dreams and giving purpose to your waking hours, are not dead. They've just been sleeping for a while.

Acknowledgments

Books don't get published without the support of people who believe in them, and for me, these people are my publisher, Faye Boer, and my editor, Kathy van Denderen. Each has helped shape this book into its present form and made it possible for me to achieve my dream of sharing it with you.

But way before anyone else saw this book, my greatest ally, my wife, Gabriela, read it and offered me suggestions on it. More than that, she believed in the book unfailingly. Without her encouragement, *Growing Up Hockey* might still be gathering dust in a drawer.

My family made this book possible long before I ever wrote a word. Although she wasn't a sports fan, my mom encouraged me to pursue my interest in playing; my grandmother burned the love for the Montréal Canadiens into my soul; and my dad spent years taking me to early morning practices and late-night games. My sister, Sandra (Kennedy) Reimer, took part in many of the events that appear in this book, and her husband, Phil, is my ultimate reference on the game and its history.

I also owe thanks to my mentor, Jack Falla, author of *Home Ice*; Kevin Greenstein, the publisher of *Inside Hockey*, who offered me my first shot as a hockey writer; Mark Hardy, who granted me my first NHL interview; and Jim Fox, forever a Kings fan favorite, and a truly gracious man. The L.A. Kings and Anaheim Ducks organizations have each allowed me the chance to cover games, giving me access to their facilities, coaches and players.

Friends and colleagues also deserve credit. My pal Tim Reid read the draft and offered me helpful commentary. At Pasadena City College, Darryl Distin convinced me that I had a book on my hands. Beverly Tate, Chris McCabe, Lynn Wright, Michelle Banks and Martha Bonilla were my cheerleaders.

To you all, I extend my heartfelt appreciation.

PART ONE

Learning the Game

chapter one

Becoming a Hockey Player

Winter comes early in Montréal. Sometimes, according to my folks, we'd have snow before Halloween when I was growing up. Taking us out trick-or-treating was a tag-team endeavor, with each parent taking a turn and trying not to freeze. But along with the cold, winter brought outdoor ice and, with that, hockey.

Every afternoon before I was old enough to go to school, I would stand in front of the windows in our living room and watch the "big kids" walk past, their skates tied together and slung over their shoulders and their sticks swinging at lumps of ice on the sidewalk. I knew they were headed to the corner rink, a place I could never go on my own. My world was limited to the edges of my yard, and even then, I had to stay inside until my mom felt like letting me go out.

Like seemingly every mom in those days, mine stayed home to take care of me and my tot sister, Sandra, 27 months younger than I. Who knows what chaos we had been causing one lunchtime when Mom asked us, "Do you want to go skating?" I doubt Sandra was old enough to give any kind of meaningful answer, but I was struggling into my snowsuit before Mom could get there to help me.

Beside me in the hallway of our house were my blades. Not skates, they were what every kid in my day started out on—the two-bladed things that strapped onto your boots. We called them "cheese cutters," and they were the on-ice equivalent of training wheels for your bike. You were a definite newbie with those on, but you didn't know it. You just knew you were skating, and you had a clear sense that if you did it right, soon you'd be getting a shiny pair of brown leather skates with the single chrome blades like your dad and the big kids had. Next thing, you'd be on the rink chasing the puck around like they did.

It probably took Mom half an hour to wrestle us into our warmest clothes. Then we headed out the door. Instead of walking down the street to the rink in the park, we piled into "Suzy Q," my mom's 1960s Austin Mini, red with a black top. Mom drove. She was great at everything except driving. Sandra and I sat in the back seat, unrestrained by seat belts or car seats, and watched the road through the hole in the floor. I wanted to know where we were headed, but all Mom would say was, "Somewhere special." Ten minutes later, we approached the building that she told me would soon be my elementary school.

We parked on the side of the lot next to the teachers' cars. As we got out, I looked over at the school, keenly aware that the big kids were inside the red brick building adjacent to the parking lot. Then my focus was diverted the other direction as Mom pointed to the playground and what I would soon recognize as an official hockey rink.

Mom let me run ahead, directing me to the players bench to get into my blades. She caught up, with Sandra under one arm and our wooden sled dragging behind in her other hand. Sandra was too young to skate and would have to be pulled along. Mom strapped my blades on for me and then put on her own, white figure skates that must have been a decade old. They were around the house in a closet my whole growing up, though I don't recall her wearing them again.

We went out onto the ice, me shuffling along and Mom pulling Sandra. We made slow circles around the rink, passing the nets left there for the elementary students and skating over the blue and red lines. I wondered how they got there, inside the ice so that I could see them but not trip over them. My feet scraped at the snow left by the older kids, who must have used the rink at recess, my progress more walking than skating. The cold nipped my face and made my breath freeze on the scarf wrapped around my nose.

Soon Mom glided up behind me, Sandra in tow. "OK, you two, you each have a penalty," she said, and took us to the other side of the rink, where there was another, smaller bench. All smiles, she opened the door and told us to climb in, then shut it behind us and skated around the rink on her own. I sat there looking down at the old wooden bench, painted red. I tried to run my mittened hand over it but couldn't; the wood was too coarse and splintered. As we sat there, the boards almost completely blocked our view of the ice, but Mom came back to rescue us after a couple of turns on her skates. She was pretty good.

"Skate over here. I want to show you something," she said as she motioned to the other side of the ice. She took us out of the penalty box, set me back on my blades and bundled Sandra up in the blankets in the sled. I skate-shuffled over to the corner, where a field mouse was scurrying along the edge of the boards. It had somehow managed to get onto the ice and was hurrying to find its way back through the crack it must have used to enter. We watched it without getting too close.

"Can we keep him?" I asked. As I said it, I looked over toward the walls and windows of the school to see whether the big kids were aware of our presence. I had the instinctive playground fear that someone larger would come along to spoil the fun for me just when it was getting good.

Mom must have known I would ask. "No, Brian. He needs to go to his home. We need to go home, too," she said, breaking it to me gently. I, of course, would have done anything to keep the fun going, though not so long that the big kids would be released from school.

"Mom, I want another penalty," I stated. To me, that was the highlight of the experience. So Mom skated me and pulled Sandra, who was freezing cold but mutely enjoying the day, over to the box. "Two minutes each," she said. How my mom knew it was two minutes, I don't know. I don't think she ever watched a hockey game.

Mom skated some more, probably glad for the chance to do this one thing for herself, then she came for us. Our day was almost over.

Before we were bundled back into Suzy Q for the ride home, we took a final turn on the ice. I skated over to the boards, which were higher than my head, and stared at the black indents made by pucks. At the time, I didn't own a hockey stick, but those puck marks were both fascinating and familiar. I knew that someday I'd make some just like them on this rink, or another one like it.

It was in that instant that I became a hockey player.

chapter two

Giving Up the
Cheese Cutters

In my era of growing up, two things happened to every Canadian boy at age five. The beautiful tranquility of being at home all day, every day, was broken. You were taken, shoved, or you flew out of the house to the school bus stop as a matter of course every morning. Your life now included the social bonding and educational ritual known as kindergarten. And in winter you learned to play hockey, if it's fair to call what most of us did at that age by the sacred name of our greatest sport.

For me, growing up without an older brother as a tutor, hockey consisted of going to the corner rink after my morning in school was over and chasing after the puck with my dad. He'd pass it to me, and I'd shuffle after it and try to pass it back. Like every other kid my age, I held my hands up high on my stick, golf club style, in a combined effort to handle the puck and to balance. Most of the time, the puck went right on by me, and I chased it and tried to shoot it back. It would go off the heel of my stick, off the toe, or stay right where it was while I fanned on it and ended up on my backside. Anything but what I was trying to make it do. But my dad was patient. He wanted me to learn, though he never told me why, exactly. To me, hockey practice was just a part of our routine during that glorious year before I had to be in school all day.

In our daily ritual, Dad timed his homecoming to coincide with mine. He had his own business and could take a lunch break whenever he wanted. Even though the rink was only three or four blocks from our house, we drove to save time. Once there, Dad parked the station wagon, and we dashed across the snowy park to the rink. Every day it would be the same: us, and one girl and her mom on the smaller rink, which was by custom more than anything reserved for skating only. No sticks or pucks allowed. Like me, the girl practiced a kindergarten version of skating, only she had fig-ure skates on, and her mom led her in long, graceful circles, trying to get her to pick the ice with her toes.

The ice was good in Montréal parks from December through March, so there were many days of "training" for me to enjoy, but my dad and I never actually talked about what we were doing. These days, a dad might see dollars dance in his head as his future NHLer scraped his way from side to side on the rink, but not back then, and not my dad and me. It was only years later that I realized that he'd lost his own dad the previous summer. I haven't asked him, but I guess our sessions out there had something to do with his trying to deal with that, to create a bond with me that would carry on what he was missing.

Sometime during that winter, Dad helped me to tie on my first pair of single-bladed skates. Cheese cutters now left in the distant past, I proudly stood while he pushed me from behind, then leaned forward onto my hockey stick for balance once the speed got to be more than a crawl. When I had some momentum up, he stopped pushing and encouraged me to "Skate, skate!" For me, that meant taking tiny, chopping steps, trying to get up some speed of my own. I pumped my feet but didn't go much of anywhere, the ice staying still beneath my thrashing blades. Seeing that, Dad would skate over and give me another push to get me moving. As the year went on, I got better, and the pushing became less.

Ironically, at these same instants in the late 1960s, the kid who would come to be our national hero, who is about a year older than I am, was doing the same thing with his dad in Brantford, Ontario. Our drills, and my skill level, looked nothing like the video footage I've seen of Gretzky at that age, but by the end of the year, I could stand up on my skates, carry the puck from one end to the other and turn without falling down too often. I was ready for the big leagues.

chapter three

The Coach Scouts His Prospect

My playing debut, unlike that of a lot of my schoolmates, didn't happen during grade one. But shortly after the next school year began, in the fall of 1970, a man showed up at our house one evening. I didn't recognize him when he came to the door, so when Dad invited him in, I was surprised. I stood there, the early evening light mixing with that of the floor lamps of our living room, while the man took a seat on our couch. My impulse to flee the room was checked by my dad's invitation that I also sit down. The man looked at me. "Well, this is your hockey player, eh?" he said.

I glanced at my dad. He was purposely trying to be matter-of-fact about the whole thing, while I was groping around frantically to sort out what was going on. "Hockey player?" I repeated to myself.

Thinking that I had grasped the meaning of what the man had said, my mind flashed ahead to school the next day, to what I would say to my friends. But I waited; I wanted to be sure. I stared at my dad, hoping he would say something. Finally he did: "I signed you up for hockey. This is your coach," he told me.

The other boys at my school were already signed up. They bragged about it to every audience who gave them an instant of attention. I had come home from school with this news and the feeling that if they were signed up, I wanted to be too. The problem was, I had no idea how you got signed up. When I had feebly asked my dad a few weeks before this night, he had said, "We'll see." It was one of those things I knew I couldn't argue about with him, or my mom.

Thinking back on it, I realize that Dad didn't have any idea how to get me signed up either. The other parents had figured it out or done it before with their older kids, but nobody in my family had played hockey before, and so we had missed the deadline. Dad, though, had somehow gotten in touch with the right guy, and he'd squeezed me onto his roster. Hence the visit on this night.

"You've missed training camp," the coach commented. I had no idea what he was talking about. Later, I learned that these evaluation sessions, which he kindly called "training camp," were held every fall by the organization sponsoring the teams as a way to sort out the few good players from the mass of the rest of us. No sense in having one team "stacked" with the only kids in the league who could actually skate and pass the puck. For my coach and his new player, stacking was not going to be a problem. I wouldn't light Brossard, Québec, on fire with my goal-scoring prowess just yet. Well, not ever.

And knowing my dad, I doubt that he oversold my talents, but I can imagine him saying, "Yeah, the kid has had some work. Yeah, his skating's coming along. Yeah, he's eager to play. Cheese cutters? He got rid of those years ago." No big promises. I'd just be a grinding, dig-it-out, playmaking right-winger. Actually, that was years later, too. For now, I would just manage to learn my position, play with vigor and survive.

The interview ended with the adults exchanging some more words, then we all stood up, me copying my dad. As the coach took his leave, I watched him, anxious for more signs of what this all meant. I had only a vague idea of the significance of what was happening, but I felt that my hockey experience was bursting its confines of playing after school at the corner rink. I was on a team. I was a hockey player, an official one. I would have a sweater with a number on it.

My new coach's parting words confirmed it. "See you at practice on Saturday," he said to me. I mumbled out a reply, but my mind was busy framing the story I would start telling the moment I got to the bus stop the next morning. No more listening to all my classmates go on about their teams, the color of their uniforms, the million goals they would score.

I didn't have all the details filled in, but I had a practice in four days, and I could build a whole story around that. Before it even got started, my career would be filled with the prospect of glorious goals and come-from-behind wins.

chapter four

Space-Age
Sticks

I was an unremarkable kid, nearly eight years old—not big, not small. My appearance shouted neither bruising defenseman nor wiry winger. I have no idea what my coach thought of me the night he first met me at our house. But neither of us had to wait long to see what I could do. The preseason was over, so the first time I would be on the ice was in a practice designed to get our team organized before our first game. In the meantime, I had school time to brag up my newfound career.

The first kid I encountered the next morning was a friend named James Modell. I got right to the point. "I'm playing hockey," I said. "My dad signed me up."

Now, Jimmy was no dummy. He had older brothers, so he'd been around BS lots of times. His dad, too, was unlike mine. He was hard-edged, the kind that stood next to the

boards and encouraged his boy to shoot the puck every time
it was on his stick. Maybe he wasn't as intense as the parents
of today with their dreams of NHL glory and riches, but he
was aggressive. I once went to one of Jimmy's baseball games,
where he hit a long fly ball to center field, and his dad yelled
and yelled to keep him running. The ball dropped as Jimmy
rounded second, and Mr. Modell screamed for a home run.
Jimmy ended up getting thrown out at the plate, by a pretty
wide margin, but as we walked back to their car after the
game, his dad told him he'd done the right thing by going for
it. This made no sense to me whatsoever. I'd always been
taught that it was better to play it safe.

Conditioned by his family to be pushy, Jimmy greeted
my news with some skepticism. Every boy in our grade who
played hockey had been talking about it for a couple of weeks.
Someone coming late with the news had to be making it up.

"For who?" Jimmy asked. It was a natural question. He lived
in the suburb next to mine, St. Lambert. He played there, too.

"LNDB," I said, naming the league that my dad had
joined me up with. It was the house league for my small suburban city, and the initials stood for something that, roughly
translated into English, meant "Our Lady of Notre Dame's
Leisure Society." The answer satisfied my friend. How could I
have invented this? "My coach came to my house last night
and told me I was on his team," I said, beaming as if I'd been
picked in the NHL draft.

"You get your equipment yet?" Jimmy added. He knew what was going on, this kid. I, on the other hand, hadn't given this any thought. Maybe seven-year-olds don't think that far ahead—but now my heart sank into my stomach. What was I going to wear on Saturday when we had our first and only practice before the season began? It was only three days away.

"Where'd you get yours?" I asked, wanting to know what to do and not sure whether I could trust my dad on this kind of thing. I was certain he hadn't ever bought hockey gear before.

"My brothers. I wear their old stuff," Jimmy replied. He couldn't help me. I would just have to hope my dad would come through.

"Just be sure you get a good stick. Get a curved one. Fiberglass," he said. I didn't really know what he meant, but I couldn't let on. I stored the words carefully in my mind. *A curved stick. Fiberglass.*

A day or two later, my dad took me to Canadian Tire, or Miracle Mart, or some other store nearby, to get suited up. But there were two items we didn't buy—the socks, and a stick. The socks were supposed to match my team's colors, so I would get them at the practice. The stick, my dad said no to. The one I had would be fine.

Saturday, the day of my first practice, began with us getting the socks in the arena pro shop: green, black and white. On the ice, the team skated around and attempted passing drills—the puck as often as not going right under our sticks as tape to tape. As we practiced, the coach looked us over. I guess he determined that I shot right, realized that I wasn't fast enough to be a centerman and made me the third-line right-winger. My dad, the coach would come to know, wasn't the type to be angry that his kid wasn't starting. Dad just let me have fun with the game. His one piece of advice was that I listen to the coach and do what I was told.

As we skated around, I looked at the other boys on my team. We had a ragtag collection of helmets, some white, some black. The gloves, too, rarely matched our team's colors. But one thing that most of the other kids had was a stick like the one Jimmy had described. Looking at what they were carrying, I knew my stick would in no way serve to make me a star. I was using the one that I'd had on the corner rink the two winters before. It was all wood, with a blade as straight as the highway between two Prairie provinces. It was wrapped with black electrical tape. My dad had done that.

The other kids had sticks with beautiful hooks and blades covered with dimply fiberglass that, it was said, made them impossible to break. I couldn't possibly go on with my antiquated piece of lumber, and I told my dad that on the way home.

He disagreed. "How will you learn to stickhandle with something like that kid playing center has? He can't shoot a backhand with that stick!" he said. It was curved like the road that snakes up a mountain. Glorious. Maybe his dad had taken a blowtorch to it the way we've all seen Bobby Hull do in that famous picture. At the time, of course, I had no idea about any of that. Neither did my dad, and his reaction may have been based on his just not knowing. He had signed me up for hockey, but he hadn't watched a professional game, probably, in years, if ever. To him, hockey was still Teeder Kennedy playing for the Maple Leafs, and the only reason he knew that player was because Dad had been called "Teeder" by his history teacher back in high school, in anger at my dad's always tipping back in his chair during class.

Hockey, to my dad at that stage, was still the game played in the '50s. Curved sticks with space-age materials reinforcing their blades were things he had no clue about. He probably didn't even know where to buy such a thing. But if he had the best of intentions, or a well-earned ignorance about things like this, to me, the stick I carried was a tragedy, an embarrassment. I didn't care if I had a better backhand than anyone on the team. I had a game coming up, and I couldn't go out there and play with that stick. I resolved to do something to fix the problem, and soon. In the meantime, I had a bag full of official hockey gear, and between the practice and my first game, I didn't miss a day of trying it on, then walking around our living room in anticipation of my league debut.

chapter five

The Stick that Would Make Me Guy Lapointe

B eing in grade two, I lived in the fog of incomprehension that every kid does. I went to school; I came home. My grandmother came over every once in a while and drank a cup of my mom's horrible instant coffee, or she had dinner with us on Sunday. Sometimes we went to her place, an old house in Westmount where my dad had grown up.

Sometimes when I was at my grandma's, I'd see her watching the Canadiens on TV. It never occurred to me that at our house, my parents never watched hockey. It was almost as though, for me, NHL hockey existed only through my grandma, a special gift that I could glimpse at in those few lucky moments when our visits happened to coincide with a game.

That was the case the Saturday evening after one of my early season hockey games. My family was at my grandmother's for dinner, and with the meal concluded, Sandra and I were taken upstairs to change into our pajamas. The plan was for the adults to stay for a bit and talk, and for my sister and I to go to bed in the sitting room. Later, we would be carried to the car for the drive home, fast asleep. While my mom was helping us get changed, Gran, as we called her, came in and turned on the TV. "Just for a peek at the game," she said. Montréal's team came to life on the black-and-white screen, and as it did, I studied the images for a long minute. Then I piped in with more about my game, which I had been encouraged to talk about at dinner.

"Hey, Gran," I said. "Look at their sticks. Look at how they curve." I was focused on this one thing and had been ever since my season had started. I couldn't really tell much about the sticks the players carried, but it only made sense that if they were on TV, their sticks must be even better than the best one any player on my team had.

"Do you have a nice stick?" my grandmother asked, not realizing the importance of her words.

"Mine's straight," I said. "And wooden. Theirs have fiberglass. You can't break them no matter what you do." I wasn't really sure about this, but it sounded good. It was what the other kids all said. "Some players on my team have sticks like that...with fiberglass." I tried to reinforce the point.

"Hugh will just have to get you one like that, then," Gran said. It always confused me when she called my dad, her son, by his first name, but my ears immediately perked up.

Here was an adult agreeing with me about the stick. "The more like Guy Lapointe's, the better," she added. Why she picked the Montréal defenseman as her example I don't know, but I didn't care. I just knew that she saw the value in the sticks these players on TV had, and because of that, maybe I had a chance of getting one for myself.

I asked my mom to leave the game on for a few minutes after my sister and I were dressed for bed. Gran volunteered to stay with us to see us to sleep, saying she'd turn it off and come downstairs shortly. I lay there in the glow of the screen, Sandra at the other end of the couch, already half gone. It was the beginning of my love affair with the team, though I didn't realize it at the time.

All I could think of was to plot some way to get my grandmother to tell my dad about the stick. I suspected that if she said it, there was no way he could refuse me. My logic was twofold: I figured that, as his mom, she had the power to tell him what he should do. And I sensed, even in these early days, that her connection to hockey was deeper than my dad's, and because of that, he would have to defer to her on such matters. I dropped off to sleep expecting that in no time, I would be carrying a fancy stick like the ones most of my teammates had.

chapter six

Delay of
Game

I didn't get the curved stick that I wanted in my first year playing hockey, and the season went by with me scoring just one goal. When it happened, I acted like an NHL player would on scoring his first or 500th goal—I grabbed the puck after it had gone in the net. It's tucked away in a box at my house, its edges chipped, hardly looking "regulation" anymore. There's no orange Cooper lettering on it, or anything else, except what I painted there with pale blue model paint: the date, "Mar. 4, 1971," and the score, "7–3." Beside the "3" is a little star, hand-painted as well. It's a reminder that I scored the third of my team's goals. I now realize that it was a completely meaningless tally, but at the time, the goal was my grand triumph.

We weren't a very good team, except for a player or two. Serge, a "French kid" in the parlance of my surroundings, had blond hair that stuck out the sides of his helmet, like wings, when he sweated. He was our star, and he scored almost all the goals. We came to count on him to get us out of any jam. This strategy worked for a while, but we made an early exit from the playoffs. I wasn't particularly focused on the tragic loss, however. In fact, when I got home from the game, I was intent on going outside to play, since it was a Saturday afternoon. Instead, my dad steered me into his downstairs office. He sat in his desk chair and motioned for me to take the other one, the one my mom used to do the accounting for our family business.

I fumbled with the paperweight on the desk in front of me, and my dad fidgeted in his chair. I felt as though I was going to get into trouble for something, but I couldn't think what I'd done.

"You know, everyone can't win," my dad began. I nodded. This was obvious to me already, probably because my team had done its share of losing that year. "And your team won't be playing any more games this season," he added. This, too, was self-evident. I was sad when he said it, though, because while losing in the playoffs bugged me, what bothered me way more was that I wouldn't have any more games to look forward to.

Actually, I hadn't particularly counted on us winning anything. I didn't really understand the idea of a season's championship or the passing of time from winter to spring in the adult sense. I was just focused on what was happening at the moment. Losing meant no game next week and nothing to brag about at school when the other boys recounted the miraculous plays they'd made in their games the weekend before. That would be hard. I didn't realize that their seasons would end as well. I figured I was the only one. "I know this must be a disappointment to you, but how we learn to deal with these things is an important part of the game, too," my dad continued.

I listened to his words, and as I thought them through, I watched my dad. His nervous posture and hesitating voice told me as much as what he said. I had a moment of clarity, seeing into his adult mind and discerning his intentions, how important it was for him to say what he'd said. Whatever message he was trying to convey about hockey, he was more intent on teaching me an important lesson about life. Still not sure I understood the gravity of the speech in the way he wanted me to, but sensing that I had to do something to show him that I saw the point, I nodded and tried to look sad. "I know, Dad, hockey's over." I cast my eyes downward as I said it, for effect.

"You'll feel better in a couple of days, and there's always next season," he said. He was doing his best to salve the wound that he saw more clearly than I felt.

"Can I go out to play?" I couldn't hold it back any longer. "Frank and Billy said they'd be out later, I mean now, when I got home." The Cameron brothers more or less ran the street hockey game in front of their house by virtue of their owning the net we used. When they were out, we all wanted to be there. Playing hockey with the net was more fun than anything in the world to me at that age.

"Sure, but if they say anything about the game, remember that you played well. Sometimes things just don't go your way. You've learned something for next year," my dad said. I listened to his words with one half of my brain, while with the other half I calculated how long it would take me to grab my gear and be in front of the Camerons' house.

"Thanks, Dad. I know you just want me to feel better," I said. It was the best I could do, and it worked. He stood up, brushed his hands together as if he'd just eaten a cookie and was shaking off the crumbs, and reached out his arms. I moved a half-step toward him, letting him hug me. I hugged him back, then asked a question I'd been holding in for months. "Dad," I said, "Next year, do you think I can get a curved stick. With fiberglass?"

"We'll see," he replied, the speech forgotten. "You don't want to sacrifice that backhand. It's just starting to come."

chapter seven

Saving My
Yellow Wonder

A couple of seasons into my minor hockey career, when I was nine, I finally convinced my dad to buy me a curved stick, despite his argument that having it would never allow my backhand to develop. I did it by promising to practice that shot as much as my wrist shot. I would be Maurice Richard and Jean Beliveau wrapped into one.

The stick's blade was covered in clear fiberglass with a net-like texture to it, and it had a painted yellow shaft, which was the other big attraction, having just been "invented," as we said at my school. So all in all, my "yellow wonder" was a huge improvement over my former all-wood, straight-blade model. Like every other kid, I had images of Bobby Hull floating in my head. I had wanted what we called a "wicked hook," the kind that could produce a slapshot you could barely control, but I was happy. I used my stick all that year and into the next, always being careful not to do anything that might put it in danger of breaking.

One afternoon during the winter, I decided that it would be a great idea to take my stick outside to play on the rink at the end of our street. This was strictly against my dad's orders, the stick being reserved for game duty, but I was motivated by the fact that some of the other boys in my neighborhood didn't believe that I had it at all. All they'd ever seen was the old wood CCM clunker with an arrow-straight blade that I reluctantly carted to the rink every day after school. To overcome the embarrassment, I had at one stage had my mom fake a Tony Esposito autograph on the shaft, but my story about how it got there was never fully believed, and so now, to many of the boys who played on the rink where I did, I was a double liar. I had to do something, and taking the curved stick out for them to see seemed like the only way out of the mess.

So on this particular afternoon, before my dad got home from his Montréal sales calls, I managed to get out the door without my mom seeing that I had my yellow wonder, and I walked to the corner rink, my skates over my shoulder.

Once I got there, I shoved the stick's shaft into the snowbank beside me, as we all did, to hold it while I put on my skates. There it stood, proud testament to my truthfulness. A couple of kids came along, after having hurried home from school to grab their gear. "Whose stick?" one older boy asked. I was sitting on the bench and called out to let him know it was mine. "Nice hook," he said. I figured he was just being polite, but when I went over to pick up the stick, I noticed that the curve did look bigger from the underneath side. I grabbed it and walked toward the ice.

"Hey, nice stick," a voice from beside me said. I turned, and there was the kid everyone loved to hate in our neighborhood. An only child, Kenny was perpetually the outsider. Skinny and with ears that stuck out, he reminded some of us of a clown, others of something much worse. He showed up at the rink every afternoon, but not to play. He skated circles with the girls on the small ice sheet next to the one we played hockey on.

"Yeah, it's curved," I replied. "My dad said I shouldn't bring it here." Kenny was the kind of guy you could confess to. He didn't have any power to hold the truth against you.

I forgot about him as our game started. The big guys picked the teams, of course. I was surprised to be selected while there was still a decent pool of talent standing in a cluster waiting, but I should have known that something was up when the big kid who had said something about my stick a minute before motioned to me. "Yellow stick," he said. Anyone older than you never acknowledged that he knew your name. I took my place beside him, our captain.

Play quickly turned into the usual melee of shouts, scrabbling after the puck and disputed goals. I was a forward, and the big kid was on defense. As play paused, he motioned me back to him. "Hey, kid, let me try that stick. I shoot right, too," he said. My heart froze. I knew I wasn't supposed to have the stick out there, and because of that, I had vowed that this would be a one-time thing and that I'd be extra careful with it. No going toward another guy and smacking his stick to free up the puck. No getting too close to someone who might slash me and damage the yellow paint on the shaft. The prospect of an older boy using the stick was terrifying. He'd play rough with it, probably even more so since it was not his. I couldn't let this happen.

"Uh, my dad said I couldn't let anyone else use it," I stammered. It was a time-honored excuse. As I said it, I cast my eyes back and forth to see if anyone would help me. Everyone stood there looking at their own sticks, as if afraid that he'd go for theirs next.

To any kid my age, my excuse would have been a warning shot across the bow not to ask again. But Neal, as I had heard someone call him, was unfazed. "Oh, come on. Your dad isn't here. Let me try it," he said. He was right in front of me now, persuading me with his size as well as his words. I had no choice.

"OK, but only for a couple of minutes," I said. "And you have to be careful with it. It's my game stick." He ignored these words as he grabbed my yellow wonder out of my hands. "What will I use?" I pleaded as he did so. Instead of giving me his stick, he motioned over to our skate-tying bench. There were a couple of extra sticks lying there, crappy ones that kids brought with them just to look like pros, carrying an extra to the rink. I went over and grabbed one. It was exactly like my old one—plain wood, no hook, no fiberglass. The game resumed.

A few minutes later, Neal, still holding my stick, ordered a halt to play. It was time to clear the ice, and he motioned me to do it, along with a kid on the other team. It fell to us because we were the smaller, younger players.

Grabbing a shovel, I watched out of the corner of my eye as Neal, and my stick, went to sit down. I scraped the ice as quickly as I could, going from one side of the rink to the other, covering my half before the other boy finished his. I crossed the imaginary centerline and helped him. Then I went to find the big kid. I knew I had to start the next part of the game with my stick in my hands, play a few minutes and then split. This guy was not going to use my yellow wonder for long.

I went over to where Neal was sitting, noticing as I got there that in his hands was not the yellow shaft of my stick, but his own, a wood CCM, albeit with a wicked hook. "Hey, where's my stick?" I asked.

"Your stick? I put it over there," he said. He motioned to the opposite side of the ice. I quickly turned my head to look where he was pointing. I didn't see anything.

"Where?" I asked again, my voice rising. I was sure that something was up, and I felt shaky inside. "Show me where you put it," I demanded. My bravado surprised me, but I valued my stick, and I was worried not just about losing it, but also about what my dad would say.

He led me to the other side of the rink and stepped off the ice, motioning me to follow. We were about halfway between our rink and the girls' rink when he stopped and pointed to a hole in the snowbank. It was about as big around as a fist. "There. I put it in there, like you did beside the bench earlier," he said. "It must have fallen all the way in. You just need to dig it out."

Now, I knew this was what we called "bullcrap." And he did, too, but he was counting on me, as the smaller kid, to go along with it. I was supposed to dig into the snow, and while I was preoccupied, he would grab my stick from wherever he'd hidden it and hightail it home. We both knew this, but I couldn't point out the more than obvious fact, or I'd be asking for trouble. So I started digging, pushing snow this way and that in a phantom effort to regain the stick I loved so well, and to escape with my life intact besides. Meanwhile, he started inching away from me, his plan working exactly to form.

What he hadn't counted on was Kenny, who now came over to the edge of the girls' rink nearest us. "No way. There's no stick there," he half screeched. Both the big kid and I looked up.

Kenny was the last person you'd expect to get involved in such a dispute.

"Shut up, kid," Neal snarled at him. "You just keep skating with the girls."

I giggled in fear.

Kenny stiffened, a look of resolve on his face. "You're a liar. There's no stick there, and you know it." I was glad for an ally, though not sure whether Kenny challenging the guy would do any good. It wasn't likely that the big kid would back down on account of a figure skater.

Neal sneered at me. "I put it there, and that's it. I'm going back to play." And he walked back to the edge of the hockey rink, skated on, and called "Game on!"

I stood there staring at the snowbank that supposedly held my stick. My brain told me the stick wasn't there, but half hoping in my heart that it was, I continued in my attempt to knock the top off the drift, thinking that I'd dig down a foot or so, just to be sure. While I was doing this, Kenny left the ice pad he'd been skating on and disappeared.

Just as I was giving up my quest, he came trotting back, smiling, my yellow wonder in his hands. "I saw him. He put your stick behind the bench, there." He pointed toward the spot. "I got it back for you. Neal's still playing," he said. He handed my stick to me, and I grabbed for it, my companion that had almost been lost forever.

"You'd better get going," Kenny warned me. We both knew that if the big kid saw me with the stick, it was all over. He'd make me give it back to him at best, rough me up at worst. If I could get out of his sight with it, I could return tomorrow with my old practice stick, and the whole thing would be forgotten. It was the logic of the kid jungle.

I scoped out my path, a wide swath around the back of the hockey rink where the snow was piled highest and where Neal, playing defense in the game, would have his back to me. I'd have to grab my boots on the way and hope to make it to the street, maybe 20 yards away, on my skates. Then I could sit on the sidewalk out of sight and put on my boots. It was a calculated set of maneuvers that would save my life, and my stick.

I made it past the end of the rink and had just grabbed my boots when I heard a shout. "Hey, kid. Where do you think you're going? The game's not over." He wasn't threatening me. He was going to play this cool until the end.

"Uh, well, I gotta go. I've got hockey tonight," I said as I dashed for the street.

I got about halfway to the sidewalk, and what I thought was freedom, when I dared a look back. I expected to see the big kid hot on my tail, bent on having that stick in his hands once more. But what I saw was Neal, over on the girls' rink, skating in desperate circles after Kenny, who was dancing around, dodging him with all the skills that he'd acquired during hours of practice while we played our games of shinny. I didn't stay around to see whose abilities were superior.

While I walked down Victor Hugo Street toward home, the streetlights started to turn on, and I realized that my dad would be there. He always got home right around this time. He would see me come in, and I'd be grounded for sure for having taken my stick down to the rink. I contemplated the punishment, probably a week with no TV. That meant missing the Canadiens game on *Hockey Night in Canada* on Saturday. It would be sad, and I'd have to make up details at school on Monday, pretending to my classmates that I'd seen the game. But no punishment could have been as bad as having to play with my old, flat-bladed, no-fiberglass stick again. As I turned up the driveway of my house, I gripped my yellow-shafted friend with a renewed feeling that together, we were going to make hockey history.

chapter eight

The Day I Got "Called Up"

G rowing up in the Montréal suburbs, I played in a league called the LNDB. The jackets were blue, with red and white flashes on the sleeves and a huge crest on the front. Every kid I lived near, French and English, played in this league, including many of my schoolmates. Other kids we went to school with played in a league in the town next to mine, which was more predominantly English-speaking in those days.

Sometimes, teams were short of players for some reason or other. Maybe it was Christmas vacation and kids were gone, or maybe some other holiday kept certain kids out of games. Anyway, in order not to forfeit a game, a team had to dress a minimum number of guys, so occasionally they would tap teams in the next-door league to fill out the roster. We termed it getting "called up," though technically there was no "up" involved. You still played with kids your own age.

One night in my third season, I got the call. Getting called up was one of the honors that let every other kid know you were pretty good at hockey. It was always certain kids that other teams borrowed, kids like the cool guy Lucho, my friend Jimmy Modell and a Philippino kid named Henry. Guys like me didn't get called up. I was a rather undistinguished right-winger, though there were a couple of seasons when I tallied a handful of goals and assists. Maybe the coach who called me had seen a stat sheet where I'd had a multi-point game. That, for me, would be two points, probably both assists. I hated to shoot the puck. I always figured there would be someone closer to the net than I was.

Anyway, by hook or crook, I received the call. It came a few days before the game, so I had time to drop the fact into the conversations at school. I worked it for all I could. By the time Friday came, the night I was to play, everyone that I cared about knew. That would be all the boys in my class.

Game night began with me sitting in the back of the coach's early-1970s sedan. My dad, who normally went to every game, was on one of his twice-yearly trips to Toronto with my mom. My grandmother was looking after me and my sister, and so the coach had agreed to give me a ride.

It was the dead of winter, and the vinyl of the car's back seat squeaked when I got in. The coach's son was sitting in the front seat. I had never met either of them, nor had my folks, but in that more innocent time, it was acceptable to have a stranger

pick up your kid, I guess. Off we went to get one more boy—
a French kid who lived a few streets away and with whom I'd
played hockey a season or two before. Then we headed to the
rink.

The arena was across a few large boulevards from our
neighborhood. These big streets served as mental barriers to
us in thinking about where the rink was relative to our houses,
making it seem miles and miles away. In fact, it was close
enough that I could have ridden my bike there. Although not,
of course, on this night.

When we arrived at the arena, it was snowing pretty
heavily. We came to the game fully dressed, with just our
sticks, helmets and skates in tow to put on before we hit the
ice. As we got out of the car, I realized why.

"We're playing out here," the coach said. He motioned
to the outdoor ice just beyond the edge of the parking lot. I
had always thought of this as a practice rink. My heart dipped
into my stomach. *Called up for a practice?*

I was a polite kid, so I didn't complain. I was also
smart, so I phrased my question diplomatically. "Is this a real
game, Coach?"

"Sure. We just got scheduled out here because of the
tournament." Now it made sense. The ice inside was being
used for back-to-back games all weekend. We had to play outdoors because there was no time for us inside. I did the rest of

my suiting up. As I put on my skates, I noticed the snow piling up on the bench. The coach tied my laces, pulling them tight like my dad would have. At that age, you didn't do this for yourself.

I stepped out onto the ice and realized that it was more than snowy from use. There was a heavy dusting of snow everywhere. We'd have to clean it off before the game, everyone grabbing a shovel. It was a huge indignity. I was already wondering how I'd explain this to the guys at school on Monday. This wasn't feeling much like how the glory of being called up was supposed to feel.

Being outdoors wasn't the only indignity we were going to suffer this night. The opposing team's goalie hadn't shown up, and there was no equipment for his replacement to put on. Normally the coach kept the gear precisely to keep such a mess from happening, but this team apparently didn't do things that way. Thus it was declared that neither team would play with a goalie, but for that reason, the game was forfeited to the team I was to play for, and the ice time would be used for a scrimmage. This was great for my adopted team—they had their two points in the standings. It was bad for me—I'd been called up to a game that wasn't real. It was nothing more than a practice, and not an organized one at that. How would I ever explain this to the boys in my grade? Monday, the first thing they'd do is ask, which I'd assured by all that I'd said over the past few days. How could I defend myself against the accusation that I'd made the whole thing up? I was in a pickle.

The game finally started, and it progressed as games at that level do, the play going back and forth, into the corners, probably more a shuffle of players than anything else, especially given the ice conditions. Then, as I was standing in front of the opposing team's net, the puck came to me, unexpectedly. I bashed at it, and it went in, sort of. It was somewhere between being just over the goal line and not, when the coach, who was playing a kind of roving-netminder-on-boots, kicked it back out. "No, No!" he said. I was in the middle of raising my arms to celebrate, but play went on.

In the next few seconds, someone froze the puck in the corner. I went over to the net, the snow trail of my shot still visible. "It went in," I said, as I looked at the coach. His boot had left a print of its own, halfway across the goal line. There was really no way you could tell how far the puck had gotten.

He looked at me, my face betraying my desperation. "Yeah, OK, but we're not keeping score anyway."

He was right. I had a goal, but I had nothing. The game continued, and it finally ended when the snow, which fell all through our play, got in the way again, and nobody felt like clearing it once more.

I should have gone home that night dejected. My grand moments of the call-up and the goal had both been taken from me. But my mind wouldn't allow it, so by the time I got home, my goal had become real. And it wasn't just a scrubby shot that went under some stupid coach's boot. It was an end-to-end rush in the style of Bobby Orr. I had taken the puck behind my own blue line, worked it through the opposing players, deked their defense and then moved in on goal. Being a right-handed shooter, I had swooped left first, then pulled the puck back to my forehand just as I got their goalie to buy my move. He hadn't been able to catch up with me, and I'd scored into practically an open net. The last part was true, and it made me feel that the whole story was, too. I had just extended the details of how the puck had gotten to that point, on my stick in front of the open net.

I told the story with conviction, and my grandmother believed it. Now, she had never seen me play hockey. The goal as I described it was exactly like the ones she saw on TV all the time while she watched her beloved Montréal Canadiens. It didn't occur to her to question whether a nine-year-old could display such a burst of skill and speed. Or maybe she was pretending. Either way, my confidence was bolstered. I could report on my call-up on Monday morning. My classmates would have no choice but to buy it.

Late Saturday night, my dad and mom got home from their business trip. I didn't see them until Sunday morning, and the first thing Dad asked me was how the game had gone. I told him the story, just like I had told Gran: swooped in on goal, pulled the shot to my forehand and banged it into the open net for a goal.

My dad had seen almost every game I'd ever played. He knew I didn't play that aggressively. He knew I'd have passed the puck before I got it out of my zone, rather than carrying it. He knew that if I'd had it in the neutral zone, I would have sent it over to the centerman, rather than taking it in myself. "Did it really happen like that?" he asked, his smile saying, "Confess or live with your story forever."

"Yes," I said. I gave him the most sincere face I had.

"Just like that, the whole thing?" he asked again. I guess, like most dads, he would have loved to believe it. How must it have felt to stand there watching your completely mediocre son play, game after game, just hoping for an assist or one of the rare (3 or 4 a season, my best years) goals?

It was too late to back out. "Just like that," I said. I stuffed the memories of the outdoor rink, the snow, the lack of a goalie and the coach standing there in his boots to the back of my mind. "Are we going to church this morning?" I asked, quickly changing the subject, and I split back to my room to get my suit on.

Later that day, strategizing for the onslaught of BS that always marked the start of a week at our school, I took a lesson from my dad's doubting. Maybe the guys wouldn't believe the story either if it was that glorious. Although we all embellished our tales to a considerable degree, you had to be able to withstand serious scrutiny if you were going to dish out too stretched an account.

With that in mind, my goal became a quick shot from in front of the net that beat the goalie on his glove side. If there had been a goalie there, that's where the puck would have gone, though goodness knows if he had been there, a quick flick over with the blade of his stick probably would have knocked the shot into the corner. But who could say?

What I do know is that I got called up, the puck went over the line and I scored. It should have counted.

PART TWO

Living the Game

chapter nine

Breaking Into the Real World

For every kid, there's a moment of waking up, realizing that there's a world outside of the family. I think that these days, kids get that wake-up call earlier than in my day. For me, life was one long round of school, friends and various forms of hockey—street, corner rink and league. And like everyone I knew, I loved the Montréal Canadiens, though I didn't quite grasp their intimate connection to the place I lived—until one day when I was nine. The moment of realization wasn't so much due to an event as to a person, and he was not just anyone; he was an NHL goalie.

The change came when I was with my dad in Montréal on a sales call. He often took me along when he went into gift stores to service the racks that held our family's livelihood—small woven bookmarks imported from the U.S. and distributed out of our basement. When we went into the stores, he

would say to the clerks by way of introduction, "Oh, I brought
the vice president of the company with me today," while I tried
to act what I thought to be businesslike.

Sometimes, he'd get some value out of me by having
me sit in the car while it was double-parked on a downtown
street. If the cops tapped on the glass, I was to tell them that
he'd be right out. I guess he figured they wouldn't ticket a car
with a company executive in it. But this one day, I wasn't outside. Instead, I marched beside him when he went into a card
store, proudly carrying his briefcase for him. Eventually, I'd
get my own and take it everywhere. His held samples and
order forms. Mine would carry our lunch.

While Dad picked through the bookmarks and
recorded what the store needed on a reorder form, I poked
around. I twirled a rack with little books in it that sold for
75 cents and were more souvenir than reading material. Then
it caught my eye. Or rather, *he* caught my eye; for there, on the
cover of one of the books, was Ken Dryden. He was on one
knee in front of his net, that characteristic flat white mask
covering his face, just as I had come to idolize him.

I was stunned. I grabbed the book like an adolescent
grabbing at a girlie magazine and flipped through its pages.
Every page told the story of the 1971 Stanley Cup playoffs,
including a section on the rookie surprise from Cornell. The
pictures, in full color, were as glorious as the saves Dryden
had made that spring.

Living in Montréal, I was starting to watch hockey, urged by my grandmother's interest in *Les Canadiens*. As such, I had seen bits and pieces of the 1971 playoffs on TV, at least when I could convince my parents to let me stay up. The Canadiens had won the finals in seven games, over Chicago. Now, a few months later, as I was standing in the store devouring the images and text in that little book, I was aware for the first time that this team didn't just play on TV—they played in my city. They were my team, and the city where I lived was their city, and I knew that somehow, life was bigger than I had ever realized before. I felt as if the words had been written just for me, that the photos were seen not through a camera lens, but through my eyes. It seemed as though I had been there for every moment of the Canadiens' march to the Stanley Cup that spring. In that instant, a thread suddenly connected my kid world with the world outside.

I didn't even have to ask my dad to buy me the book when he came to get me. He must have seen on my face that I had found something magical. I left the store carrying his Samsonite briefcase again, but this time, it had the story of my hero and my team in it, and so I clutched its handle carefully, making sure that my book would still be there when we got home. I wanted to study it over and over, to take it to school and show it to the other boys in my class. Sure, we all loved the Montréal Canadiens, but now, it would become my mission to make my friends understand that there was nothing more important than the Habs, and that by virtue of where we lived and the air we breathed, they belonged to us. It wasn't really all up to me, of course. But I didn't realize that. What I did know was that this book held truths that it was my special job to spread to all the boys I knew.

chapter ten

Hockey Cards
Before the Boxed Set

Hockey lived for me, and the boys in my school, in more ways than just playing the game in leagues or on corner rinks. We also had the NHL as a constant backdrop to our days, and one of our most important ways of experiencing the game at that level was through hockey cards. For me and my friends, the cards had a magical effect, like tarot cards, with power to conjure up the great plays and glorious goals of the guys pictured on them. They weren't commodities with monetary value. Instead, they brought us close to the players we loved. We read the stats on the back sides over and over, arguing the merits of players' past seasons or the virtues of their teams. The cards were our reference point in these discussions. We relied on them as we relied on our moms making our lunches and sending us to school with them—they never failed us.

Back then, hockey cards were something bought in packs, five cards at a time plus a flat, soapy-tasting piece of gum.

There was no such thing as buying the entire NHL in one box, as kids and parents do nowadays, nor was there a sports card store, so to make our buys, we went to our corner store. Once inside, we stood there, eyeing up the waxy paper coatings of the packs lined up in a box on the counter next to the till. Impatient while the adult in front of us paid for white bread or cigarettes, we waited our turn, maybe touching a few packs before finally choosing the one we wanted. It was essential to get a feel for what was inside. Did this pack have a Guy Lafleur, or just another Dave Keon? It seemed that we always got an abundance of cards with the hated Toronto Maple Leafs on them. It was a rare miracle to come up with a Canadiens card. But we did what we could to get some card karma going, and then selected a pack and plunked down our money.

Opening the pack was like discovering some unknown tribe for the first time. You didn't know what would be there when your canoe rounded the bend in the river, but you had so much invested in the experience that your hopes were sky high. Usually, the protocol was to get outside the store before you unsealed your fate. No sense getting your bike stolen because you were standing inside looking over the goods.

My ritual was the same as that of all my friends every time I bought cards. I hurried out of the store to the sidewalk, ran my finger along the back of the pack where the wax paper folded over and sealed, and popped the seam. Then I unfolded the paper, made sure each side was out and creased back, and grabbed the gum. The whole works had a kind of powder coating, too, for some reason. I shook that out. Then I stuffed the gum in my mouth, more to get it out of the way than anything. It was nowhere near as good as Bazooka. Probably the card executives didn't chew it, so they didn't know. It was something that I and my buddies always questioned at one level in our heads, but accepted.

As I held the cards in my right hand, I crumpled the pack in my left and threw the paper ball into the garbage can outside the store. I wasn't even aware I was doing it, because I grabbed for those cards with my left hand as soon as the ball of wax paper left it. I looked, almost afraid. Whoever was on top would set the tone. Marcel Dionne? Good, but where was L.A., anyway? Gordie Howe? Wow! A goalie—almost any one—was jackpot. Also highly favored were special cards like "JC Tremblay, 1st Team All Star," or "Checklist" cards that let you keep track of what you had and what you should try to trade for.

If I saw a Canadiens player on top of my stack, I knew that I'd reached the Promised Land. It didn't matter what else was in that pack. I had all I needed. The rest was just good fodder for trades. Of course, even if I found a Canadiens player, I still held a faint glimmer of hope of scoring a double by finding another Montréal player in the pack, but I wouldn't expect it. That would be like getting an extra $5 in change at the movies or something.

If I opened my pack and saw a Maple Leaf on top, I felt doomed, but there was never any sense in making the judgment too soon. It was a mistake to condemn the whole pack out of hand just because the random gods who ran the packing machines had doled out a loser right off the opening faceoff. So no matter what was on top, I kept digging and thumbing through the pile until I got to the end, pronouncing each one good or bad by saying "got it" or "need it," almost like a chant. If I got lucky, the Maple Leafs player would be offset by something at least tradable, if not by something that I desperately needed.

Outside the store, the scene never varied. As the pack came to an end, so did my frenzy of discovery, or my disappointment of getting skunked. I got back on my bike to pedal home. But before I got very far, my brain would be going as fast as my pedals. *Who was it that wanted Rod Gilbert? What could I use to get Lucho to part with Phil Esposito? A Tony Esposito would be cool...I already have most of the other goalies in the NHL.*

On the days I bought cards, such scheming carried me home, which was where I laid out all the cards I had: the ones carefully stashed in my desk, plus the cards in my carry-around stack, plus my new ones. I deftly worked deals in my head, always slightly in my favor, of course, and I imagined my riches growing as I tricked and cajoled my friends into making foolish trades. It was like being the general manager of a team.

Then, the next time I was in school, I tried my maneuvers on my buddies—careful double trades where for a few brief, but terrifying, moments, I held a card I didn't have any need for in order to complete the swap with a third guy to get the one I ached for. It was science and art all at once.

Some kids were good enough to trade a Butch Goring for a Bobby Orr. I was never so savvy, though occasionally I came out on the winning end of a trade. The one thing I and all the boys in my grade knew, though, was that you couldn't swap a Toronto Maple Leafs card for anything. Although there was no logic to it, everybody I knew hated what we called the "Maple Laughs," so their cards had no value to us whatsoever. We stood them up against the fence when we played topsies at school, flinging cards against the boards and trying to cover the kid's cards we were playing against. We didn't mind seeing Leafs cards creased, frayed, even lost.

Yet as much as we hated them, it seemed as if we got tons of Leafs cards in every pack. Every kid I knew had them coming out his ears. It was almost as bad as getting cards featuring the St. Louis Blues or Minnesota North Stars. Sometimes I thought that if I got another Bob Plager or Lou Nanne, I'd quit buying packs forever. But I was always motivated by the hope that in the next one might be a Serge Savard or Yvan Cournoyer.

Often, my friends and I argued over why there was such a limited supply of cards with our favorite players on them. To us, they were diamonds that had to be mined, not merely ink on paper. It didn't occur to any of us that if they'd wanted to, the O-Pee-Chee Company could have printed 10 million Peter Mahovlichs and given one to every kid at every school in the country. We didn't think of it as a giant capitalist game to get us to buy more cards. We just knew we wanted every player on the Canadiens team, and every player in the league, if possible. Not because we wanted to complete the set for its monetary value, but to have command over every man who skated in the glorious NHL. In our endeavors, the cards' worth had no bearing. The only thing we ever did with them was trade them for other cards anyway.

One time, my dad suggested that if we were getting a million Maple Leafs cards, the kids in Toronto were probably getting a million Canadiens cards. Maybe trading with them would be a good idea. These days, a kid hearing a suggestion like that would go to his or her bedroom, jump on the Internet and find someone in another city to swap with. Back in the '70s, though, the idea of finding another kid in a distant city and striking up a correspondence, then making a deal through the mail, was like the hope of meeting Jacques Lemaire coming around the corner of your street—it was beyond belief.

So we just kept the players we hated, not bothering to treat them with any care at all. Soon, these cards had edges so frayed that the corners were rounded. It was at that point that we clothes-pinned them into the front spokes of our bikes. If they weren't much good as cards, we figured that the noise they made could turn our two-wheelers into motorcycles, at least in our imaginations.

chapter eleven

Consolation
Cards

It seems impossible now that things have changed so much in a generation, but when I was growing up, very few kids had parents who were divorced. In Preville Elementary, at least in my grade, I remember only one such kid. Brad Chambers, unlike the rest of my friends, lived with just his mom. Brad's dad was a shadowy figure who had been gone before we ever knew him. We sometimes pondered where he lived and what he did, but the only answer we could come up with was "he's somewhere else." Anything that happened outside the few streets we lived and played on was a complete mystery to us. But we did know one crucial fact about the man. He was what we called "generous." The proof was that Brad Chambers had more hockey cards than anyone we knew.

Back then, most kids had some kind of small allowance, or money from shoveling driveways or mowing lawns. But a pack of five cards cost 10 cents, so buying a couple, maybe three, a week was all anyone could afford. Still, if you started in the fall, by Christmas you had a decent-sized stack, which you carefully hoarded. Your favorite players' cards were carefully tucked away in your drawer at home. These were your "savers." For most of us kids in Montréal, the savers included all the Canadiens, plus players we grudgingly respected from other teams: Bobby Orr, Stan Makita, Johnny Bucyk, Gerry Cheevers. No Toronto Maple Leafs players were ever savers.

After the savers were stowed, we carried around what was left over. Of these, what we called "decent" cards were ones that we would trade if given the chance to pick up some- thing good—stars from another team or a special card like one depicting the "NHL Shutouts Leaders" from the prior season. Plus we carried our doubles, cards that we'd deal at any good opportunity to get Canadiens players. The carry- around stack also included cards that we didn't care about at all, ones that we used to play games at recess or after school. All in all, the stack that most kids had with them at any one time contained 15 to 20 cards. We carefully guarded them, of course, since allowance money had been sacrificed for them. Yet while this was true for most of the kids I knew, Brad Chambers didn't have to go through any of this trauma, because his dad bought him all the cards he wanted.

Brad's dad visited him on the weekends, and every Monday morning Brad came to school and announced, "My dad bought me some cards." We all knew what that meant. It wasn't the slim pickings of our weekend purchases, but packs upon packs. More cards than most of us would buy all year. Enough so that Brad didn't have to hoard them or guard them, since they flowed like water through his hands.

We liked Brad, and we admired his power, but we resented him too. We imagined him standing in the store with both hands full of packs, trying desperately to hold them all long enough to get them to the counter so his dad could pay. We visualized the frenzy of opening that must have followed. We pictured so much gum that no one person could chew it all.

We angled to be with Brad when his dad came to visit, to see the buying spree firsthand. Everyone believed that whoever was lucky enough to be around him would go home with a considerable bounty of cards to keep. But when we asked Brad about the experience each Monday, all he would say was, "My dad bought them for me, and I opened the packs when I got home." He neither offered further specifics nor invited anyone to participate next time. Whether his vagueness was because there was no truth to the story of his plenty or for some other reason, we couldn't guess. But whatever happened on those weekends, on Monday morning, with the huge stack in his hand, Brad was envied, worshipped even. And he knew it.

As we all gathered around him in a tight circle, he'd pull a stack that was as high as five of ours out of his school-bag, the pile held securely with an elastic band. He was no fool.

On the top was always something that he knew we all wanted—Frank Mahovlich (in the Montréal era, naturally) or Jean Beliveau. Even when we asked to see them all, he'd be demure. He wanted us to believe that the whole stack was Montréal Canadiens, that he'd either had the luckiest streak of card buying ever, or that his dad had bought him so many cards that just these, this whole glorious pile, were the Canadiens players. We could only imagine the thousands of rejects left in his bedroom. It was a score that only a rich kid, a really rich one, not like anyone we knew, would ever see.

For the kids I went to school with, cards were a means of power, the currency of the playground. By virtue of his incredible collection, Brad Chambers was the bank. He could get into any game using cards as his entry tool. He got picked first for our floor hockey games. He got on the good team when we played soccer. All it took was a flash of the giant stack of cards that he seemed to carry at all times. The rest of us would stand back, shaking in awe no matter how many times we'd seen it. And we would wait, because to get what he wanted, Brad was always willing to dole out some payola.

When we picked teams at recess, Brad would pull out his stack and deftly flip the top card to the bottom. What was underneath was always something good, but not primo perfecto like the one on top. He would thumb through the deck for a minute, thinking, or pretending to, grabbing cards as he went. Pretty soon he'd have five or six in his hand, the top one showing, the others a mystery. He would hold the cards forward, showing them to the guys doing the picking. They were the same guys who chose the teams at every school—better at sports than most of us. Later, they'd be the first ones to get the girls.

There Brad would stand, inviting the captains to defy logic and pick him. He wasn't bad at sports. He was just like the rest of us—in the second tier. The guys picking would normally have been indifferent to the idea of having him on their team. They would have grabbed the good athletes, then divided up the other kids. "I'll take you three. The other three go over there." Under any other circumstance, Brad would have been assigned to a team like this, with the rest of us. But the cards were the lure. "You," the captains would say. They almost never said your name if you weren't one of the stars, but Brad would be chosen before we were.

He would walk over to the captain's side, handing over the cards as he went. None of us cared that Brad was making a payout or understood the unfairness of it. We would have done it if we could have. We would have taken the loot without shame, too, if it was offered to us. Only an idiot would refuse it.

A brief flurry of excitement would erupt while the captain thumbed over his new cards. Sometimes, if there was something really good in there, deal-making immediately started. Usually the other captain, the one picking second, grumpily put a stop to it with, "Come on, guys, the bell's gonna ring!" They'd reluctantly go back to choosing up sides. But everyone would be mentally thumbing through his own card collection, wondering what deals might be made for what Brad had given away. We repeated this routine every time we picked teams.

Given the chance, every kid I knew during those years would have traded places with Brad Chambers, at least for a while. To be able to handle the precious commodity of hockey cards without thought was a dream life all of us envied. But thinking back on it now, I can imagine the sadness Brad felt when his dad left him back at home after spending a Saturday or Sunday together, the cards a sorry consolation prize for not having a family like the rest of the kids he knew. Maybe opening pack after pack of cards, oblivious to the allowance money they cost everyone else, wasn't the euphoria we envisioned it to be.

I realize now that Brad's parents used the cards to make him feel better about what had happened to his family. But to my friends and me, Brad was the luckiest kid in school. We never thought to ask him what it felt like to be a "divorced kid" or not to have a dad to take him to hockey practice. These sentiments were out of our range as primary schoolers. All we saw was a mountain of hockey cards adorned with images of our heroes, even if they were only cardboard representations.

chapter twelve

Gran to the Rescue

wo types of grandmothers exist. One kind is similar to you—the grandchild—whoever you happen to be. If you're from the suburbs, then your grandma is, too. If you're from a farm in rural Saskatchewan or Minnesota, then so is your grandma. The other kind of grandmother is the one who is essentially different from whoever you are. That's the kind of grandmother I had.

I grew up in a then-new suburb of Montréal. My grandmother lived in Westmount. After moving from the house my dad had grown up in, she lived in a high-rise apartment building that had a doorman. She did things my parents never thought of doing, like playing bridge with friends or having lunch at the country club. My parents were people for whom such extravagance was impossible. Needless to say, I was completely fascinated by my Gran.

One time, when I was a teenager, we went to McDonald's together somewhere near the old Montréal Forum. We had been out shopping for the day and were riding the subway. I suggested a burger, and she agreed. We walked into the restaurant, and she immediately looked around for someone to seat us. I told her that we had to order first, at the counter. Standing there, she read over the menu, and when it was our turn to order, said very regally, "I'll have one hamburger, cooked medium." And then, noticing the puzzled look on the kid's face behind the counter, she quickly corrected herself. "Or however you cook them," she said. She was the greatest.

But if we were divided by culture as well as age, the one thing we shared was our love of the Montréal Canadiens. Sometimes when my folks were out of town, Gran stayed over to babysit us, and she watched the games, frequently yelling at the screen to try to get the players to do what she wanted. My grandmother was in love with Jean Béliveau, never more so than in the spring of 1971. But then again, so were millions of other women in Québec.

Our mutual love of the game had come into play in a big way earlier that same 1970–71 hockey season, thanks to Esso gasoline and something they invented called "NHL Power Player Trading Cards." These were one of the only things a kid could collect in my day, aside from hockey cards themselves. For this reason, the Power Players became an obsession for everyone in my school.

There were three essential components to the deal. First, you got a book in which each NHL team had a two-page spread with spots pre-assigned for their roster players of that season. The idea was to stick the players' images in the appropriate spaces as you got them. Then you got a wallet, a blue plastic fold-over deal, with two compartments on each side for the cards. Finally, there were the cards themselves, which were about the size of a hockey card cut in half from side to side. But unlike hockey cards, the Power Players were flimsy, more paper than cardboard. You could play topsies with a hockey card, but not with the Power Players. They existed purely for their own sake, and it was my ambition, as well as that of many of the boys I knew, to have a complete album of Power Players. The problem was, we were at the mercy of our parents' need for gas in order to get more Power Players. You couldn't save up and buy them. Even Brad Chambers was locked into the system.

When the promotion started, my dad obligingly procured the wallet and the book, and I began working my way slowly to getting the pages filled. Just as with the hockey cards, it seemed that the Power Players were overflowing in Dunc Wilson and Andre Boudrias cards, along with a plethora of other Vancouver Canucks, who were new to the league at the time. The players we really wanted, like Jacques Lemaire and Bobby Hull, were in short supply. But I had hopes of completing my set. That's where an important misunderstanding, and my Gran, came into the picture.

One October day, my dad and I pulled into an Esso station in Brossard, where we lived, to fill up. Naturally, I jumped out to go with Dad to pay and to get my package of Power Players, and as we walked back, I started to rip open the pack. The cards were similar to stamps in that you had to tear the seams open and then separate the six cards at their perforations.

When we got back to the car, I found that I'd improved my situation only slightly. There were a couple of "got its," but one of them was a Bernie Parent, and I had a friend at school who was looking for him. My friend seemed to have an over-abundance of Boston Bruins, this being the odd luck of the game. I needed a Johnny Bucyk and a Derek Sanderson. I commented to my dad that it would be really nice if I could finish my collection. He nodded his assent.

"But what I really need is the deluxe album," I said, hoping my dad would catch my hint. It hit like a bomb. The basic album was paperback, with blue, black and white on the cover and the words "NHL Power Player Saver" lined up with "Esso" in a little white circle beside them. Almost every kid had one. You could spend a little more money, though, and get the deluxe hardcover edition. Brown with gold-accented lettering, the deluxe edition promised a world of wonders above what the cheapo paper album offered.

"I was hoping I could get it?" I offered. It wasn't a question, but I phrased it as one.

"It will be a long frosty Friday before I do that," my dad said. Now, I was seven, and my skills at recognizing irony were, to say the least, probably a little underdeveloped. So I asked what, to me, was an obvious question. "When will it snow for the first time?"

My dad looked at me a little puzzled. "Probably some-time around your birthday," he replied. *Bingo,* I thought. *He'll buy me the album then.* My birthday was in early November, and it was October now. I was home free. I immediately vowed to cease pasting Power Players into the softcover album I'd been using. No sense trying to get them out again when it came time to fill the deluxe book.

Early November came, and we were spending a Sun-day afternoon with my Gran at her place in Montréal. I made sure to have my Power Players album and trader's wallet with me, to show her. And, of course, I chose this exact moment to reveal the promise that I thought my dad had made to me.

I explained the system of one set of cards with every fill-up as I flipped through the pages. My Gran's first question to me was a natural one. "Do you have Jean Beliveau's card?" I had the book open to the Canadiens page. Most of the spots were empty.

"Not yet. He's hard to get. Plus I don't want to put any more cards in here until my birthday." I looked at my dad, not daring to say another word.

His ears perked up at hearing that. "What's going to happen on your birthday?" he asked me.

I was reluctant to say anything, sure that if I did, my dream would be lost. I had already figured out that parents hate it when you ruin surprises.

"You think I'm saving some cards for then?" he asked. He really didn't know.

I was cornered, and I had to say it. "The big album. The deluxe. I'm getting it for my birthday." The words look more confident here on the page than they felt coming out of my mouth that day.

My dad was always big on honesty, so he followed up with, "What gives you that idea?" He thought he could see a con coming, I'm sure. I had a way of working out deals to get what I wanted. It was how I would get my street hockey goalie pads a year or so later.

"You did. You said when it snowed, you'd buy me the deluxe," I said. I guess he knew that I meant it, because his only reply was a look of puzzlement.

"What gave you that idea?" he repeated. And, of course, what ensued was a guessing game as to where we were at the time and what he had said. Since he'd just tossed the expression out—the equivalent of saying, "Never in a million years will you get that big book"—he now didn't remember anything. Finally, I convinced him by coming up with some version of his "frosty Friday" comment. By this time, all the adults were laughing. I don't know if it was from the misunderstanding or my complete gullibility. But it wasn't funny to me. I'd made plans on his word, and done a pretty good bit of bragging at school, too. If he didn't go through with it, I'd be sunk. At my school, you just didn't go back on such a boast.

"I have no plans to buy that big album. What you have is fine. Anyway, your birthday presents are all bought." He said it as nicely as he could.

Great, probably another snowsuit, I thought. It was the kind of present kids are forced to say thank you for but don't really appreciate. My face wrinkled up, and though I tried not to show my hurt, Gran must have seen it, and she jumped in with a suggestion.

"If he can't have the deluxe album, at least I could help him fill the book he has. Maybe I could buy Esso gas, too, instead of my regular brand," she said. I cheered up at the idea and looked to my dad for the OK.

Dad smiled. "That's a great plan, but Gran never goes very far, so the fill-ups won't come very often," he cautioned me.

But Gran was on a roll now. "What if Marnie buys Esso, too?" she suggested. She was talking about her lifelong friend, Mrs. Wallace, who lived a couple of floors above her in the apartment building. Motivated by her love of Jean Beliveau, Gran pressed on. "Maybe the two of us, plus the Wilsons from the bridge club, plus Paul, the doorman, could all buy Esso gas for a while." My dad looked on while she waved her arms in excitement, her charm bracelet dangling and clanging with energy.

I was ecstatic. The terrible misunderstanding was turning into a grand triumph. I would have my Power Players, and probably so many left over that I could trade them for hockey cards, more Power Players wallets and who knew what else!

Then Dad chimed in with another doubt. "But you buy Shell," he said to Gran. Switching to Esso was more of a commitment than it seemed. Gran had been going to a Shell station in Westmount for as long as it had been there. The guy didn't just sell her gas, he also kept the car maintained, which eased her fear of it breaking down. She was, at the time, already pretty old—over 70.

"If you suddenly stop turning up at the Shell, you'll break some of that loyalty that keeps the guy there doing things for you, like making small adjustments to the car without charge, or looking the car over every time you go in for a fill-up," my dad added. As the responsible son, he couldn't let that kind of thing go without comment. "I don't think the Power Players are worth that risk," he said, looking at me with an apology. He didn't want to ruin my dreams. He was just being sensible.

But Gran was a woman of purpose. She and I had never shared much, so maybe this was her chance to do something for me that I would appreciate. It's not that I didn't appreciate the snowsuits and ski jackets I got from her as presents, but maybe she sensed that this was different. "Rene at Shell will understand. He has a couple of boys himself. I'll go back there when the album is filled," she said. With that, she silenced my dad, and a plan was born. She and her friends would form a small old-lady army of Power Players collectors, with one mission between them: to get me enough cards to fill my album. They would be relentless.

I left that Sunday excited about the prospect of a bounty of Power Players to come, and I was not to be disappointed.

Gran showed up at our house for coffee a few weeks before Christmas, and her purse was stuffed with Power Players in their "NHL Power Player Packet" envelopes. She took them out and put them on our kitchen table while I watched, my fingers eager to rip open their seams to see what they contained. But I was polite enough to wait until she told me I could start.

Opening the packets was like an early Christmas, and while Gran watched me and chatted with my mom, I filled my album, all except for a couple of stubborn players, whose spaces remain blank to this day. The extras I gathered into a pile, like a stack of hockey cards. There were so many that I couldn't fit them into my Power Players wallet.

At school, I turned my loss of the deluxe album into a win. The big book was hard to carry around, not like our paperback versions, and the only kid who had it was Brad Chambers, and his was mostly empty. His dad might have been able to buy him stacks of cards, but I had a dedicated grandmother who could get Power Players by the millions.

chapter thirteen

"Topsies" and Diplomacy

S ometimes, rather than a stick-and-ball game taking up our recess or lunch hour, my friends and I played with hockey cards themselves, a game we called "tops" or "topsies." We'd draw a line on the pavement facing the fence that bordered our playground, and two combatants would stand behind it. Everyone else gathered along the sides, forming an imaginary box that constituted the field of battle. Someone would set up a line of cards, leaning them against the fence. The goal was to flick a card out of your hand, throwing it at the ones standing up and attempting to knock them down. You claimed as prizes any of the opponent's cards that you covered with yours.

There are various ways to play this game, but we used the strict version of the rules, giving nothing for a "bridge," when a card covered the opponent's but also touched another card, or for "edgies," which was an incomplete cover—or one that touched the other just slightly. Bridges and edgies didn't count; only a clean "topsy" won you that card.

The objective, of course, was to win as many of the other guy's cards as you could. If you had to lose, you hoped that the opponent covered your worst cards. That's why you always carried a bunch of your reject cards with you. But there was some etiquette involved in the selection of which cards to play. Nobody would go up against a guy who didn't put at least some good ones at risk. You wouldn't chance your best stuff against a kid who played a whole stack of Toronto Maple Leafs.

You would think that Brad Chambers, who had more cards than any other kid in our school, would be the king of this game. In fact, he almost never played. Maybe to him there was no thrill in winning. He had all the good cards already, and risking a few of the thousands that he had, or seemed like he had, meant about as much as a professional poker ace playing nickel slots in Vegas. What would be the point? So instead of playing, he blended into the mass of us who stood alongside the game, watching, calling the doubtful tops as edgies or bridges. Sometimes Brad staked cards to kids, giving them some of his to play and then watching while they gambled with his collection. It wasn't that he needed to win anything. He just liked the power of it, everyone watching him while his player took his turns, throwing recklessly and taking every risk he could to win because he didn't have any of his own stack to lose.

One morning, the game got hot. Normally, the "big" guys, the ones who starred at the recess-time baseball, soccer or football games, wouldn't play cards. Instead, it was always the vast horde of the others, the "normal" kids, who were most absorbed in watching cards knock over cards and then be claimed by the shooter who had topped his opponent. But on this day, it was a kid named Jeff against a guy I claimed as a friend, or better yet, who claimed me, Lucho. Our friendship was my only small hold on being "in." Jeff and Lucho were excellent athletes, but this morning they had started a game of topsies, which naturally attracted a large crowd of onlookers. We were as curious about their motivations as about the game itself.

They had not begun the game in the usual way, with a bunch of cards standing against the fence to be knocked down. Instead, they were playing a simpler version of the game, called "bouncies." The object was to bounce your card off the fence that marked the end of the playing surface and then have it come back into play and cover the other kid's card. Normally in this game, you'd never play anything all that good. Why would you, when you knew pretty much for sure that your cards were going to get all bent up at the corners after hitting the fence?

But in an act of desperation or sheer bravado, Lucho had played a Guy Lafleur, which was way outside the bounds of common sense. He knew it, but he was cocky. He expected

Jeff to do the same. It was the unwritten rule—if you put something like a Canadien up for the taking, the other guy should try for it with something at least close to as good. It didn't have to be a Canadien. A goalie card would do, or a star from another team, or a special card of some kind, like "League Scoring Leaders." Even what's now called a "rookie card" might work if it was the right guy. But never a Ken Dryden. Nobody had any of those.

So when Jeff pulled out a Brian Glennie, we all gasped. For some reason, this guy, who ended up playing for Toronto for about 10 years, was in every pack we bought, or so it seemed. Maybe it was the result of some kind of print overrun of his image or a particularly bad streak of luck for the guys I knew, but we all had three or four Glennies. You couldn't trade them for anything. You couldn't give them away. They were the cards you used over and over to practice topsies. Every one we had ended up with its edges frayed like the corners of an old library book.

Jeff had no business playing for the Lafleur with a Glennie, and we all knew it. But these were the big guys playing, and none of us peons dared do anything to enforce the accepted rules. If it had been anyone else, our chorus of boos would have shamed him into putting his Glennie back on the bottom of his stack. He might even have overplayed the next card to compensate for the breach of tact. At the very least,

Jeff should have gone with something like a Vic Hadfield, maybe a Phil Esposito. But there was nothing but a gasp.

Lucho looked at Jeff, then surveyed the cards on the ground in front of them. A couple were lying next to the fence. They were nothing cards, easy to win. All Jeff had to do was flick the Glennie at the fence and let it fall. It would very likely top one of them. The Lafleur was pretty safely out of reach, Lucho having given his wrist a good hard flick that bounced the card way out, close to halfway between the fence and the line he and Jeff stood behind.

Standing there, I wondered whether Jeff was just teasing with the Brian Glennie. Maybe he wanted to work Lucho up; maybe he'd just give the card a casual flip and let it land where it might. So what if he took a St. Louis Blues card that was lying close to the fence? We all had too many of those too, and since the Canadiens had beaten them for the Stanley Cup a year or two previous, we saw them as the vanquished, almost like a minor league team next to our mighty Habs.

Jeff put his feet in position for his turn. Right foot in front of left and knees bent, he held the card in his right hand. Then, in a move we'd all anticipated but dreaded, he took a step back with his right foot. We understood what was coming. He was going to play for that Lafleur card.

He flexed his arm over his head and adjusted the card in his hand, holding it between his forefinger and middle finger with just the upper right corner sticking out. He had it where he wanted it, and he stepped into the throw, giving his wrist a strong flick. The card sailed true and straight, hit the fence about a foot and a half high and came back out. It fluttered and then landed. We all strained to see, but no one dared cross the imaginary line that marked the left and right edges of the playing surface. Jeff's Brian Glennie had come to rest with just the barest edge overlapping the edge of the Lafleur. "Edgies!" someone yelled. I guess Lucho yelled it, since it was his foul to call. But the rest of us called it too.

Jeff was having none of it. He scrambled onto the playing surface, all of us crowding around. "Is not!" he said, almost screaming as he stood up. "Is not, and I get it!" He turned to deliver the true force of his bluster at Lucho.

By rights, Lucho should have had the chance to have a look. The cards had borders printed on them, and the rule was that covering this border was not enough. The opponent's card had to overlap the player photo itself in order to be called a legal topsy. Lucho had the right to check it out, since he stood to lose the Lafleur. They would settle the dispute fairly, or at least that's how we always did it. Lucho tried to move past to kneel down and scrutinize the cards; Jeff blocked him.

"Hey, I have to see it!" Lucho said, his voice betraying his tension. The rest of us instinctively took a breath and a step back. Whatever happened between these two was not our business. We didn't dare try to settle the thing the way we always did—by appointing someone from the crowd as mediator. Nobody had as much power as the two now in dispute, and so there was no point in trying to get things fixed diplomatically.

Lucho straightened his spine as he bumped up against Jeff. He wasn't a bit afraid of him. These were the type of guys whose nature it was to be brave. "Let me look, or else," Lucho said. His threat hung in the air. Our collective eyes shot from him to Jeff. What was to come next would be the decider. They were on the edge of a scuffle.

Suddenly, I was aware of a movement beside me. As I turned, I saw Brad Chambers take the oversized rubber band off the giant stack of cards he always had with him. He bent down, flexing his knees. So far, I was the only one whose attention was diverted from what was sure to be a punch in the nose from Jeff to Lucho, or Lucho to Jeff, in the next millisecond. And then Brad yelled at the top of his lungs.

"Scraaambuuullle!" It was a word we knew well. When you wanted to play a joke on another kid, you walked up behind him when he held his cards loosely in his hand in front of him. If he saw you, it wouldn't work, but if he didn't, you positioned yourself just behind his back and reached around his body. Then with your open hand, you smacked the underside of his hand, sending his cards flying all over the place. As you did it, you yelled "Scramble!" and took off running. Everyone else would gather like moths to a light, trying to grab the flying cards. Most of them would land on the ground, leading to guys diving all over the pavement or grass to get whatever they could while the frantic kid yelled and kicked in a vain effort to save his collection.

Usually at the end, the kid forced everyone to give back what they'd picked up. We all knew it wasn't right to keep a guy's cards after a scramble. Sometimes the victim would let some go, cards nobody much wanted anyway, as a way of showing that he didn't care about being the victim of the prank. He could save face that way.

But on this day, Brad didn't smack the cards out of someone else's hand. He flung his own gigantic wad to the wind, letting what seemed like hundreds of them hang above us and then flutter down to the ground. I can still see them spotlighted against the red brick of the two-story building, then covering the black pavement of the yard. They obliterated the comparatively few cards that Jeff and Lucho had played in their game, including the Lafleur.

Everyone, including Lucho and Jeff, realized at the same time what was happening. We forgot about the disputed Guy Lafleur and Jeff's major breach of etiquette in playing a junk card. We flung ourselves about after the bounty, grabbing all the cards we could in hopes of getting something good. We were seized with the ecstasy of it, knowing that a chance like this would likely never be repeated.

By the time we had finished, pants bore the marks of the playground's pavement, elbows were scuffed and shirts were untucked. Everyone's but Brad's, that is. He just stood by and watched. What did he care? He had a thousand more cards at home, or at least that's what we all said whenever we talked about it afterwards. Nobody ever thought to ask him why he had done it. All I know is that it was the greatest act of playground diplomacy any of us at Preville Elementary School had ever seen.

chapter fourteen

Placing My Faith
in the Cards

As a kid, you're always being someone in your imagination. When you're playing street hockey, you might be Guy Lafleur. When I lived in Ontario, all the kids wanted to be Borje Salming. I never understood why, but it did leave me free to be whatever Canadien I wanted. When you're not playing sports, you're still acting out roles, like Evel Knieval. These days I suppose it's cartoon superheroes.

In my day, acting out the role of cowboy was always a favorite, and back then, toy guns were miniature versions of the real thing, silver with white plastic handles molded to represent the pearly grips of the gun a sheriff from the Lone Star State of Texas would use to round up the worst outlaws. This was the glorious un-politically correct 1970s, and every kid I knew had a pair of six-shooters and a holster set, or at least one gun and a holster attached to a belt that had spaces for spare bullets. Most of us also had cowboy hats, and on one agonizingly long Saturday, I decided to wear my hat and gun all day long. Deputy Brian was on the job.

Mid-afternoon, my friend Tracy Pearson happened over. He didn't have his cowboy gear with him, but it was OK. I wasn't necessarily into playing cowboys and Indians all day. But I was determined to have my trusty sidearm ready in the event of an Apache attack.

We were playing some kind of tag game, me running after him but falling behind. As we crossed my front lawn, I felt a wicked impulse that told me to draw my gun. If he'd had his six-shooter, I would have shot at him, hitting him between the shoulder blades, in my imagination of course, and dropping him. As soon as Tracy heard me yell, "I shot you," he'd have to play dead. But since he had no gun, the game couldn't proceed by those customs. Instead, I reared back and threw my gun at him. It spun out of my hand, going end over end like one of those knives thrown at human targets at the carnival. Only instead of whistling by him, like I'd wanted, as a way to get him to slow down, it struck him with a solid thump, right in the back of the noggin.

He stumbled and put his hand to the back of his head. As he did so, I caught up with him. That sick feeling that you get when you're a kid and you're about to get in what we called "big heck" started to wash through my body. Instinctively, my devious kid mind started searching for a way to make it

OK, even as my eyes darted to the front windows of my house. My plan was to get Tracy calmed down before my mom realized what had happened and insisted on calling Mrs. Pearson. Then we could go on playing, and I'd be saved.

What my brain landed on was hockey cards. They would be the ticket to making this problem go away. All I had to do was start babbling a mile a minute about hockey cards, then somewhere in there throw in the offer that Tracy could come up to my room and look through my stack and take as many as he wanted. He'd forget about the welt rising on his head, and things would go back to how they had been a few seconds before.

He was half bent over, my gun lying on the ground beside him. I picked it up and holstered it. No sense having that kind of evidence screaming out my guilt if my mom happened to look out the kitchen window. His face was puzzled. We were good friends. He was obviously wondering why I had done this to him. I saw that he was starting to panic, his head probably beginning to throb. So I blurted it out: "Let's go to my room and look at hockey cards. You can have anything you want out of my stack. It'll be like I have a penalty." It was the closest thing to an apology I could give.

But wait. I have to confess that I was practicing what a Catholic might call "mental reservation" even as I said it. I was not lying, but I wasn't exactly telling the truth, either, because I knew that my stack didn't have anything good in it.

Some kids I knew would never carry around a stack with nothing decent in it. They were the ones who didn't care about cards so much, or who were willing to make frequent trades with their cards and didn't want to get caught flat-footed when someone showed up at school with something they desperately wanted, or who played topsies at recess and would risk good cards to get good ones back. I wasn't like that. I was ultraconservative when I made my stack, always making sure that it had enough cards in it to look credible, but nothing that I would mind losing if someone "scrambled" me on the playground. I knew that what I'd had in my stack when I last went through it was a bunch of junk, none of which would be fair compensation for my stupid move with the gun. Of course, I wouldn't mention the box in my desk drawer, which held everything really worth anything.

I tried again, being careful not to sound pleading. "C'mon. It's hockey cards. Let's get outta here and see what's in my stack."

If Tracy had been anyone else, the immediate crisis of a head injury would have passed while he greedily took up my offer, but even as I made my desperate gesture, I knew it was flawed. Tracy was one of the few boys in my class who didn't play hockey. He could hold his own in a street hockey game, when he was around to play, but he wasn't on a team. Nor did he have much interest in hockey cards, and he never played topsies. He didn't place much value in carrying a stack, which to the rest of us was like a measure of our self-worth. So my offer of cards was not the lure to him that it would have been to just about every other boy that I knew.

Still, I had no choice. Offering him hockey cards was the best plan I could come up, and I was already committed to it. If I changed tactics now, I'd be doomed. He'd know that I was scared. So I put on my most nonchalant face and persisted, saying it over and over like a mantra as he alternated between suppressing sobs and looking at me like I had tried to kill him. I could only imagine the punishment I'd get if my dad found out what I'd done. Having my gun confiscated would be just the beginning.

"Come on, let's go look at the cards. You can have any of my cards you want. I'm sick of tag anyway. Let's go inside," I pleaded.

I knew that I was making an offer that was not in good faith. But I had seen the power of hockey cards to fix problems, and I believed in the efficacy of their diplomacy the way the UN believes in the Security Council. I couldn't forget the scramble that Brad Chambers had done over the disputed "edgie." It had averted a fight between the two toughest boys in my class. Heck, it might have saved us from an all-out schoolyard riot.

Now I was placing my faith in the cards once again, desperately hoping that they were stronger than the pain of the welt rising on the back of my eight-year-old friend's head. "Come on, Tracy, let's go inside now. The cards are..."

His look stopped me in mid-sentence this time. "I'm going home. You can keep your cards," he said. It was the ultimate put-down in our world, leaving a guy all by himself in the middle of the afternoon. He straightened up and started to walk away, and I just stood there. Now what? Nobody else was home to play with. If they had been, I might have been playing street hockey instead of tag, anyhow. I watched him go, glad in one sense because I knew I was now safe from my dad finding out what I'd done. Then I looked around me. There was nothing but stillness in the neighborhood.

I wasn't allowed TV at this time of the day, but I realized that there was something more important I had to do. I decided to go inside and re-sort my stack, putting a Canadiens player in there, or at least one special card, like a team photo or "JC Tremblay, 1st Team All Star." I didn't want to get caught out if I ever had to use the cards to get out of a tricky situation again.

As for Tracy, I don't know whether he was being generous in forgiving my transgression without sizing up my cards, or whether he just didn't care. Either way, the cards had given me something to say while he got used to the aching in his head, proving that on the playground or at home, their magic was untouchable.

chapter fifteen

Dryden's Goalie Crease

For every collector, there is a holy grail. For me at nine, it was the Ken Dryden hockey card from the 1971–72 season. These days, we'd call that the "rookie card." In fact, it's on eBay right now, going for about $40 US for a decent example. But in 1971–72, the year Dryden played his first full season, it was just *his* card, not something whose value equated to dollars and cents, and I had to have it. Ken Dryden was my hero. I had fallen totally under his spell in the spring of 1971, when he led my team to the Cup. In the September 1972 Summit Series, I would lose my awe somewhat, but in the interim I was obsessed, and my mania focused on getting a Ken Dryden card. The problem was, nobody in my school had even seen a Dryden, let alone owned one.

By seeking a Dryden, I wasn't trying to complete my set or gather the full Montréal Canadiens team. Marc Tardiff and

Rejean Houle were local guys who turned up with regularity when I bought packs of O-Pee-Chees. Guy Lapointe and "Pocket Rocket" Richard were a little more rare. But buying a pack at a time or even five or, in rare cases of unbridled excess, 10 packs for a dime apiece, I had faith that eventually I would get all I needed. I just didn't define "need" as equaling a full team or league set. Although getting the entire NHL would have been nice, it was hard to compile the cards of every player, even in a 14-team league. There were always so many doubles, and so many Vancouver Canucks. When I did have gaps in my collection, I resorted to trades. The Dryden card was different.

Not even Brad Chambers, despite his enormous collection as represented by the three-inch thick stack he had with him at all times, could help me when I asked him to trade me one. However, his being unable to answer my request threatened his position as the king of the cards, and that made him uneasy. He had always been able to answer any and all requests, and we counted on him as a stabilizing force when we were drowning in a sea of Dennis Hextalls and Gilles Marottes. Only Juha Widing seemed to turn up with greater regularity in the packs we bought.

It was after school one afternoon when my desire for Dryden's card came face to face with Brad's self-appointed role as hockey card maven. We were supposed to be standing in what our teacher called a "neat and proper line" waiting for

Jack, our bus driver, to pick us up. I was standing behind Brad who was, as usual, waxing on about the cards he had at home, ones that made those he was showing off to the little crowd gathered around him look like nothing at all. "Here," he said to one kid as he shoved a Guy Lafleur card at him. "Take it." It was pretty rare. It too was a "rookie." But Brad did this kind of thing from time to time, suddenly gifting one kid with something spectacular. It's why the crowd gathered in the first place.

I shoved in a little closer when the free card went out in Brad's hand. I had to see what he was giving, just like everyone else. "Hey, you still want Dryden?" he asked, half turning to face me. I almost choked. He had a Dryden? It would be mine in a matter of seconds? You never knew with this guy. Sometimes he would say something like this just to make you go, "Yeah!" then laugh at you and say something like, "Then get your dad to buy you more cards!" It was his only power over us, and we accepted it.

So now, I didn't know what to say. I decided to play it cool. "Sure, to trade. You got one?" I knew I didn't have anything on me that was worth trading for Dryden, but I was willing to bluff to see what he was up to. Maybe he'd just give me the card. If not, I wasn't going to look like I was begging for it.

"No, not today. But I can get one," he replied.

How? I asked him with my eyes rather than my voice. Card dealers didn't exist back then. At least, they weren't on my radar or that of anyone I went to school with. The only way to get a card you needed was to buy more packs, but everyone I knew had been buying packs all year, and nobody had the magic card.

"My dad says he knows a guy with one," was Brad's reply to my mute inquiry.

Was this true? Who knew? I took a quick look around me and saw only stunned faces. We all wanted to see that card. It wasn't clear whether or not he really had a line on it at that moment, but I was smart enough to follow up with a question. "When do you want to make the trade?" It put him on the spot. He'd have to come through now.

"Monday after school," he said. It was Thursday. He could have been buying time to somehow get the card, or playing to the dramatic, but I couldn't chance it. I had to go along with the game. It might be my only opportunity to see a Dryden, or get it.

"What do you want to trade for it?" I asked. It was a ridiculous question. Brad had hundreds of cards stacked everywhere in his bedroom, unopened packs lying around the house, or so we believed. But this was to be a trade, so I had to offer.

"You just bring your stack, and make sure it has good stuff in it. I give you the Dryden—I take what I want," he said.

It was a crazy offer, but I squeaked out an "OK." Then I went home to plan my strategy. I knew that I had to show up with something decent. Coming to school Monday with a bunch of "got its" that weren't even worthy of topsies would not only void the trade but also make me the laughingstock of my class. So I planned my attack carefully, putting together a stack of 20 cards. I made it thicker than normal as a way to suggest both the plenty of my resources and my generosity. I stacked some good cards on top, a Johnny Bucyk, a Bobby Orr and a Stan Makita, and then filtered some other great stuff in between some junk. I didn't dare put in a single Maple Leaf. It would have been the death knell.

I spent practically the entire weekend in my bedroom, going over various scenarios in my mind, building and rebuilding my stack, changing its order and composition. Finally, I was happy with what I had. It would be enough to pry Dryden loose from Brad's hands.

On Monday afternoon, the boys in my class departed from the normal after-school routine. Usually, we tried to beat the girls outside so that we could be first on the bus, claiming the strategic seats. This day, we were all at the back of the line, Brad and I standing beside each other like two combatants ready to go to war. When our teacher went back inside, trusting us to the oversight of whoever was on monitor duty that day, we each pulled out our stacks, as if they were pistols and we'd be dueling at 10 paces.

By now, my lust for the Dryden card had blinded me to all sense, and I showed my hand first. It was an honest mistake, born out of my eagerness to get this done. Just to make sure of things, at the last minute, I had shoved a last-year's Jean Beliveau onto the bottom of my stack. My trump card. Now, I showed Brad the good stuff at the top, hoping he'd jump at what was there and that would be it. But he was smarter than that, a better negotiator than I.

"What if I want anything in there?" he asked, pointing to all the cards in my hand. I nodded. "What if I want it all?" he added. My face fell. It was my worst-case scenario. I would not be losing my whole collection, but I'd be giving up my cream-of-the-crop and almost nothing that I didn't have at least some attachment to. But I pressed on.

"Maybe. I have to see the Dryden first," I replied. He hadn't even flashed the prize. How did I know it was even there? "Where did you get it?" I asked, hoping he would reveal the jewel. I held my cards tightly in my hand, close to my body. A scramble right at this moment would ruin everything.

"My dad got it for me. He knew I was going to trade it," Brad said. It was an important point to make. Nobody wanted to have a dad void a trade afterward, and Brad couldn't leave open even the possibility. It would weaken his bargaining position. "What else you got there?" He reached out for my cards, but I pulled them back. "What's on the bottom?" he asked. I groaned. I would have to show my Beliveau. Instead, I fanned the stack, and what appeared in the middle was one of my other tempters—Eddie Giacomin.

Brad was impressed. "OK, OK," he said. I smirked inside to hear it.

The other boys were starting to press in now. They wanted to see Dryden, too. "So?" I asked. I didn't have to say any more. He knew what we all wanted.

"My dad got it off some guy." Was it a stall tactic? "It was his best one," Brad said.

Sure, sure, we all thought.

"Let's see it," some kid intoned. The pressure of our coming bus was starting to weigh on our minds.

"What'll you give me for it?" Brad asked. He started to thumb through the pile of cards in his hand, as if he didn't know where the Dryden was. It was just another play for time.

"These, plus your pick, but not Beliveau," I said. I indicated the good cards on the top of the pile and then let him see the rest, again fanning them out in my hand, including Beliveau, waiting patiently there on the bottom.

"OK, but I might want Beliveau anyway," Brad said. He was going to drive a hard bargain, and I had made the mistake of letting him see the desire dripping off me. I didn't know anything about hard-core trading, and I didn't care. I just wanted that card.

And then he pulled it out, somewhere from the middle of his stack. I wasn't the only one holding his breath. This was the card none of us had seen. It might be the only one we'd ever lay eyes on.

Ken Dryden stood there in his equipment with the red Canadiens sweater on, that skinny-bar mask on his face. He was kind of floating on an orange background. There was no net behind him. The kids around me pressed even closer. We let out our breath in a group gasp as the truth crashed down around us—the card had a huge crease right down the center, as though it had been folded in someone's pocket for days.

It should have been the crowning moment of my card-collecting career, and here I was, face to face with a card I would have rejected out of hand had it been anyone else in the entire NHL. I quickly recalculated the value of the card, my heart sinking into my stomach as I did so—I would have Dryden, but a compromised version, not the perfect holy version I had envisioned, all crisp edges and shiny colors. I wanted to say something about the fold in the card but didn't quite know how. Plus I realized that if I did, everyone would see that I had traded for a card that wasn't, in all reality, worth risking in a game of topsies. But it was a Dryden. The condition was just something I would have to live with.

"OK, but no Canadiens, and no goalies," I stated. That was my only recourse. He could have Makita and Bucyk if he wanted, and the rest too, if it made him feel any better getting 8 or 10 cards for this one. But the crease made the other Habs cards off-limits.

The boys gathered around us looked from me to Brad. He had delivered all right, but not quite like what any of us had expected. Now, he had a choice. Try to get more for the card, which was unlikely, or go for my deal, which everyone knew was pretty fair.

"OK. Deal," he said. He took my stack, sorting out everything but the Habs and Giacomin. When he gave back what was left, he handed over the Dryden. I turned it over in my hand, reading the back. I couldn't believe I had it. As I stashed it safely in my diminished stack, Brad turned to the boys in the group, handing my cards out to them one by one as if to prove that none of this meant anything to him. He was the king of cards, and the very fact that he'd been able to come up with a Dryden had to be respected.

When everyone had a card, he gave the remaining couple to the nearest kid. The best of my collection was now dispersed, and to Brad Chambers this was a triumph. But I didn't care. I would love my Dryden, treasure it and never bring it back to school again. Within a few weeks, I would have that crease down the center mythologized away to a faint line, and nobody would really remember enough to say it was any worse.

chapter sixteen

The Dream
Save

Hockey invaded every corner of our lives as kids. It wasn't just playing on the ice and card collecting but road hockey as well that took up time and gave us a space to fantasize about being one of the great NHLers we saw on TV every Saturday night.

Every kid I knew had a dream save. It didn't matter if you were a goalie or not. Somewhere along the line, you decided what the most glorious goaltending move was, and you practiced it over and over, not just in net, but everywhere.

One spot that worked the best was the smooth vinyl floor of a 1970s kitchen. At least that was true in my house, where every morning, I would run down the stairs in my pajamas, then do a half turn to slide sideways on my sock feet across the floor. While sliding, I would gradually extend my legs into the splits, or as close to them as I could get, then stretch my left arm out as far as I could over my toe as if I was catching the puck in my trapper. I would partly extend my right arm too, as if the imaginary blocker and stick I had there were ready to knock down any rebound that might squirt loose. It was the Canadian version of playing the air guitar, and it amused my dad as much as it did me. My imaginary saves became one of the stories he would tell about me. I think that he mistakenly thought that I was the only kid who did this. No one ever bothered to correct him.

Once, we were in Shrewsbury, Massachusetts, visiting my parents' friends, people who were so close that my sister and I called them uncle and aunt. When we arrived, I was surprised to find out that my three "almost" cousins, all boys slightly older than I, knew about dream saves. I just hadn't expected this from a bunch of Americans.

The first afternoon, my dad looked at their kitchen floor and said, "No dream saves for a few days, eh, Brian?" Their kitchen floor was carpeted.

Like every kid, I hated it when my parents did this kind of thing. I figured the other adults wouldn't understand anyway, but my Uncle Stu jumped in. "You guys can make your dream saves out in the driveway. No hockey in the house." He hadn't understood that my dad was just making nervous conversation. But in saying what he did, he opened an interesting window onto American life for me.

Bruce, Bryan and Perry played hockey? They lived in the U.S., so this didn't make sense to me. Somehow, I had inherited the myth that their whole country was in love with baseball. So when Bryan asked if I wanted to go play hockey, I was shocked. Of course I did! One of my regrets in taking this trip was in missing out on the games that would be played on my block. On my street, every kid was a Montréal Canadien in his imagination. Now here I was, in Boston, and the chance to play would let me show these guys how the greatest team played. It would be like the Stanley Cup playoffs all over again, but instead of beating Chicago, we—in the form of me—would beat the Bruins. Then, I would raise the Cup in victory. "Sure, I'll play. But I get to be Jean Beliveau," I said to Bryan. I doubted he would care, but I called it anyway, just to be sure. It was never this easy on my street.

Bryan and I went to the driveway. Bruce and Perry had gone through the garage ahead and now had a net out, a real, regulation-sized one. I was amazed. The one we played with on my street was the silvery-looking aluminum square model that everyone had back then. It didn't have the rounded back of a real net. This one did. These American boys were rising in my estimation.

Bruce went into the garage once more, to close the door I thought, but came out with his arms full of equipment. Goalie pads. My heart jumped. On my street, no kid had pads of his own, and it would have been unheard of to use the ones a team issued for play on the ice, even if any of us had been a real goalie. Instead, we played with pillows and baseball gloves. I had a goalie stick, a street hockey one, that I used when it was my turn. But here was the whole kit—right down to a regulation blocker and trapper. The trapper even had the holes in it that let you see through to the hard, white plastic piece underneath.

"So, you're a goalie?" I asked with surprise. Bruce had a real mask among the equipment too.

"I'm Gerry Cheevers!" he replied. He was probably just like every other kid in this Boston suburb in his idolatry of the great goalie with all those stitches in his mask, marks of every puck that had ever hit him in the face.

"So what's your dream save?" I asked without thinking. When you're nine, you assume that what you do is pretty much what everyone does. I didn't know whether we had made that term up in my neighborhood or whether it was universal. I had already forgotten the conversation in the kitchen. He looked at me as though it was something that he'd thought about but had never put into words. This surprised me, but I waited for him to answer.

"Are you a goalie?" he asked instead.

"No, not on the ice. Sometimes on the street. But I have a dream save. Everyone does," I stated. I'm sure that I said it with the confidence of a colonizer conquering an unknown land. I was younger than all three of them, and a foreigner. I must have looked like a cocky little man, but they were tolerant.

"Show me," Perry said. All four of us were standing right next to the net now while Bruce suited up. The others nodded in agreement. The game could wait a minute.

I cleared them out of the way, and then for good measure, I grabbed the goalie mitts. Putting them on felt like being a gladiator taking up his spear. They were heavier than I had imagined them to be, and my hands got lost inside them. Bruce was, after all, the oldest of their bunch, at least 15 to my 9. I shrugged the gloves back off. It wouldn't be as glorious if I couldn't lift up my arms properly.

Standing in the net, I scuffed my Adidas across the rough surface of their driveway, approximating the splits I had done every morning for what seemed like years. I got my legs far enough apart to be convincing, and then let my left hand fly up toward an imaginary puck. When my hand was about shoulder high, I made a motion to show that I was snatching a wicked wrist shot right out of thin air, and then pulled it back into my chest. I waited for an instant—as if the referee still hadn't blown his whistle—then hopped up onto two feet again and looked around. They had to be impressed. "That's my dream save," I said. I tried to be big like they were as I said it.

I waited for their reaction. Bryan spoke first. "Hey, let him put on the gear," he said to Bruce.

"Yeah, put all the pads on little Brian," Perry said. It was a diminutive formed of necessity, to distinguish me from "their" Bryan, as the parents sometimes said. Actually, it was the closest I'd ever had to a nickname, and I liked it.

Bruce had by this time strapped on the pads, but he looked at me and asked a question I could never have anticipated. "You want to make that dream save for real?"

I looked up at him, then at all the equipment. "Do I get to wear the pads?" I asked.

He nodded.

"The gloves too?"

"Sure, except why don't you use my baseball mitt. You'll be able to lift it up to make your save better. It's way lighter," he said.

I almost didn't dare to ask the next question. "The mask?" I could see now that he had a mask a lot like the one Cheevers wore, including some stitches painted on it. The chance to wear any regulation mask was something I wouldn't turn down.

"Why not? Here, get these on," he said as he knelt to remove the pads, then put them on me. Even with the straps done up tight, the pads flopped back and forth on my legs. I grabbed the blocker once more, and the stick, then put on his first baseman's glove. Last, Bruce put the mask over my head and cinched the straps. It pressed on my face and obscured my vision, exactly like Jacques Plante's coach had said it would when Plante first asked to wear one in a game. But despite the discomfort, I was ready.

I stood my full height, the regulation-style net behind me, and positioned myself for the first shot. The three boys each took a stick from the garage, and Perry opened a can of old tennis balls and dumped them on the driveway. The balls had once been white but were now basically brown from having gone through a million puddles during games. The fuzz was almost completely off a couple of them. Perry, Bryan and Bruce each took one onto the blade of his stick and backed up to a distance that I suppose to them represented Phil Esposito standing in the slot.

These guys were all older than I was. If they had wanted to, they could have pounded and pulverized me with the tennis balls. But that wasn't the idea. Instead, over and over they took turns, each one gently lifting a tennis ball toward my outstretched glove. Time and time again I dropped into my fake splits and shot my glove up, grabbing the ball in the nick of time before it went into the net. I felt like a hero. Each time the ball plunked into my mitt, one of them would yell out "Dream save!" I would stand there a minute in the pose, and then struggle back to my feet, the pads weighing me down. I may have looked like Gerry Cheevers on the outside, but in my heart I was Ken Dryden, suited up to play the Bruins for the Stanley Cup, and those dream saves were the key ingredients to a shutout.

That day in Boston, three American boys turned me into a goalie and gave me my first clue that the love of hockey wasn't just confined to my neighborhood, or my country.

chapter seventeen

Goalie Pads and a Grown-Up Job

Almost every time we were at the arena for one of my games, my dad and I would stop by the pro shop. Sometimes we bought a roll of tape, the proper white kind that let the puck leave a mark on the blade of your stick each time you touched it. Often, we stopped at the pro shop to get my skates sharpened.

Each visit was like a trip to a wonderland, because even though the shop was tiny, it was stocked to the ceiling with equipment. Roch, the guy who ran it, always seemed to have something new to tempt my imagination. I think my dad enjoyed looking at the goodies as much as I did.

Sticks with even more glorious curves than what I had were always the first thing I looked at. But one day, as soon as we were through the door, my eyes were drawn to something I knew right then I had to have. Hanging from the beams just

over my dad's head was a pair of goalie pads. They were unlike
any pair of pads I'd ever seen: black vinyl with canvas bolsters
on the sides, and a rough canvas bottom near where your feet
would be. Every goalie I knew, from the kid who played for
my team to Ken Dryden, the greatest goalie ever to play
between the pipes, wore leather pads. I couldn't help asking
why this pair was different.

"Street 'ockey," Roch answered in his French-Canadian
accent. "Extra tough at de bottom, so dey don't ruin on de
street." As he said it, I saw a window of opportunity open.

I had been a street hockey goalie for a while now. This
wasn't the only position I played, and it wasn't that I had been
stuck in there because I was either the youngest kid and therefore a sucker, or the fat kid who was too slow to be any good
playing another position. I was in net because I had been the
one to invent a crude set of pads out of some seat cushions
from my mom's car.

Even though my mom drove an Austin Mini, the
smallest car you could get in Canada, maybe in the world, she
still had trouble seeing out the windshield. My dad was always
trying to find ways to make it easier for her to see, so that she
could drive better. Her driving skills never improved, but the
result was a constantly growing pile of pillows in our garage,
discarded whenever Dad found something more comfy for
her to try. So, at one point, I grabbed a set of red vinyl cushions with yellow foam in the middle, about two inches thick.

Every player born before about 1950 has a story about playing hockey on some pond in the Maritimes or on the Prairies, wearing a pair of shin pads made from the Eaton's catalog. No one I knew ever had to do this. At least, not the forwards and defensemen. But you might say that my red pads were my generation's equivalent of the catalog; although homemade, they served their purpose. I used the same elastics that were used to hold shin pads on, on the ice, and my red pads reached from about my ankles to just over the top of my kneecaps. Having them on not only made it possible for me to go down, therefore increasing my repertoire of saves immensely, but also allowed me to feel more like a regular goalie—with my baseball glove, street hockey goalie stick and old leather glove of my dad's on my right hand in a crude imitation of a blocker.

My homemade pads were great, but while I stood in the pro shop I sensed that having these, the ones hanging up here, would change everything. I would be able to fill the net like no other kid on my block. And they would look official. I would be unstoppable, closer to becoming Dryden than I had ever imagined possible before—except maybe when I had put on my cousin Bruce's pads and played "dream save" in his driveway. I nudged my dad, pointing to them, but he had already seen them, and my fascination with them.

The only problem was the price: $24. That was about a year of allowances at my rate of 50 cents a week. I had a few dollars saved in a green strong box, but I was nowhere close to that amount of cash. There was no way my dad would lend me that much money, either. My mind revolved a mile a minute as we waited for Roch to finish my sharpening job. I had to have a plan to get those pads.

"Could I work for them?" I asked my dad.

My dad had a small business that he ran out of our home, and one of his product lines was woven bookmarks that he imported from a place in Philadelphia. For a while, I had been poking around in the basement when he was picking orders from numbered cardboard bins. I helped him to secure the boxes of bookmarks in preparation for shipment. Sometimes, he let me pull orders on my own, then he checked them to make sure I got everything right. Certain bookmarks, the ones that didn't sell so well, he kept on the highest shelf, and I'd have to ask him to get those for me. All in all, I was as much trouble as help in these endeavors.

But now, I saw a way. I would be the chief order puller. My dad could put all the bookmarks down at a level where I could reach them, and after school, before he got home from his sales calls, I could pick orders. They'd all be in boxes, waiting for him to fill out the invoices and finish the packing when he got home. With a system like this, we could work twice as fast as normal. We'd sell so many bookmarks we'd get rich, and it would all be thanks to these beautiful black goalie pads. I had always been something of a schemer, but this plan made sense. It was no con.

I nervously floated the idea to him. His reaction was more hopeful than what I thought it would be. Instead of saying no outright, he looked at me and said, "How much do you think you should get paid an hour?"

I hadn't thought about it, but I quickly blurted out a number. Half my weekly allowance seemed like a fortune, but I said it, "Twenty-five cents." My wages plus the cash I already had saved plus my allowance filling in the gaps would get me those goalie pads in a matter of weeks.

A short time later, as we walked down the hall to my team's dressing room, my dad mulled over the venture. "OK, we'll try it," he said. "When you get halfway to the pads, I'll lend you the rest, but you have to keep working once you get them. You can't just go out and play street hockey all day." I didn't pay any attention to the last part of his sentence. I was already calculating how different my life would be as an official street hockey goalie.

My excitement didn't last long, however. My dad refocused my attention on my game as we got to my team's dressing room. "You're here to play hockey," he said. "Forget those pads for now. We'll talk about it when we get home." Talking about something when you got home normally meant big trouble for a kid, but this time, the words sounded good to me. I grabbed my skates from Dad and headed in to get ready for my game, secure in the knowledge that life on my block was about to change forever.

chapter eighteen

Are You
Ken Dryden?

F or weeks, I worked for my dad at the rate of 25 cents an hour so that I could reimburse him for the pair of black street hockey goalie pads that had captivated my imagination since I had seen them at the pro shop. Each week, I got a pay envelope, and a day or two later, my dad would give me my allowance. I took whatever I felt I could spare from these two revenue sources, leaving some money for necessities like hockey cards of course, and paid down my debt. We kept track of it on a piece of paper that Dad kept in his dresser drawer. Toward the end of the agreement, he pulled what I now see was his plan all along.

It was a Sunday, allowance day. He gave me my two quarters and sent me on my way. I went to my room, opened my green strong box and counted what was there. Then I took a dollar to his room. When I got there, he had the account sheet out, and as

I gave him the dollar, he took out the Cross pen he always had in his dress shirt pocket and drew a big line across the paper. "Paid in Full," he wrote. The pads were mine, free and clear.

Having them was glorious. I became the king of our street hockey games, at least for a while. We'd all seen "real" goalie pads in our league, of course. But the idea of having pads for the street was beyond our collective imaginations, until I made it happen.

Naturally, everyone wanted to give them a try, and I let them, but just once. After that, they were mine to wear. I was going to keep them perfect forever, and I didn't want anyone else carelessly throwing himself to the ground and scratching up my prize. For my part, I would carefully kick any rocks away from the crease area before I played, even if we were just taking shots on net.

But if I was the king of my street, some of our circle were not so content. Maybe it was because they didn't play in a league, a mark against them as far as all the rest of us were concerned, but Frank and Billy Cameron were insanely jealous of me and my pads. And as soon as the furor of excitement died down, and the Cameron brothers had had their try with them like all the other kids, they started in on me.

"You're a regulation goalie with your regulation pads," they chimed as they came in on net when we practiced penalty shots. "He thinks he's Ken Dryden," one of them would say to whoever happened to show up to our game. "Ken Dryden, number twenty-nine. Are you Ken Dryden?" When they ran out of things to say, they'd go back to the first. "A regulation goalie with his regulation pads."

As a matter of fact, with my new pads on, and using a trademark stand-up style, I was a pretty convincing street hockey version of my idol. Where before I had been good in goal, now I was almost unconquerable. The net we played with was an aluminum affair, by no means regulation size. With my pads, I filled a good portion of that net, and with a little side-to-side movement, it was pretty hard to get a tennis ball by me. This was partly due to my great catching hand, which in my one summer of baseball, played around the same age, was the only thing that kept me out of the lowest level of the league.

Now I flashed that mitt whenever I needed to make a truly spectacular save. Otherwise, I could pretty much just stay in position and kick out one leg or the other in classic Dryden style and be nearly invincible. The problem was, as I got better, the Camerons got meaner. It all came to a head a few weeks later.

"Shoot high, shoot high!" I heard the words one morning just after we started playing. The forwards—that is, everyone but me, the lone goalie on our street at that moment—were all huddled about 15 feet from my net, ready to start their breakaways. The routine was pretty familiar to me by now. I'd be able to stop most of the one-on-ones. When we later played a regular game, my team would win despite the handicap of having to keep their shots on goal on the ground, a rule we enforced because there was no goalie in the other net. I, meanwhile, kept them in the game. Apparently, this had reached the point of frustration for some kids, and so they had a brand new plan.

The first guy came in on me, tennis ball held out in front of him on his forehand. I saw a deke coming, so I started to shift for it. Sure enough, he went to his backhand, but instead of putting one into my pads, he followed through high, throwing the shot up into my chest. I flinched but kept my position, and the ball fell in front of me. I flopped on it to end the play.

The next kid came in on me and did the same thing, only his backhand sailed past me and over the net. I had been out of position, and he would have scored except that he couldn't control the shot. We were all at that point in our hockey careers when we had learned to lift the tennis ball and could even get pretty decent momentum on our slapshots. Wrist shots, too, would rise on command at times, but they were wobbly affairs, and like the slapshots, never quite hit the target we intended them to.

Next up was Frank Cameron. He wasn't a great player, being one of the few kids on our street who had no experience on a league team, but he was just enough older than I was to be a little frightening. The kids he hung around with at school were noticeably bigger than our group here on the street.

Except for Frank, the kids we played hockey with on the Camerons' deadend street were my age or younger.

Frank started toward me, then about 10 feet out he stopped, teed up the ball and slapped it as hard as he could. The shot went wide by five feet, but it wasn't on the ground, either. By this point, I was starting to feel a slight creep of panic.

"Hey, you guys, no fair," I pleaded. "No fair always shooting high." It was directed more or less at Frank, but my gaze took them all in, including the four or five kids waiting their turn behind him.

"What's the matter, Ken Dryden? Your pads no good anymore?" Frank asked. His sneering face made the question more frightening than it should have been. It was more like a promise to keep the ball sailing up near my head.

I replied to his taunt in my head. *What a stupid question. Of course my pads are good. They're great!* They had changed everything on this street, and all of us knew it. But what could I say, especially to Frank Cameron? I wanted to know what was going on, though.

"Why are you guys shooting high on me? It'll just go over the net," I said, trying to put a spin of logic on the thing. No sense sounding scared.

"You're a chicken!" Frank yelled. Of course, he had jumped to the very conclusion I least wanted him to. "You're no Ken Dryden." He turned to the others and said, "He's no Ken Dryden.

It's just like my dad said. When we shoot high, he cries." He stood there with his stick in his hands, looking back at the group, including his younger brother, with scorn on his face.

This was getting bad, fast. Accusing a guy of crying, especially when he hadn't, was an insult amounting to a knife in the heart. But in trying to hurt me, he had given away a crucial fact, and I jumped on it.

"What's your dad got to do with this?" I asked. As I said it, I could see by his face that he knew he'd made a mistake. I had taken all the air out of his challenge by showing everyone that he'd gone home and talked to his daddy because he couldn't score on me.

He knew he'd blown it, so instead of escalating his accusations of my fear, he turned to logic. "We can't score. We can't score on those pads," he said. No sense giving me any credit for being decent in net. "So my dad said to shoot high. He said to get you thinking about that. Then we'll be able to shoot low again and score."

Mr. Cameron was Mr. Logic, an engineer who diligently tuned a 1961 Plymouth Valiant in his driveway, keeping it running long after my family had traded up to a 1967 Ford Country Squire. He probably didn't know much about the game—like I said, his sons didn't play on the ice—but he had figured out how to defeat me. Standing there in net, I knew that the glorious moment that the pads had given me was over, unless I could think of something, fast.

"Will not. Try it," I said. Feigning bravado was my only choice. I hoped that by challenging them, I could call their bluff. For one thing, I knew that they couldn't get their shots to go where they wanted to consistently. The last few minutes had proved that. But I also knew that Frank was right. I'd be able to stand in for a couple of shots, but pretty soon, my fear of getting one in the face would have me flinching every time anyone shot a ball that wasn't right on the road. I wouldn't be able to stop anything reliably.

I felt as though I was at the edge of a cliff, looking over into the canyon below. At the bottom were the goalie pads, thrown there in frustration that my moment of triumph had ended. There was only one conclusion I could draw, assuming I got through today's game alive. If I wanted to keep being Ken Dryden, I needed a goalie mask. I didn't know whether Roch at the pro shop had something that would do the trick, and I had no idea where the money would come from since I had just paid off the pads. But without a mask, the pads weren't going to be much good anymore, and then it all would have been a waste. I returned to the game, but with half my mind on my next scheme—the plot to get a mask.

chapter nineteen

The Last Goalie
with a Human Face

Everyone knows that Jacques Plante is credited for having invented the goalie mask. The story goes that he was playing around with the idea, and using a mask in practice, when he got creamed one night in a game. Photos show him with his nose all taped up, and the reports say that his schnoz was practically ripped off by a shot. Hockey being what it is, his coach told him to get back out on the ice once he was stitched up. How crazy is that?

It's not totally nuts, especially when the game is on the line and there's no backup goaltender. Back then, the roster didn't include one, so the guy in net was it. In the rare case that he was too hurt to play, they'd suit up a replacement if someone in the crowd was a minor-league player. If nobody could be found, then someone like the equipment manager had to go in. Kind of makes you glad you're not carrying the bags for a living, or weren't back in the black-and-white days of hockey on TV.

Anyway, on the day of his injury, Plante agreed to go back between the pipes, but only if he could wear his prototype mask. The coach said it would obscure his vision, but reason prevailed. I mean, what could possibly bother a guy more than having his nose taped back on? So on went the mask, and back to the net went Plante. But in those days, the mask wasn't a helmet or a cage like you see now. It was a curved piece of fiberglass that sat directly on the skin. Ouch. That mask would press right onto Plante's damaged flesh and fresh stitches. But better that than another puck to the wound.

Following Plante's example, other goalies started to don the protection, and soon afterward not many were left without a mask. As we all know, this changed the game, making it possible for netminders to do things that previously were impossible, if "saving face" was the goal.

When I came to the game in around 1970, Plante's exploits were a thing of history, and all the goalies wore masks, except for one—Gump Worsley—and for that reason, he became an oddball hero to me and the boys I knew.

Gump played barefaced for a decade or more after Plante changed the literal face of the game. It was what made him famous for kids of my generation and gave his Minnesota North Stars the added attraction that maybe sold a few more tickets. I watched him play on TV, sometime around 1972, with his pudgy face showing every expression, and his mouth opening and closing to yell instructions to his players. He represented a past that I knew only from the hockey books that I had started to collect at a young age. At school, my friends and I talked about him, even though we hated his team, or more accurately, didn't care in the least what they were doing and didn't even have much of an idea where they played. None of us remembered that Gump had played for our Canadiens until early in 1970.

Part of our fascination was that he wasn't known by his name, "Lorne," but by his nickname. "Gump" just sounds like something that a tough old guy would be called. Someone who does things his own way. Someone who would rather stand right in front of the shooter and grimace when the slapshot winged toward him than present to the world a face obscured behind plastic. The reason often cited for his not wearing a mask, of course, is the same one Plante's coach tried to use. Masks obscure vision. You can't stop what you don't see. Other rationale included accusations of being frightened. But in our discussions about Worsley, we didn't care about that. We just liked to talk about the goalie without the mask, and we usually prefaced the conversation the same way every time: "He goes by 'Gump,' but his real name is 'Lorne.'" It was doubly weird because we didn't know any kid with that name, or any other adult, either.

We theorized that Gump played without the mask because of his vision. But there may have been more to it than that. Maybe he was playing an intricate and calculated game of chicken. Everything you read about hockey in the old days says that the players were driven by reckless abandon. Teeth knocked out? No problem. Play without them. Ankle broken? OK, we'll freeze it. I guess you still see that a lot today, especially in the playoffs, but the idea of facing the shooter with your face bare seems a different order altogether. It's more like being a boxer than a hockey player. You put your mug out there almost daring people to hit it.

Maybe it's just me, and maybe this is just another of the million reasons why I'm not a professional hockey player, or even a very good amateur one, but if all the goalies in the league wore masks, and one day I found myself bearing down on one who looked me in the eye and sneered, daring me to shoot high at his exposed face, I think I'd go for the deke instead. Maybe the Gumpster had a plan more sinister than just being out of step with the times.

Whatever the case, he stood out in the minds of the boys in my school for another reason. The masks of Worsley's day were white plastic things that covered the face entirely, rendering it impossible to see the goalie's expression. He became almost a robot. Take, for example, Gilles Meloche, who played for a collection of teams including Chicago, California, Cleveland, Minnesota and Pittsburgh from 1970 to 1988. His mask didn't sit flat on his face but was more like a bowl that reached almost back to his ears, leaving only small black holes for the eyes and nose, and a little round one for the mouth. His mask made him look like some kind of alien staring out from the crease. A personality may have been there, but it wasn't human. So when the guys and I talked about Meloche in my school, it was with a kind of strangeness, as if we were discussing an automaton.

Gump Worsley, however, looked out over the game with eyes open, hair slicked over in '60s style, and a mouth that could open to breathe, cheer, or, we imagined, to scream. He was real. He was a person, a man. Vulnerable in a way that seems nuts today, but a goalie with a human face. We felt somehow that we knew him.

Maybe it was the same for the players who faced him back then. Maybe in the opposing team's room, the players marveled at the guts or nuts of the guy they were about to play. Maybe they wondered whether they'd have the nerve to shoot high on him. Maybe in the moment out on the ice when it was time to pull the trigger, Gump got a flash of hesitation to go through the shooter's mind when he squared to—very literally—face him. I bet he did, though as kids in elementary school, we were never quite able to put that kind of a theory into words. We just knew that we were lucky to see him play, because after him, there wouldn't be another.

Oh, and what finally drove Gump from the game? It wasn't the fabled Bobby Hull slapshot or the change in velocity of the shots from the newly invented curved sticks. It was airline travel. The goalie who could stare down a shooter and dare him to wing the rubber right between his eyes hated to get on a plane, and with the expansion of the league outside of the little geographical triangle of the original six teams, airplanes became a part of life in hockey. Gump was the John Madden of his day, but unlike the football commentator, who has a week between games to ride his luxury coach to his next assignment, it was impossible to wheel it from Oakland or L.A. to Minnesota for games a day apart.

Of course, we didn't know any of this. We did, however, feel a kind of funny absence in the fall of 1974, the first fall that Gump was no longer in net. And our hockey card collections were somewhat the poorer for not having him as a part of them. But we still talked about him, though now we started the conversation with a question. "Do you remember the last goalie to play without a mask?" Actually, we were wrong, because a guy named Andy Brown came along in the 1971–72 season and played a handful of games for Detroit barefaced. He bounced back and forth between the NHL and the minor leagues for a couple of years, ending his NHL career in 1973–74 with Pittsburgh, still with no mask. The irony is that in that same season, his last, Worsley put on a mask for the first time. But we didn't care. When we talked about Gump, it was as if we had ancient history at our fingertips, and all these years later, with goalies padded up like the Michelin Man, it seems that maybe we were right.

chapter twenty

Gump Worsley's Last Stand

Whenever I wanted something but was told I couldn't have it, I did what my mom called "building a case for it." For example, one spring, I wanted a new pair of rubber boots but was told that they weren't in the budget. My response was to wait a couple of days, all the while asking over and over again for the boots. Then I went outside in my running shoes and jumped through a bunch of puddles. When I came back in after playing, I was soaked through to my socks, but I didn't say anything. The next time my mom and I were at Miracle Mart, however, I subtly reminded her of my wet feet, right when we were passing by the rubber boots, on sale. I got my boots. I may have been a spoiled kid, but I prefer to think of myself as having been crafty, able to devise a plan of attack that was a combination of propaganda campaign and visual demonstration.

It was this skill that I planned to draw on to get the goalie mask I desperately needed to salvage my street hockey career. I couldn't wait to save up for the mask, even though I continued working for my dad for a quarter an hour. My time horizon was probably a couple of weeks, max, before my days as a street hockey goalie were over, ruined by the wild slapshots and backhanders of Frank Cameron. Then what would I do with my pads? It would be a crushing end to a beautiful moment in my hockey life. So I was determined to find a way, and before long, I had it. An injury. If I got hurt playing goalie, my parents would have to find a way to help me.

I went to school the next day and tried out my scheme on a couple of friends. We were standing around at recess, and I said to them, "Hey, I got hit in the face playing goalie yesterday." It sounded glamorous coming out of my mouth, like I was relaying the story of a great battle in World War I or talking about Terry Sawchuck, a goalie who played in the NHL both before and after the mask was in common use. The guys I was talking to, Tracy and Jimmy, looked at me, puzzled. They both knew I didn't play in goal for my team in the LNDB league.

"But I thought you played right wing," Tracy said. He wasn't even on a team, but everyone knew what position a kid played, whether you were in his league or not.

"I do, but I'm talking about street hockey," I replied. Their faces changed, reflecting their boredom. They didn't say it, but they might as well have. *So what? Street hockey is street hockey. Injuries there don't count.* Now, get hurt on the ice and need a cast or something, and you'd be a hero. A broken leg or arm would be glorious. Your reputation for that entire school year was set.

So I had my reaction—my first strategy wasn't going to work. I had to switch tactics. I went home that night with a new plan. It was a desperate long shot, but it was my only hope.

That night around the supper table, I started by saying how great things were going with my goalie pads, but that playing in net was dangerous. I hadn't realized it when I'd gotten the pads, but I was putting myself at great risk by letting anyone and everyone on the street take shots on me. "I could get a black eye if one of them got a shot high enough," I said, looking at my mom to gauge the effect. "And Frank Cameron is almost good enough to do that," I added.

Still, her face didn't show much more than a casual interest. So I went for the zinger. "He said that some of his friends might come over and play with us after school one day soon. The big boys." Letting her have it with the threat of a big kid, and an unknown one at that, who could hurt me was the scariest thing I could think of to do. "The only way to protect myself is to wear a goalie mask," I concluded.

My dad thought that he saw through me. "You just want to look like Ken Dryden." He was right that I would do anything to get closer to my idol, but really, I was more scared at this moment than living in some street hockey fantasyland.

I abandoned my campaign of deception and decided just to let out the secret of my fear.

"Frank tried to hit me in the face. On purpose. He shot a backhand that would've bonked me right on the nose if it hadn't gone wide," I blurted. I didn't bother to mention that the shot had been about a million miles wide—the next one might very well hit me right in the head. The tone of panic creeping into my words wasn't faked.

My parents looked at me. They understood the forces of a neighborhood and the constant threat that kids older than you represent. Plus, I think that they had a vague suspicion that the Cameron boys were just a little bit antisocial, like their parents. But their imagination on how to handle such a problem had lost something in the years since they'd grown up. "Well, just don't play with Frank Cameron," said my mom. A brilliant idea.

"Oh, sure," I replied. *Tell a kid older than you that he can't play. Fat chance.* But I put my thoughts in language she would understand. "Then Billy won't be able to play. Then we won't be able to use their net." The net was the key to the authenticity of our games, and I was telling them the truth. If we didn't have that net, playing out there wouldn't be the same; I mean, how was I going to look wearing regulation pads and standing between a pair of old shoes or bricks or something? My moment as a street hockey hero would be ruined.

Maybe it was the look on my face that convinced them, or maybe it was that I'd worked so hard to get my pads in the first place.

"Where would you get a mask, anyway?" my mom asked. Her question betrayed her sympathy and put me one step closer to my goal.

I blurted out my prepared answer. "Roch. I'm sure he has some masks." I hadn't been in the pro shop very many times of late. On game days, the lineup for skate sharpening was so long that my dad waited in it while I went directly to my dressing room to change, so I hadn't had a glimpse of the pro shop's newest goodies. But I was certain that my friend would not let me down. He always had a stash of amazing and tantalizing things in that tiny place.

"And who's going to buy it?" my dad said.

"Maybe Gran?" I said, my voice rising in question mode. "I was going to ask for an early birthday present?" Desperation showed in my tone.

My birthday wasn't for weeks, but I thought that if I approached it right, my dad would see that it was better for Gran to buy me something I wanted than something I needed— in the grown-up sense of "need." She was generally the one to give me and my sister things like a winter coat or new clothes to wear to church. We appreciated these gifts, but what kid wouldn't rather have a toy, or a goalie mask, as a birthday gift?

"We'll look next time we go for a game. You're playing on Friday," my dad said. *It had worked!* His words confirmed that he would work the birthday present details out with my grandmother. I couldn't quite believe my ears, but I didn't dare to ask for more particulars. As a kid, you just have an instinct about when you've said enough. Saying one word more at that point puts the entire plan into question.

I was going to have my mask, and all I had to do in the meantime was survive a couple more days in net, barefaced. I would have to hope that Frank wasn't around when we played. Or else I could pretend I was Gump Worsley, bravely playing without a mask while, all around him, NHL goalies covered their faces.

chapter twenty-one

Joining the Brotherhood of Goalies

I t was Friday, and I had all my teeth and no nasty bruises to show for my goaltending duties during the week. Of course, I didn't dare point out my healthy condition to my dad, since I had no intention of letting him have a moment of regret for promising to get me a goalie mask. My whole week had focused on my hope that Roch from the pro shop had a mask that would suit me, and the days couldn't go fast enough. Finally Dad and I were at the arena once again for my game.

In we went, Dad carrying my stick and me lugging my hockey bag. As I walked into the pro shop, I noticed that there was another pair of pads hanging from the same rafter mine had hung from some weeks earlier. I was surprised. I guess like every kid, I thought that mine were it, the only ones, not one of a run of who knows how many, each waiting for a kid like me with a big dream of street hockey glory and an accommodating dad to help make it happen.

"Hey, Roch," I said. He was one of the only adults I got to call by his first name in that more polite era. "Got any goalie masks? I mean, something good for the street?"

Secretly, I hoped that he would have an exact replica of Ken Dryden's mask. It would be just like in the picture I liked the most from my Dryden book—a close-up of his face that showed the tiny V-shaped fiberglass cross pieces and the holes for his eyes and mouth. But I knew that wasn't possible. There was no other mask like that in the world, no matter how much money a person might have.

Roch pointed to the counter next to the skate sharpener. There under the glass, along with the laces and tape, and tiny replica skates that you put on your jacket zipper to pull it up and down, were the masks. There were four or five of them, each a version of the flat, white plastic style worn by nearly every goalie in the NHL in those days. But he only brought one out and set it on top.

"Dis one fit you best," he commented. "Not like dis one." He pulled another mask out and put it on the counter beside the first. Ignoring the one Roch liked more, I held the second one up to my face. With my dad standing beside me, I was kind of afraid to try the one Roch recommended. If it didn't fit, I was sunk.

The second one must have been for an adult, because as I held it in front of my face, I had the choice of either seeing through the eyeholes or breathing through the mouth hole. I couldn't do both at once. I set it down and grabbed the other one. I held it to my face, tentatively, and discovered that it conformed to the curve of my cheeks and jaw and didn't stick up high above my forehead or hang down below my chin.

"You like de pads?" Roch asked, recalling my earlier purchase. "Dey make you unbeatable on your street?" He understood the eternal rhythms of road hockey. Wherever he lived, the game probably went on exactly the same way it did on the street just north of my house, where I played. I nodded my assent, still holding the mask in front of me.

I tried the mask again. "This one, like Roch says," I told my dad.

"Try it on all the way, with no hands," he said. I'm sure he was as curious as I was to see what it would look like on me.

I held the mask out to him so that he could loosen the elastic straps. It apparently hadn't been out of the case before, because the straps were all cinched up tight so the mask would lie flat on the shelf.

My dad got the straps loosened, and I pulled them out with my right hand as I grabbed through the eyeholes with my left, just like I'd seen NHL goalies do on TV. I raised my arms over my head and put the mask onto my face. Quickly, I darted my eyes right and left. *Wow. How did goalies see anything out of these things?* I had a moment of understanding for Gump Worsley and his barefaced style of playing net.

I felt that I should crouch into my goaltending stance to get a really good idea of what the mask allowed me to see, but I was too embarrassed to do it with my dad and Roch looking on, so I bent slightly at the knees and tipped my head down while I again tried out the vision. It wasn't perfect, but I was so excited at the prospect of having an official goalie mask that I didn't dare say anything. If I gave the slightest hint of a doubt, the moment to get my mask would be lost. I could already tell that my dad was anxious to get down the hallway to my dressing room so I could suit up for my game. I said just one word: "Perfect."

My dad nodded to Roch. "I'll come back when he's changing. Put it away for me until then?" I would rather he just paid for it right away, so it didn't get sold to someone else. But adults had a way of handling these things that kids learn not to get in the middle of.

As we left the pro shop, my dad walked beside me, my stick still in his hand. Normally, Dad would take this opportunity to talk to me about the game and my position at right wing. He hadn't played organized hockey himself, but he wanted me to get the most out of my games. I didn't have to be a star to satisfy him, but I did have to show that I was learning. On this day, though, I did all the talking.

As we walked through the arena area where two older teams were playing, I gave him a detailed analysis of each goalie's style, reciting everything I'd ever heard on *Hockey Night in Canada* about the difference between the butterfly, modeled of course by Tony Esposito, and the stand-up style of Ken Dryden. In my mind, it was as if I were watching those two compete, instead of a couple of 13- or 14-year-old kids.

My analysis was flawless, my understanding of their technique complete. I spoke a mile a minute while my dad feigned interest in what I was saying. He let me go on, driven by my excitement at having come one step closer to being just like these goalies and everyone who ever played the position through possession of the mask. I felt like I had joined an exclusive fraternity, even if nobody else had any idea what had happened except me, my dad and Roch. But my secret would be public before long, because the next morning, it would be Saturday, and I would make my official debut with the mask on my street as soon as I could round up enough guys to have a game.

chapter twenty-two

Giving Tony Esposito
His Due

On Saturday, I went outside with a sense of barely contained glee. It was still early, but it was more important than ever that I rustle up some guys to play road hockey. I rang the usual doorbells, and pretty soon had a few players, including the Camerons and their net. Once we got going, other guys would show up to play, like they always did. With the crowd gathered, I left them warming up and went to get my pads. At least that's what they thought. When I returned, I was holding my gloves and my stick all in my left arm, and my pads were held in my right hand by the straps. Tucked under my right arm was my brand new goalie mask.

I wasn't the kind of kid who did a lot of bragging. Some guys would seize a moment like this to make a grand entrance. For example, when a kid got a new bike, he would wait until he knew we'd all be gathered in a group on the sidewalk, as we were every morning of the summer. Then he'd come zooming around the corner, streamers flying from the handlebar grips, and skid to a stop in front of us. It was his moment. Me, I'd be subtle about it, cruising from my house as if I'd had the bike a thousand years. There was always an awkward moment before the other kids would realize that they could say something. Then they surrounded you and asked a million questions. That was my strategy for the introduction of the mask. I was going to casually slip it on and take my place in net for the warm-up shots. We'd see then what everyone would say, especially the Camerons.

As I knelt on the Camerons' front lawn to strap on the pads, I laid the mask down in the grass. Nobody paid me any attention. I got the straps done up like I wanted and picked up the gloves. Putting them on, I realized that I had to have my hands free for the mask, and so I reversed the procedure. Laying them back down alongside my stick, I picked up the mask, my back to the street, and stretched it over my head. I was too nervous to adjust it to fit, but the night prior I'd had it on and off enough to have it pretty close. After making sure I had the maximum view out the eyeholes, I grabbed my gloves and stick, then turned around and marched toward my place in net, a gladiator entering the Roman Forum.

On the street, Frank Cameron was in the middle of winding up for a slapshot. His stick stopped in mid-air. I could see on his face a combination of horror and surprise.

"Stupid-Idiot-Damn-Sh**," he said. It was our street's special made-up swear word, one we saved for the most dire occasions. The other boys just stared at me.

I stuck to business as usual, taking my spot in the net and kicking aside the gravel that would nick up my pads, then giving the area in what was my goal crease a sweep with my stick. I positioned myself between the aluminum pipes and set my feet. I stretched my arms out into their ready position and faced the shooters. They looked smaller than usual, and far away, through the eyeholes of the mask. I panicked for just a second but kept cool. Luckily, no one could see the expression on my face. This mask was good for more than protection.

"Come on, what're you waiting for?" I said to Frank. "Shoot the thing." He resumed his wind-up and let fly. The ball came off his stick straight, for once, and I squeezed my pads together in classic stand-up style. It thumped off the spot that would have been what hockey commentators call the "five hole," had I not closed it. My first save. I looked down for the rebound and realized that I had to adjust the angle of my head to see the ball at my feet. I could get used to the mask, but it wasn't going to be entirely natural.

I turned toward the next shooter, but nobody else had the mustard on his shot that Frank did, being a year older than the rest of us. This was going to be easy. Their shots gave me a chance to get used to the head position I needed in order to deal with rebounds. By the time Frank's turn came around again, I had a pretty good feel for the mask. I wondered if Ken Dryden had had a similar period of adjustment when he had started to play goal.

A couple more guys joined us, and each had something to say about the mask. Everyone wanted to try it, naturally, but I said no. The straps were adjusted to fit me, and I didn't want them stretching them out. They did talk me into taking it off though, and then each guy held it in front of his face and looked through the eyeholes. Everyone agreed that it was harder to see than they'd imagined. I didn't let on that I had doubts of my own. No sense making Frank or any other shooter more confident. Plus, I already felt more used to it than I had been just a few minutes before.

The game started, and I was stopping most everything. That wasn't much different from before, but with my face protected, I wasn't restricted to playing stand-up like my idol, Ken Dryden. I could go down, too, in the flopping style of his 1971 Stanley Cup finals opponent, Chicago's Tony Esposito. I was caught up in the greatest controversy of the day, trying to decide which style was better, but I opted for a bit of both, going down when the shots came in close, standing up for ones from the imaginary blue line. Even Frank was amazed at what the mask did for me, but he wouldn't let me have the satisfaction of saying so. Instead, he turned on me and tried to rally the others to his cause, a primitive version of a strike to get me to take the mask off in hopes that I would be beatable once again. And he posed it in the language we all used on the street.

"We have to go in now," he claimed, though it was barely 11:00 AM, and his mom hadn't called him and Billy for lunch.

Normally, when they had to go eat, whoever was left was allowed to keep playing with their net, on the agreement that the last kid to leave had to put it beside the porch in front of their house. Usually, if the Camerons were called in first, they'd be the first out again, so the game would just continue as players came and went. Eventually, we'd all be back for the afternoon. But now, he changed the routine.

"We're taking the net," Frank declared. "And nobody can use it again until Brian stops bringing his junk over to play." We all looked at him in surprise. *My junk?*

"Aw, come on," some kid protested with a wail. Others joined in. Losing the net would ruin everything. We'd be back to playing with shoes as our goalposts, and it wouldn't be anything like being on *Hockey Night in Canada,* which was the fantasy that fueled our passion for these road games. Whether Frank realized it or not, his net and my equipment made the whole situation on our street seem much more like NHL hockey than it would have without a real goaltender. The only thing better would have been a regulation-style net like my cousins in Boston had. Someone tried an appeal to Billy, but as the younger brother, he kept mute.

"I'm sick of him wearing all that junk." Frank said the word again. I stood there, still in my mask, trying to muster an answer. I had gone from being an unbeatable Dryden–Esposito super hybrid to being the reason for the end of our street hockey games, all in a flash of Frank Cameron's cruelty, and I had no idea what to do. Hockey cards, the usual answer to trouble between kids in my world, would do no good. Frank and his brother were two of the only kids I knew who had no collection whatsoever, so the idea that flashed through my mind, a bribe-trade kind of deal, was out of the question.

I could try to marshal the group to my side, suggesting that we play on the street one over, also a dead end, but none of us lived there, and there was a strict territoriality about such things. So it came down to a choice. My mask, or the net. Everything depended on me. Then I had an idea.

"Hey, why don't you play goalie for a while," I said, pointing to Frank. He hadn't tried the mask with everyone else, but I knew he wanted to. He just hadn't wanted to lower himself to do what all of the younger kids had done. I also knew one other thing: whether or not a kid was crazy about being a goalie, every guy had fantasies about becoming Ken Dryden or Eddie Giacomin or Rogie Vachon. But Frank wasn't going to let me, a younger kid, see that he was jealous because the mask put me so much closer to being like an NHL goalie.

"We'll take shots on you, and if we can score, you let me keep playing, plus we use the net," I suggested. It was a crazy gamble, way outside my usual low-confrontation way of doing things, but I had to protect my dream.

I was smart enough to know that Frank had a natural assumption of his superiority as the older kid on the playground, so to speak. If I could stop shots with the goalie equipment on, it would be simple for him. That might have been true with just the pads and the gloves; they were pretty big, more or less filling the Camerons' undersized net. But that mask had changed everything, and I knew that the combination of it and the newness of wearing the heavy pads would have him standing there flat-footed and half blind. So we might have a decent chance of actually scoring on him.

He took the bait, and as I watched him change the position of the straps on the back of the mask, I cringed. I hated to see my stuff get abused, but this was for the good of our whole street.

Frank got the pads on and shuffled toward the net. He adopted the classic pose that we all practiced a thousand times in our kitchens or in front of the TV watching a game, and then he adjusted the catching glove on his left hand. We each got a tennis ball and lined up. Anything would count, breakaway or slapshot.

As I steadied the ball on my stick, I prayed that I could work magic with it, but when it came my turn, that didn't happen. I just took my shots like the rest of the guys, and after a few minutes in which Frank did a more than credible job of stopping us, he tipped the mask up onto the top of his head. We had scored a couple of goals but not enough, really, to win the bet. We all waited for him to say the words that would change life as we knew it.

Instead, what he said was, "OK, you can keep bringing your junk. This isn't as much fun as I thought." With that, he turned and clomped to the lawn, knelt down and took off the pads. I looked around at the guys standing there, their faces showing a mixture of surprise and relief. It was my cue to retrieve my stuff and take my position in goal once again. I watched as Frank took off my mask and dropped it onto his lawn, hoping it wasn't being scratched by a stray rock. I silently congratulated myself. My gamble had worked, in part because I'd been smart enough to give Frank the last word. I retrieved my goalie mask, reset the straps, then suited up. I could once again be Ken Dryden. With all due respect to Tony Esposito, that is.

chapter twenty-three

Sure, He's My Friend

When I came alive to NHL hockey in the spring of 1971, one of the greatest players in the game, Montréal's captain, Jean Beliveau, was having the last glorious season of his career. He helped lead the team to the Stanley Cup that spring and then retired after the victory parade. My dad tried to explain to me what his retirement meant. It didn't make any sense to me, because Beliveau is exactly the same age as my dad, and at the time, there was no end in sight for Dad's working life. Plus, Beliveau had scored his 500th goal that season. He was the fourth guy ever to do it, and at that time, it was a huge deal. Why would he just stop playing?

But stop he did, and when the next season rolled on and I watched the team that I now counted as *my* Canadiens, I kind of forgot about him in the excitement of Lafleur, Cournoyer and the Pocket Rocket, Henri Richard. There were just so many great Canadiens players to worship.

One Sunday, my dad told me that after church we would stay downtown in Montréal to have lunch and then go visit a friend of his and my mom's, Mrs. Walker, who lived in a rehabilitation hospital. He tried to prepare me for the visit by telling me that she was crippled by arthritis. I now realize that he didn't want me staring at her deformed hands when we went into her room.

He was trying to prep me to be mannerly, but all I heard was "Lunch at the Chalet Bar-B-Q," which was my favorite chicken place in all the world, and still is. Thinking of their French fries had sustained me through church, but as lunch wound down, Dad repeated his caution. "Mrs. Walker has terrible arthritis, but she's a nice lady. You and Sandra talk to her, and then you can go down the hall and see if there's anyone in the TV room. You'll stay there, and we'll visit her for a while before we go home. If anyone else is in the TV room, you don't touch the set." Pretty standard advice given the circumstances.

Spending an afternoon in a hospital isn't exactly what a kid wants, especially when it also means looking after his younger sister, and I was grouchy about it. *Why did my dad always have to be doing stuff like this?* To this day, he spends countless hours visiting people like this elderly woman and doing things for people with special needs. I now recognize this as evidence of a life well lived, but on that Sunday, all I could see was an afternoon stretching out endlessly into boredom. I hoped that at least they'd have a color TV there, instead of a black-and-white set like we had at home. If only there was a hockey game coming on! But I had no hope of that in the middle of the afternoon at this time of the year.

Mrs. Walker was just like Dad had described her. She was sitting on her bed when we got there, a pen held sideways in hands that looked like old tree branches. She was doing a word puzzle, but she set it aside when we came through the door. I semi-tiptoed into her room, trying to be as nice as I could because I was already feeling sorry for her. The other people we'd seen as we came down the hallway were pretty old and broken-looking, at least to my eyes.

I was standing on a rug made of wool, staring at my shoes so I wouldn't focus on her hands, when she said, "That's a lovely rug. My granddaughter made it for me."

"Yes, Mrs. Walker," I said, glancing up for a moment before immediately refocusing on my feet. Then, gathering my courage while my parents greeted her, I took an inventory of the room. There was the usual old lady stuff, including some knitting needles and yarn that I couldn't quite imagine her being able to use. I didn't see a TV, but there was a radio on the bedside table. I wondered what she listened to. To me, radio was AM broadcasts of the news on CJAD. That's all we ever had on in my house. She saw me looking around and asked if I wanted to see her photographs, which were sitting on top of the dresser.

Being the politely raised Canadian boy I was, I said yes and walked over to them while my dad helped her off the bed. She stumbled over to me with the help of a cane and began going through the pictures. When she got to one in particular, she picked it up, kind of squeezing it between her fingers. It was the only way she could hold it.

"I think you know who this is. He's a friend of mine," she said to me.

As gently as I could, I took the picture out of her hand, being careful not to touch those fingers, in a combination of fear of hurting her and worry that the disease might rub off, and I looked at it. In faded color, Mary Walker was standing beside a man in a cardigan. He was leaning over, being far taller than Mrs. Walker, and he had his hand on her back like a kindly nephew. At first, I couldn't quite place him. It seemed as though I knew the face, but all the other pictures had been family shots, so I stumbled for a second. Then it came to me. I knew that smile. The truth exploded into my brain. This was a Montréal Canadien!

"Jean Beliveau? You're related to Jean Beliveau?" I knew he spoke French, and that Mrs. Walker "was English," as we commonly said, so it didn't really make sense that they'd be related, at least to my kid brain. Maybe someone in her family had married someone in his? It was the only thing I could think of.

"That's Jean Beliveau, all right, but I'm not related to him. He's just my friend," she said. I looked at her again in disbelief. *Friends? Jean Beliveau has friends? Old lady friends? This lady has friends who used to be Montréal Canadiens?* It was something a kid would make up at school, but so outlandish that nobody would believe it. But adults didn't lie, and anyway, here was the proof right in front of me.

"He comes to the hospital to visit us. That picture was taken in the TV room down the hall. He was here for my birthday. That's why he's helping me to blow out the candles on my cake," she explained. I looked at the picture again. There was a cake in the foreground.

I didn't quite know what to say. Until then, hockey players to me were like teachers. They existed in one role and didn't have lives outside of what they did. I couldn't imagine Jean Beliveau being here, or anywhere else for that matter, except at the Montréal Forum or some other arena playing in his Canadiens sweater. He wasn't a real person to me, but a figure of myth. To think that this little old crippled lady knew him, and that he had been in this room, or in the one down the hall, was not something I could make sense of.

As it sunk in, I was beside myself. My Gran and I had cheered Beliveau in the playoffs the previous spring, though truth be told I was more crazy about Ken Dryden. But Beliveau had been her favorite player—tall, handsome, dignified. And he was one of the greatest scorers in history. All of this went through my mind in a flash. I should have asked a million questions, but I could think only of one.

"When's he coming here again?" I didn't ask it so that I could meet him or for any other reason than to test Mrs. Walker. If she had an answer to this question, then her story was true. She really was his friend.

"I'm not sure, dear. He does come by often. Next time, I'll have him sign a picture for you," she replied. Her answer wasn't what I had expected, but in that instant, I knew that Mrs. Walker was telling the truth.

I wanted to ask her all about him, but the only thing I could think to say was, "Why isn't he wearing his Canadiens sweater?" He was dressed almost exactly like my dad. This also made no sense.

"Well, he has his Canadiens pin on. You can see it in the photo," she said, pointing a gnarled finger at the picture. Sure enough, there was a little "CH" logo on his lapel. Maybe that was enough to identify him to whoever saw him and didn't know who he was, like, I imagined, most of the old people in this hospital.

"Of course, he wears his Canadiens sweater when he plays. I'll make sure he has it on in the picture I send home to you," Mrs. Walker said. It was more explanation than I expected from this lady, who to my mind couldn't possibly have known anything about hockey or the Montréal Canadiens. I only realize today how wrong that assumption was.

With that, my dad shooed my sister and me out of Mrs. Walker's room, sending us down the hall to the promised TV. It was a color set, but as I had suspected, there was no hockey on.

A few weeks after our visit, Dad came home with my autographed photo of Jean Beliveau. It was even inscribed to me, though he spelled my name "Bryan." But I didn't care, I knew he meant me.

Of course I took the picture to school, carefully guarded by a plastic sleeve my dad gave me for the purpose, the sleeve that's still on it today as it rests in a memory box at my dad's house. My friends were both disbelieving and impressed at my acquisition, but in truth, neither what they thought nor the fact that I had been touched by the greatness of one of the greatest hockey players in history was the real magic of the photo. The picture's true worth was in how it transformed an old woman into the person she really was, someone with a life far greater than the confines of a hospital room containing family photos and macramé carpets.

The photo was a bridge connecting two people who couldn't hardly have been more different on the surface— a nine-year-old boy whose whole life was hockey and a little old lady with a life that was, it turned out, more about hockey than that kid would have guessed. I never saw Mrs. Walker again, but every time I showed anyone that picture, I thought about her, and Jean Beliveau standing behind her with his hand on her shoulder.

chapter twenty-four

The Goalie with All the Stitches in His Mask

Hockey in the '70s had a lot of colorful characters. The personalities of Gump Worsley, Serge Savard, Dave "The Hammer" Schultz and many others lit up the game, but no such list would be complete without the name Gerry Cheevers. He played for Boston for the better part of 20 years, wearing a mask of white plastic, shaped somewhere between the saucer of Jacques Plante and the bowl of Gilles Meloche. It would have given Cheevers a soul-less stare, except that he wasn't content to present the white blankness of the mask to the world. This was before anyone came up with the idea of painting elaborate designs on masks, as today's goaltenders do.

Although Cheevers played before the era of painted masks, he adorned his with stitches to show the damage that would have been inflicted without it. In time, the mask became criss-crossed with black lines for cuts and smaller lines representing sutures. By painting up his mask in this way, Cheevers was not only pointing to the danger of his profession but also saying something about the human being who wore the mask. And it wasn't, "Look at me—I'm brave." It was more like, "Look at me—I'm terrified. This mask is the only thing keeping me from becoming disfigured like some kind of Frankenstein's monster."

But to us as kids, his design showed that he was a gladiator of the highest order, and it made us wonder about how it must have been to play goalie in the day when nobody wore a mask. This, of course, only made Gump Worsley, who played without one well into the 1970s, an even bigger curiosity. We knew that in seeing Worsley we saw the past. Instinctively, perhaps, we felt that Gerry Cheevers was the future. But since my friends and I were between 9 and 10 in the spring of 1972 when the Bruins won the Stanley Cup, we couldn't actually put such abstract thinking into words.

What we could verbalize, though, was our conviction when we thought we saw a new scar appear. One recess in grade four, a group of us were discussing the mask, which we had all scrutinized the night before when Boston played the Canadiens. Jimmy Modell claimed in a defiant voice that "The ones under his eye are new. They must have come from Bobby Hull's wrist shot that Saturday on *Hockey Night in Canada*." He talked about the painted stitches as if they were real, as we all did. Every time we discussed Cheevers, the grotesque image of a cut-up and scarred human face hung in front of our eyes. We felt as though it was our faces that were saved from near annihilation by that mask.

We all stared at Jimmy, scorn coming out of our mouths in a collective "Naaahh." Everyone was sure that those stitches had been there for a long time.

Naturally, such a negative reaction couldn't just be left to lie unchallenged. Jimmy would have to defend his claim. We all knew that the only way to tell whether that scar had been there since last season was to consult the cards. Hockey cards with Cheevers' picture on them would reveal the truth. Brad Chambers, often the last line of recourse in such a situation because of his all-powerful hockey card collection, would be the mediator. "Show the card—that'll prove it," said a voice in the crowd.

Brad, ever on the ball, took out that giant stack of his and flipped through it one card at a time. It wasn't clear whether he knew he had a Cheevers in there or not; he acted as if he was going through the pile for the first time, a look of discovery adorning his face. The guy had so many cards that he could bring any old huge pile on a given morning with no idea whatsoever what was in it. This was a long way from my carefully chosen stack of 12 to 15 cards.

Finally, he found the card we needed, but as he showed it, a collective groan went up. It was not an action shot, but a studio photo of Cheevers in his uniform. This would prove nothing. Along with the others, I puzzled over the problem facing us, and being a hockey history nerd even at that age, I offered another solution. "We need the 'NHL Goalies Wins Leaders' card," I said. "I'm sure Cheevers is on there."

Once again, Brad went to his deck, and sure enough, in another minute, he had that one, too. We stifled our amazement at the guy's resources as we crowded around to see. But we were skunked again. The card had just head shots, all four of the wins leaders—Tony Esposito, Ed Johnston, Ed Giacomin and Cheevers—smiling for the cameras that had captured their images.

While Jimmy tried to muster an argument, the cards were passed from hand to hand anyway, but before he could get his case together, the bell rang. We had no choice but to obey it, since not to do so risked the strap back in those days. We took off on a run to line up and re-enter the building. Brad, diligent about his collection in ways that he was not always, pressed to get his cards back. He probably knew that they would be the focus of attention over the next day or two and didn't want anyone else having the power of holding onto them.

The argument continued the next recess, and the next, but the problem was that the verdict would never be quite certain because Jimmy couldn't show us what the mask looked like now. He could only pledge us all to memorize the pattern of stitches on Cheevers' mask the next time Cheevers appeared on TV. Then we'd see it for ourselves.

Really, this didn't make a lot of sense, but we didn't care. The passion of the case was what carried our interest. With that, the argument halted. Jimmy had neither won nor lost, but he had—or rather, Gerry Cheevers' mask had— turned a whole classroom full of hockey fans upside down.

Whatever the truth, there came a day when I would be able to verify it for myself, because my dad got tickets to a Montréal Canadiens–Boston Bruins game. It was a Saturday afternoon game in the Montréal Forum, one of only two I went to as a kid, and though it was weeks after the Cheevers mask controversy, I was still to be the eyes of my class. I was going to glimpse that mask and bring back a report on it.

My dad and I sat behind the goal, the one that was twice defended by the Boston Bruins. The seats were pretty good, but what with Cheevers' back to me and the distance up to our spot, I quickly realized that it would be tough to pick out the individual patterns of stitches, as I had hoped to do. Instead, I vowed to watch Cheevers carefully, to see how he played. At least I could tell my friends about that.

Most of the game, he was unimpressive, at least to my partisan eyes, but then he did something that I could report back to the boys in my school. Someone dumped a long shot in on Cheevers, about waist high. It was no threat, but he jumped in the air to catch the puck in his mid-section, then fell to the ground in a fetal ball, cradling it. The whistle blew. Cheevers wasn't hurt, and he confirmed it by springing up a moment later and going about the usual routine of clearing the snow from the crease.

The crowd, partial of course to the Canadiens, booed him. I looked at my dad as if to ask why Cheevers had done the big move, when clearly there was no need for it. My dad didn't have an answer, nor did anybody sitting there, judging by the curious looks on their faces, but I'll bet, knowing Cheevers, that he was grinning away under his mask. He could have been laughing like a hyena, and we probably wouldn't have known it with that mask on.

Thinking back on it, the reason for his actions should have been clear. He was telling us that, just as he'd painted up that mask, he'd play the game how he saw fit. If he wanted to jump, he'd jump. And what we, the Canadiens, or for that matter the Boston Bruins, thought about it didn't matter in the least.

Gerry Cheevers' mask was an extravagance never before tolerated in the NHL. Until then, the league was a world where rules and order were strictly enforced, both by management off the ice and players on it. Witness Gordie Howe's razor elbows supposedly knocking rookie Brad Park's teeth out the first time they went into a corner together, a kind of "How do you do—and don't forget who's the veteran here."

With the mask, Cheevers defied the management, who wanted things to look right, for the focus to be on the teams, not on the players in the way that Cheevers demanded when he put the stitches on there. Nobody who saw him could help but remember that mask, nor could the viewer ignore the personality behind it. That's why my friends and I, like kids in every school in hockey country, were so fascinated by him. He was his own little Woodstock, a personification of the "me" decade every time he stepped onto the ice.

I now know that I was doing more than watching a hockey game that afternoon; I was witnessing social history. But as I devoured cotton candy and cheered on the Canadiens, all I cared about was getting a glimpse of that mask as Cheevers skated toward me to take up his position in net. And at one point, just before he turned his back on me and started roughing up his crease as goalies do, I thought I saw a scar that hadn't been there in the past, but I knew that I'd never be able to prove it. So when Monday came and I went back to school, all I talked about was his big, jumping save.

chapter twenty-five

On the
Road

I t's commonplace that September 1972 changed forever everyone who lived through it in Canada. We went from swaggeringly confident to achingly humble to gloriously triumphant in 27 days. Most of us don't think of the process when we remember that month when hockey reigned supreme in our hearts and minds, though. What we remember is the goal. It's like the familiar American question, "Do you remember where you were when you learned that JFK had been shot?" Or more recently, "Where were you when you heard about 9-11?"

These days when important or tragic events happen, their images are played and replayed so many times that the original tends to disappear. But my memory of September 1972 is clear, because I experienced it once, live, and not on replay. Ironically, while I will never forget Paul Henderson's goal, it's not because I saw it happen, at least not then. In fact, for 25 years, the moment was reduced in my memory to the famous photo of him leaping into Cournoyer's arms. I only saw the goal on videotape in the late 1990s, when the 25th anniversary commemorative VHS set came out. But that doesn't mean that my memory of the goal on September 28, 1972, is any less vivid, for I shared the moment with one of the most significant figures of my childhood.

But aside from the goal, I remember other things about September 1972. Living in Montréal, of course, we had the first game. A columnist for the *Globe and Mail*, Dick Beddoes, promised to eat his hat on the steps of Toronto's City Hall if the team didn't win. The news in the days leading up to the series was all about hockey—our way versus the Russian way. They had crummy old equipment, and they were so scared of us, it was said, that they sat in the stands watching our practices just to get a glimpse of the greatest players in the world— Brad Park, the Esposito brothers, Rod Gilbert, Rod Seiling, Jean Ratelle, Serge Savard, the Mahovlich brothers, and of course, the great Ken Dryden. And I wasn't the only one in awe of our team. The whole world was.

On September 2, my dad and I watched the first game on the TV set in our living room. In black and white, there they were—the players who were going to bring us glory. We felt the excitement of the first goal, just a minute in, and then disbelief at how the Russians took over to win. For years after that night, every time the topic of the Russians came up, my dad commented on the magical way they passed the puck back and forth, especially how they carried it over the blue line instead of dumping it in and chasing it, like our team did.

Ken Dryden, until then my hero and a god, failed me that night, and it was the start of the end for him and me. I could not believe that he could be so bad. He looked as though he had no control, flopping around and missing the puck like he did. I didn't see it as a matter of the Russians' skill, though they did create a series of shots where the poor guy had no chance whatsoever. All I knew was that he didn't play like I had known him to before. It was a crushing feeling, and a year or so later when he retired, I was glad. Of course, he came back in 1974 and won a bunch more Stanley Cups, but that's another story.

When I now look at the first game and the others on DVD, I realize that if it weren't for Dryden and Tony Esposito, Canada never would have come close to winning four games. The Russians would have beaten us by six goals in every game. But at the time, reasoned analysis wasn't a strength of anyone living in Canada, especially me.

The intermission reports on the Russian training system also burned themselves into my mind. They made the players out to be automatons who did nothing but work out, but they also gave viewers the sense that these guys were prime athletes. One segment showed goalie Vladislav Tretiak squatted down with a rubber ball in each hand, bouncing the balls off a wall and catching them. I tried this with tennis balls, figuring that if this guy was as good a goalie as he was, the exercise would help my street hockey game. I bounced the balls twice and fell over, which only increased my sense that these guys were incredible. But none of us thought of the Russians the way we did our players. If the Russians were amazing humans, then the Canadian players, including Bobby Hull, who was up there in Winnipeg and not playing, were gods.

We had also heard the rumors about the Russians. Not that they were spies, or Communists—who cared about that in elementary school? But that they loved ketchup. We were fascinated that they put it on everything, even their ice cream. Or at least that's what we were all saying in September 1972.

The games themselves between the first and the last have disappeared from my memory, including the famous speech by Phil Esposito in Vancouver. I've only recently seen the speech again, and I suppose the adults understood its nuances far better than I would have at nine. But what I do remember is how my classmates and I sat in neat rows in the school gym to watch every game from Moscow, on TVs attached to rolling carts. During the last game, we watched, with the boys at the front for a better view and the girls dutifully not talking, having been warned by our teachers, and we glanced at the clock at the same time. The game was still going on when the buses came to take us home. The vice principal announced that he would hold the buses as long as he could in the hope that we could see the end. We got close, but finally he had to tell us to file out. The buses needed to drop us off and get to the Catholic schools to take those kids home. We were going to miss the last few minutes of play. But for many of us, hope was lost anyway. The Russians had the thing all but won.

We got onto our bus, greeted by Jack, the same guy who had taken us to school every day of our childhood. He was a happy-go-lucky fellow who was probably all of 40 but seemed like all adults to us—old. As we boarded, Jack pointed to his tiny radio, which was always beside him. "I got the game on here," he said to us, repeating it for every few kids. Maybe he was politely telling us to be quiet so he could listen. Or maybe he was responding to our mumbles that we had been forced to leave without seeing the rest of the game. The idea of videotaped versions waiting for us at home was a decade in the future.

Normally my sister and I didn't pay much attention to each other, but this day, I noticed her as I took a seat on the right, about four rows back from the driver. She was on the left, two rows behind me. Every kid on the bus was silent, for once, listening. We already felt the sting of having lost the series and with it, our world dominance of the game that meant everything to us. We never considered that there might be Russian boys listening to the games on radios in their houses who were as crazy about Valeri Kharlamov, Boris Mikhailov and Tretiak as we were for our stars. We just couldn't imagine that hockey could mean to anyone else what it did to us.

Jack turned the bus left onto Taschereau Boulevard, where he would go a mile before turning left again onto my street. His radio squawked out the call, every rotation of the tires taking us one second closer to home and to the end of the game and hockey as we knew it. As best we could, we listened to the voice coming from that little plastic box, but without hope.

Then there was a mad scramble in front of the net, "Cournoyer, Henderson, they bang at it. He, he, he SCORES!" The bus erupted. None of us had a clue who had done it; nobody cared. Jack threw both hands off the wheel and up into the air to celebrate. Every kid on that bus went mad. Canada had won! It didn't occur to us that all over the country people were going insane in various ways, celebrating the goal. All we knew was that we had done it. It was over, and Canada was still the best.

Meanwhile, 350 miles away, my future brother-in-law Phil Reimer, whom I wouldn't meet for another 20 years, and who had no idea he would eventually marry a girl from Québec, had stuck up his hand in class and asked to go to the bathroom. Phil left the classroom and saw his school janitor watching the game on TV in the hallway. Phil stood there and watched as Henderson did his heroics. He was the only kid in his school to see the goal. And every Christmas while we watch the game, he reminds me of the fact. It's a story that I will never tire of hearing.

At the same moment, the other kids on the bus and I were somewhere between Taschereau Boulevard and my street,

Victor Hugo. And we were going crazy. We yelled, clapped and slapped each other on the back. Like no other day, both boys and girls smiled at each other, the barriers between us temporarily breached. I looked back to find my sister and grinned, not so much because of the goal. I knew she didn't really care that much about hockey; she hadn't watched any of the games that my dad and I had. I smiled because even then, I had the sense that we were sharing something important.

A few moments later, we were at my bus stop, the first one on Victor Hugo Street. I got off, as did my sister. The funny thing is that my memory of the afternoon stops right there, with Jack waving goodbye to us, as he did every day. I don't recall rushing into my house to see the replay or watching the news that night.

By now, Jack has probably delivered his last load of kids safely to their destination and retired. But I'm sure that when the topic of September 1972 comes up, he tells the story of driving down Taschereau Boulevard and throwing his arms into the air when the greatest moment in Canadian sports history occurred. Although there's no way he would remember any of us who were on the bus that day, I hope he knows that there's nobody we would rather have shared the goal with. Even though Jack didn't score the goal, it's almost as if he did, because at that moment, he was the only adult around, and he took on the qualities of a hero to all of us.

chapter twenty-six

I Saw It with
My Own Eyes

Some moments in life just happen. Henderson's goal against Russia, for instance, or the winning of the Stanley Cup in overtime. You can't know when they'll occur; you just have to hope you don't miss them. Others are somewhere between planned-for and unexpected. Frank Mahovlich's 500th goal was one of those moments. We all knew it was coming, but nobody was quite sure when it would happen, so my friends and I were on the alert in the spring of 1973. We watched the march toward the moment and talked about it at school. More important, we prepped our parents for our vigil of staying up to watch the games on TV. Nobody would have dared miss it.

I was 10, and crazy about the Canadiens. Things weren't quite the same between me and Dryden as they had been before the Summit Series. I had lost confidence in his

all-conquering ability, though I still had his poster on my bedroom wall and his hockey card carefully tucked away in my box.
Other Montréal Canadiens were now catching my interest and
worship. The "Big M," Frank Mahovlich, was the most important of these. I had no recollection of his having played for anyone but Montréal. Seeing a picture of him in his Toronto uniform
from the mid-1960s, or Detroit's red and white from just before
my team got him, was like looking at a lost world. For me, hockey
had started in the season of 1970–71, which was the same year
he'd been traded to Montréal and helped them to the first Stanley Cup that I considered myself a part of.

Now here it was a couple of springs later, and Frank
was the star of the team. They were playing well, too, on their
way to another Cup, though we didn't know that at the time.
All we knew was that one of these days, soon, Frank would
score that magical goal, and that we had to be in front of the
TV when it happened. This was an era before *TSN SportsDesk*,
so you couldn't count on seeing the goal replayed, nor could
you tape the game yourself. It was up to each kid to persuade
his parents to let him stay up to watch every Montréal Canadiens game until it happened, or have to bear the scorn of his
classmates for missing what we all saw as one of the most
memorable moments of our lives.

The anticipation we felt is hard to imagine nowadays,
when 500 goals is almost a stepping stone. Currently, six players
have 700 or more goals, and 17 have at least 600. Frank doesn't

even break the top 25. Twentieth is Guy Lafleur with 560. The Big M would end his NHL career with 533 total goals. But back then, if someone from the future had come and told us of the Gretzky era that was just around the corner, we would have said he was from Mars, or maybe Russia, here to seek revenge for the Summit Series by ruining our game as we knew it. There was no way that one player would ever score almost 900 goals.

In that immediate post-expansion era, 500 was an almost unreachable milestone. Until Mahovlich did it on March 21, 1973, only four other players had, and their names read like those of the Greek Gods: Maurice Richard, Gordie Howe, Bobby Hull, and the great Canadien Jean Beliveau. So we waited, and when Frank had 499, the anticipation grew excruciating.

Watching hockey on Saturday nights was an institution, as it is today, but it was on Wednesdays, too. Most kids I knew, however, weren't allowed to stay up on a weeknight to watch a game. My bedtime was 8:00 PM, so for me, such a luxury was out of the question on a school night. Except that my parents understood the history that could be involved and let me stay up. Dad and I parked in front of the TV on a Wednesday evening—me just hoping it would happen, and he there to be a part of it with me. He's never been much of a sports-on-TV kind of guy.

Every kid I knew was in front of his TV, too, and you can bet we'd all talked endlessly about the way the goal would go in, Mahovlich's 500th becoming versions of each of our dream goals. Some kids saw a blistering slapshot. Others, a wrister. Some wanted a breakaway. I didn't particularly care. I just wanted to see it with my own eyes. I had been almost too young to be aware of Beliveau's 500th, scored in February 1971. So Mahovlich's moment was to be my first look at a great personal achievement.

My memories of the game are fuzzy in some of the details because I've embellished it with time. When I think back on it, for instance, I visualize Montréal playing the New York Rangers. The opponent that night was actually the much less glorious Vancouver Canucks. As for the goal itself, it occurred later on in the game, and Frank had already missed a few chances. But then, he got the puck in front of the net and tried that famous left-handed wrist shot of his. Only the puck didn't go straight off his stick to the top corner, which would have been endlessly reenacted on playgrounds and in driveways for weeks afterwards; instead, it dribbled off the heel of his stick. Moving at half the normal speed along the ice, the puck somehow snaked its way through the skates in front of the net and went in. As it did, Frank fell down. He had scored his 500th goal, but it was nothing like any of us had imagined or hoped.

I stood up and cheered anyway. Then I looked at my dad, because what was happening on the TV screen didn't make any sense to me: Frank Mahovlich was sitting on the Canadiens bench acting as if nothing had happened. He stared blankly out toward center ice as the announcement was made, his stick held in one hand, the other draped over the boards. It was as if the announcer was talking about a goal for the other team.

"Hey, look at him!" I said to my dad. "Why isn't he happy?" I had a sinking feeling in my stomach, having been let down by the goal. Frank seemed to be experiencing exactly the same thing. He wasn't yelling or waving to the cheering crowd. Was he ashamed that, after all that waiting, this was the goal he'd given us?

"He's just being modest. That's how he's supposed to act," my dad replied. He was trying to make sense of it by telling me what the adult code of conduct governing number 27's behavior was, but his words didn't help. We had all waited for Frank to do this great thing, and even if the goal wasn't what we'd hoped for, it would live forever for us now. It just didn't seem right that he wasn't somehow transformed the way I was, and the way I was sure every kid I knew had been in that instant, because we'd been a part of history.

Standing there in my living room, I made a vow that if I ever scored 500 goals, I wouldn't go to the bench and act modest, no matter if it was a dream goal or not. I would celebrate, my stick in the air, and a huge smile on my face.

chapter twenty-seven

Rookies Come From— Peterborough?

When I was a kid, practically everything the Montréal Canadiens did was memorable. In 1971 they beat Chicago in a nail-biting seven-game series to win the Cup, riding on Ken Dryden's back. They won all but eight games of the entire 1976–77 season. They took the Cup every year from 1976 to 1979.

When I started to read the Montréal *Gazette*, pages and pages of articles about the team awaited me, even during the summer. It was my team in my town. I even went to a couple of games with my dad. These were like seeing the Pope, highly anticipated moments, and I'll never forget them. Each game was preceded by weeks of bragging to my friends.

But at one point in the middle of all this triumph, real life took over when my parents moved us, and our small business, to Peterborough, Ontario. It was 1974. They told me and my sister that they felt bad about displacing us and worried about us making new friends and starting in a new school. To me, none of this was a big deal. The real problem as I saw it was that they didn't think about what being separated from the great Montréal Canadiens would do to me. I would be lost without them, my world turned upside down. It would be like the team didn't even exist anymore.

My friends told me before I left Brossard that Peterborough was in Toronto Maple Leafs country and that I'd be defending the Habs every time I turned around. Actually, once I got to Peterborough, I found that the kids on my block didn't have any particular love for the Leafs, though a couple were Borje Salming fans. Later, some tried to emulate Mike Palmateer in net when we played street hockey. But perhaps it was just that the team was so bad in the mid-1970s that no one got all crazy and boastful about their chances to win the Cup.

That's not to say that Peterborough wasn't hockey mad, and before I'd been there very long I learned that there was more to life than the NHL. There was also the Peterborough Petes. To people living in my newly adopted town, they were everything, though it was not until I saw a game for myself that I understood why.

Maybe I had been too young to see the bigger picture while living in Montréal. I was about 12 when we left, but it never occurred to me to ask where the NHL got its players. I knew that Ken Dryden had been a university student in the U.S.

before helping the Canadiens win the Cup in 1971. I also knew but could barely tolerate the thought that Frank Mahovlich had played for a couple of teams before he joined the Habs. But I had never asked the fundamental question of life up until that point: Where do rookies come from?

I went to my first hockey game in Peterborough with a friend from school, Johnny Walsh. One or the other of us had won the tickets in a drawing held for all the kids who served as volunteer "patrols"—crossing guards helping kids get from our school to the other side of the street to walk home. I had no idea what to expect, so I was surprised when Johnny said we should get my dad to drop us off early enough to see the warm-up. "Maybe we can stand behind the net and get a puck as it comes over the glass," he offered. He was an old pro at working the Peterborough Memorial Centre, having been to games there with his dad tons of times. For my part, I was prepared to be unimpressed. Warm-up or not, this was not the NHL.

We were dropped off well in advance of the opening faceoff. Considering the build-up I'd had all day, with friends at school wanting to know all about our tickets and our plans to see the game from start to three stars, I was struck by how few seats there were, compared to what I had seen in Montréal. To get to our seats in the Forum, my dad and I had ridden escalators that looked like giant crossed hockey sticks, with the sides all lit up white. Here in Peterborough, there was no need of an escalator. The farthest seat was still practically on top of the action.

Johnny and I stood directly behind the Peterborough net while the players took shots on the goalies. At one point, a puck went sailing past the net, a slapshot, and smacked the boards right in front of us with a thud. I jumped back, and Johnny laughed.

My shock came from never having been so close to the action before. When my dad and I went to see the Canadiens play the Bruins, we were up behind the net 20 rows or so. When we went to the Forum to see the Rangers come to town, we were at center ice, but up so high we could see the dust on the rafters. The game took place far below us, with the players' voices never reaching our seats, and their faces probably more recognizable to me than my dad, since I had them all memorized from having thumbed past their images on hockey cards a million times.

Now here I was standing within a few feet of the Petes, and the game took on a whole new life. I could see the players' faces and hear their voices as they called for pucks to shoot on net in preparation for their game.

"Who are these guys?" I asked my friend. All I could think of was that I no longer lived in the city with the greatest team in the world in it. Although the sports section in the *Peterborough Examiner* was always dominated by what the Petes were doing, it was small-town-like, kind of skinny, not like the thick pages of the Montréal *Gazette*. I just didn't get it, until I was actually standing there, looking the players in the eye.

I had been ready to dismiss this team as something other than the real thing, hockey-wise, but now I was curious. These guys were bigger and scarier than any hockey players I had ever seen, at least this close up, and here I was, pressed up against the glass with them right in front of me, something I knew I would never ever get to do at a Canadiens game. I had to figure out where in the hockey universe this team fit, so I turned to Johnny and asked him again: "These Petes, who are they. I mean, where do they come from?"

I could tell that my friend didn't quite know how to answer my question. He had lived in Peterborough all his life, and the Petes had just always been there.

At our age, nobody was a good liar—another kid could always tell when the answer was made up, so I was on my guard lest Johnny try to BS me. But he made what looked like an honest stab at a reply, and even if he was unsure of what he said, he was more right than he knew. "These guys are going to be in the NHL soon. They'll be playing for the Canadiens," he said.

I didn't know if he said that last bit because he knew it for a fact or because he thought that's what I wanted to hear. I had made no secret of my affection for my team at my new school, mostly because I was surprised that there wasn't more opposition from the Toronto fans that I had assumed would be everywhere. Still, Johnny's answer stunned me. He didn't have to tell me about the Memorial Cup or that there were junior leagues in Québec, and out West too, to get my attention. And if he had, it wouldn't have mattered. All I cared about was that here, in front of my eyes, were players who would one day wear the bleu-blanc-rouge of my team.

Then he added the real shocker. "They go to Crestwood." It was the high school we'd be attending in a few years. "My brother sees them all the time," he added. Johnny's brother Rusty was a "niner," the term used for a member of the grade nine class.

I couldn't process the information. These guys, who obviously played hockey like they already were in the NHL, had to go to school? The humanness of it didn't compute. Did that mean that in the distant past, Jean Beliveau and Henri Richard had also gone to high schools somewhere?

"Which ones?" I asked. I had to know. I wanted to memorize their faces so that when I later saw them on hockey cards, which I had not quite outgrown yet, I would recognize them.

"I don't know. Ask my dad on the way home, or ask Rusty," Johnny replied. Mr. Walsh was supposed to pick us up right after the game. Rusty wouldn't be there, but he was often around the house when I went over to Johnny's.

I had no idea how I'd be able to wait for the answer, but as Johnny and I made our way to our seats, a giddy feeling overcame me. If he was right, that meant my parents hadn't moved me away from the center of the hockey world after all. They had brought me to a place where the NHL was on my front doorstep. What was funny, at least to me at the time, was that it seemed like nobody else at the arena quite understood the importance of what they were seeing. Why, if they knew, weren't there hundreds of people behind that net with us, adoring these future stars?

Of course my ideas about the local fans' interest were wildly mistaken, and I would learn the depth of devotion of Peterborough residents for the Petes in the years to come, but for this night, I was the king of a domain my mind had created, the only one in the crowd of several thousand to really understand what he was seeing—the NHL of the future. I watched every play as if I was attending the last game of the Stanley Cup finals.

chapter twenty-eight

The Rumors Were
All True

Over time, I came to feel a sense of belonging in going to a Petes game at the Memorial Centre. In that intimate arena, fans could wander anywhere, see the warm-up from ice level as I had done my first time there, be down near the chute when the players came from their dressing rooms, get down there in time to see them go back, and even be right behind the bench when the three stars took their half-moon whirls at the end of the game. Often I'd be down there in time to see them shake hands with the announcer and take the watch that always seemed to be the prize. How many wrist watches a guy like Tim Trimper had, or what he did with them all, I couldn't imagine.

But there was never a greater insider moment for me than the night the Russian Junior team came to play the Petes. I arrived at the arena early, hoping for an up-close look at players like those we Canadians had gotten to know so much about in 1972 during the Summit Series. I wanted see for myself whether they passed the puck back and forth instead of dumping it in and crashing to get it back. I figured that the game would allow me to verify what everyone had said about the Red Army team—that the Russians played with equipment so old that Canadians wouldn't be caught dead in it.

During the course of the evening, the European style of play that I had been hearing about since the 1972 series made sense to me for the first time as I watched the Russians handle the puck. But my impressions of the game were superseded by seeing something so shocking that it confirmed every rumor I'd ever heard about this strange breed of human being called the Communist hockey player. And I saw it by going down, between periods, and standing in the hallway outside the visiting team's dressing room.

I got there just after they'd closed the door, the players having made their way inside. A second later, along came a man wearing a blazer with the logo of the Peterborough Petes displayed on the breast pocket. Behind him was a guy I recognized from the snack bar in the lobby. He was carrying a tray out in front of him. It was a time-honored tradition that I recognized from my own experiences as a player.

Everyone who has ever played hockey remembers the Cokes. Some kid's dad, usually a different one every time, would go to the arena snack bar and buy enough drinks for the whole team at the end of the game. The ladies there would put the waxy paper cups into a metal tray, all divided up into compartments, and the hero-for-the-moment dad would work his way to the dressing room, carefully holding the wire handle but still spilling the pop onto the floor as he went. He'd always make sure there were enough cups for everyone, with one left over just to be certain, and once inside the room, would go from player to player, holding out the tray.

Each kid would take one, in those days probably an eight-ouncer, and slurp it down practically before the dad had moved on to the next kid. The coach or some dad who was in the room would have to remind the kids to say thank you, and then right after warn them to pick up their cups, which were immediately crumpled into balls and thrown on the floor as the drinks were finished. It was a tradition as old as the game itself, at least to me.

Now here I was, watching as the Cokes (it could've been Pepsi, but we still called them "Cokes") were taken into the Russian Juniors' dressing room. I was picturing what was going on inside, or what I thought was, when a moment later, back came the Cokes in the guy's arms. There was no way the players could have gone through them so fast. I looked at the tray. The cups were all still there. Behind the snack bar guy, the door was partway open, and in the doorway stood the Peterborough Petes' representative. He had a puzzled look on his face.

I looked through the cracked door, glimpsing a few skates stretched out on the end of tired legs, sticks lying around on the floor. I could barely make out a few players' faces when the door opened all the way and the Petes' representative came out followed by a man in a suit. The man was obviously one of "them," and he looked like the Russian coach had in 1972, his hair in a style that seemed old-fashioned, even back then. He pointed to the tray with the drinks all untouched.

"Tea. They'd like some tea," he said to the man in the Petes blazer.

"Tea?" I said it to myself at the same time as the man in the Petes blazer said it aloud. I could tell he didn't believe it either. Tea would do nothing but make you hotter. Coke was cold and had sugar for energy. Every coach knew that this burst would do the players good. Tea made no sense at all, but in the spirit of being a polite and diplomatic host, the Petes' representative turned and motioned to the snack bar guy. "Tea," he said again, but this time as instruction. "Take these back and bring them some tea."

I looked around me. A group of adults who were standing around smoking their between-period cigarettes were also witnesses to this culturally alien spectacle. *Tea?* Whoever heard of such a thing in the middle of a hockey game? Surely, on the other side of the arena, the Petes players were sipping

Coke after Coke in anticipation of the exertion of the third period. That I knew, or thought I did, but this?

The snack bar guy trundled back the way he'd come, followed by the guy in the Petes blazer. When they returned, the tray was laden with steaming tea in Styrofoam cups. This time, the Russian coach nodded a grim, tight-lipped thank you as he took the tray from the snack bar guy and went inside with it. He didn't even let the guy back into the room. Maybe he had drawn up some strategies on the chalkboard and didn't want anyone stealing them, I reasoned as I stood there hoping for a good look at the players when they came out to start the final period. They were all about complicated strategy, after all—at the team level, and as a country. All Canadians knew that.

When the Russian team finally emerged, I didn't look at their equipment to see if it was old-fashioned, like I'd planned to. Instead, I looked at their faces and wished that somehow I could ask them why they had sent back the Cokes and asked for tea. Were they told they had to drink tea? Was their country really so poor from Communism that they hadn't had Cokes before? It was the only explanation I could come up with.

Returning to my seat for the third period, I tried to make sense of it, and I eventually settled the problem in my adolescent mind. The profiles we'd all seen in the intermissions of the games during the 1972 series were my answer. In Communist Russia, players left their homes when they were young and went to places almost like hockey factories, where they learned to play the game. It was their life. They couldn't live with their families, and their parents, forced to live in tiny apartments and to work in factories themselves, were not able to go to their games. The whole thing had a soul-lessness to it that you could see on the players' faces. It was a vast contrast to our players—Clarke, Esposito, Henderson, Cournoyer—who lived free lives and had expressions, and hairstyles, that indicated life and color.

Maybe the Russians were as good at our game as we were. Some people by the mid-1970s were even willing to admit that they were a little superior—better conditioned and able to work as a team, and less selfish—but I felt kind of sad for these guys. I realized that there were two luxuries their system couldn't afford them: the Cokes, and more importantly, having fathers who participated in their playing careers, something I and my teammates took as a given.

I may have had the logic kind of twisted, but what I concluded that day probably wasn't all that different from what most Canadians would have figured given what we knew about the Russian way of life back in the 1970s. And this newfound knowledge made me glad to be who I was, a Canadian.

chapter twenty-nine

Brian Kennedy Scored That Goal?

E very once in a while, someone in the NHL playoffs will play way beyond himself. Maybe he scored five goals in the regular season, but in the post-season he gets seven, including a couple of overtime game-winners. You watch the games, and you're amazed. The puck just seems to bounce in off his stick for some reason. Usually, as quickly as the magic comes, it disappears again, and no one ever understands why.

This happened to me in grade six on a rainy afternoon, when suddenly I became one with the game. I had the power to score at will; every shot I took was a seeing-eye shot that found its way into a corner of the net. The thing was, I was not playing on the ice, where my career was percolating along at the same steady but unspectacular pace it had been for years. My miraculous day of hockey glory took place in the gym of our school.

Lunch was over, but going outside was out of the question due to the weather. Instead, the teachers had us stay in, and the boys were taken to play floor hockey. We were divided into teams arbitrarily, not with the best guys picking, but by being numbered off by our vice principal, Mr. MacDonald, who also happened to be my classroom teacher. The "ones" went to the left and used the yellow sticks; the "twos" went to the right and used the red ones. I was a two.

Maybe I was just among the first to be numbered off and sent to my side, but for some reason, I started the game on the floor rather than on the sidelines. Mr. MacDonald dropped the ball at center. It came to me, and I had a sensation I'd never felt before when playing. It was like I was floating out there. I moved around a guy and took a shot on net. I scored, and it was barely a minute into the game. My first thought was that the game would be one of those 11–10 deals with every player on each team getting at least one goal, but that theory was discarded as I started to notice that everywhere I went, the ball came to me. Every time I shot, it seemed to go in the net. Before I knew it, I had three goals. No one else on my team had scored.

On an ensuing play, I was in the center of the floor instead of my usual right wing. The ball squirted out of a scramble between me and the opposing net. I stepped into it and took a whack. It was as if a wire were between my stick, the ball and the net, and as I shot, I had a moment of unbelievable clarity when I just knew that I had lasered it into the open spot. The ball sailed by everyone in the scrum and went in the top right corner. At the time I shot, I had been moving to my right. Now I kept trotting that way as my amazed teammates looked back at me, trying to figure out who had been responsible for the goal. It was not often that such a thing would have been credited to me.

"Who did that?" I heard one say to another.

"Brian Kennedy," someone else responded.

When kids used your full name in school it meant they didn't know you that well. If they did, they would only say your last name, "Kennedy." Thus, the guy who responded was registering a combination of surprise and lack of familiarity. It just wasn't like me to score at all, let alone score a bunch. Now here I was, on some kind of a mission from the hockey gods. I could do no wrong.

The game ended with my team winning and my goal total at four. I had been the king of the floor. I had felt like I could score at will, as if I were playing in some magical other world where everyone looked like the kids I knew, but I alone had been gifted with superior powers. Funny thing was, as we left the gym to go to our classroom for the afternoon, nobody said much to me about it. No one else seemed to believe my luck that day, either. Maybe it was because I was relatively new at this school, my family having moved to Peterborough a few months earlier. Breaking into the crowd of boys on the playing fields at recess had been hard. Most of them had been together since grade one, and the loyalties were firm.

Looking back at it, I realize I was given a moment that I could have built upon to form a basis for acceptance. But life went back to normal right after the game, and I let my chance go. I had had my moment of incredible glory. It wasn't luck, but it also wasn't something that I dared build anything on, because even then, I knew that I would not be likely to repeat it.

Hockey for me was always a game of caution. My dad was proud to tell people that as a player in Pee Wee, I had read a book on positional play and was disciplined in staying in my "lane" as a right-winger. When I was on the ice, I patrolled my side without fail, never venturing into the opposite corner after the puck for fear of putting my left-winger out of position. What my discipline got me was an unspectacular house league career. Meanwhile, other kids, like my friend Jimmy Modell in Montréal, scored all the goals. They played with abandon, the way I had done that day on the gym floor.

Being more disciplined than my teammates on the ice could be seen as a kind of virtue, but I think it also killed the magic that could have come to me more often. During the floor hockey game, I had played with a looseness that I seldom felt. I had no fear as I shot the ball. I wasn't afraid to fail. I was just having more fun playing hockey than I had ever had in my life.

It didn't matter whether I was in or out of position; I just lived the game.

Some players can cultivate that kind of magic anytime they want to. Are they perpetually gifted with that feeling that everything they touch will go in? Or do they have to manufacture the emotion? Perhaps they don't play on feeling at all, but instead have a superior athletic skill, one that I wasn't born with. At my age, I can live with that.

By recess the day after the floor hockey game, I was back to being one of the horde, hoping not to get picked last by the real athletes among us who always did the choosing no matter what game we were playing. But I'm still puzzled about why I was incredibly blessed that rainy afternoon. Had I tapped into some latent talent that I just hadn't known how to surface before? Could I have played like that again if I just let go and forgot my fear of failing? Maybe. But that wouldn't happen, literally, for another 10 years, when once again the hockey gods would smile on me. But that's a story for later.

chapter thirty

Banquet Day

Anyone who has played minor league hockey remembers the event that the adults who ran such things thought was the highlight of the year: the banquet. I played for All Saints Anglican in the "church league" in Peterborough, and it was at the banquet that awards were presented to teams representing our sponsor, All Saints, in various divisions.

For us in the church league, however, banquet day also meant something else. We had to spend a Sunday morning at the church that sponsored our team. But we weren't at All Saints that morning for the preaching. We were there because at the lunch hour, we would meet the Peterborough Petes. The excitement was palpable. It was as if the Pope and the Virgin Mary themselves were going to drop by for a visit.

After the service ended, we all filed downstairs to the basement to eat. Once there, we were told to sit with our teammates and wait for the minister to come in and say a few words to us. All we cared about was where the Petes players were. Every time someone opened a door, 100 heads turned at the same time to see if it was the players. I think we imagined that they'd be marching in a column like some victorious army, or that they'd look like Jesus in those medieval paintings, a glowing circle of light surrounding their heads.

Dinnertime came, and what seemed like a million church ladies materialized out of the kitchen to put plates of chicken, mashed potatoes and peas in front of us. As the food absorbed our attention, we forgot about our visitors and started talking about the season. My team, the Pee Wees, hadn't done anything. But the Midgets had won their championship, and they were acting like conquering heroes at the next table. I sat there with jealousy in my heart, wishing I could be part of a championship squad, but noticing, too, how much bigger they were than I. At two levels above mine, their hockey was considerably rougher. A lot of kids were washed out of the game for just that reason right about the time we got to the midget league.

The meal ended, and still no Petes. One of the coaches from the championship team got up and presented his players with their patches as league champions, and we all half-heartedly clapped on command, our minds elsewhere. Some of us started to worry that we'd been had. Were the Petes showing up or not?

Next came the entertainment portion of the program, which consisted of two things: a raffle for goodies donated by friends of All Saints, and footage of the prior year's Stanley Cup playoffs projected onto a screen at the front of the room.

We'd all been given raffle tickets as we came through the door for lunch. Prizes varied from a fish-and-chips dinner at Captain George to the grand prize, a hockey stick. Although that sounds kind of lame, it wasn't any old stick—it was autographed by every member of the Toronto Toros. The World Hockey Association, man. This was, after all, the 1970s.

As the guy at the front held the stick aloft for us all to see, I looked on, apathetically. I couldn't have cared less about the WHA. Nobody I knew really paid any attention to it. I watched only a couple of games during what ended up being the whole six-year history of the league—AVCO Cup contests featuring what looked to me like a 100-year-old Gordie Howe and his kids. My friends and I were staunch NHLers who, even at 12, resented the departure of talent from our league. The Toronto Toros, another team as lowly as the Maple Leafs in my mind, had taken Frank Mahovlich from my Canadiens. For that alone, I figured I should hate them. Little did I know at the time that the Big M would spend his last two years of professional hockey in Birmingham, Alabama, playing for the Bulls. How glamorous could that have been after winning Stanley Cups with Toronto and Montréal?

Anyway, some kid won the stick, and then it was time to see the playoffs. This was in the pre-VCR era, and the only way to review the moments of Philadelphia's Stanley Cup triumph of the previous spring would have been something like this movie version of it we were watching. Most of us had seen the games live, of course, but now we got to relive them as a narrator—sounding just like the one in the sex education films we saw in our health classes at school—retold each glorious moment. We watched and tried once again to get used to the idea that an expansion team had possession of the great Stanley Cup. And while the projector whirred and the screen at the front of the hall filled with light, I wondered where the promised Petes had gone.

Just as we got to the part where the narrator was telling us about Boston meeting Philadelphia in the finals, I had what I could have mistaken for a vision. In the darkness behind the portable movie screen, a door opened a crack. We all started to boo in derision at whoever would dare interrupt our film. Most of us probably had the notion that it was one of the kitchen staff or that minister, neither of whom, we were sure, cared at all about the game.

But then the booing suddenly stopped, for there, walking through the door, was Doug Jarvis, who would go on in the next several years to four championships with the Montréal Canadiens. He was entering from a lit hallway, so as he came in, there was a glow that emanated from behind him, creating the effect of god-like awe among those of us still young enough to admit to worshipping our heroes. The boos turned to cheers—the Petes had come, and it was like a visitation from on high. They came around to each of the tables to say hello, and then they sat up front and waited while we filed by for autographs.

I still have a piece of cardboard about 10 x 7 inches with a bunch of the Petes' signatures from that day. It's slightly bent up from the process of carrying it from player to player and from passing it around to my teammates as we compared who had whose autograph and where on the page it was. It's worth a lot to me as a memory, and I'm thankful that Jarvis and his teammates took the time to visit us that day. Seeing them and talking to them was the closest I would ever get to meeting a real NHLer, or nearly NHLer, until years later, and my impression more than anything was that Doug Jarvis was not just a hockey player, he was actually a nice guy. He wasn't scary to talk to like some of the other players, and he was clean-cut in an era of long-winged hairdos.

But I think back on that day with one regret. I wish it had been me who had won the hockey stick. If I had been, I would have taken it home with a feeling of curiosity mixed with apathy over its origins in the WHA, but I would still have it today, like I do all my other hockey memorabilia. And the stick would still be in mint condition like when I got it in 1975, Mahovlich's signature and those of his teammates serving as a reminder of a time when hockey was divided into two worlds and most of us didn't care a lot about the new league with its shiny, ultra-modern trophy.

I'm not sure which kid won that stick or what he did with it. Maybe he saved it like I would have, or maybe the stick ended up being used for street hockey, played with until it was shaved down to what we called a "toothpick," the blade so skinny that eventually a good slapshot would break it in half. If so, maybe he scored some glorious goals with it. I just hope he wasn't pretending to play for the Toros when he did so.

chapter thirty-one

The Month I Played Above Myself

I'd been playing goalie in street hockey games for years by the time I reached Bantam age, though on the ice I stuck to my position as right-winger. But one Sunday afternoon, the kid who played net didn't show up for a combination practice/scrimmage that our All Saints team was holding along with St. James United. Maybe he stayed home because it was Sunday. Back then, some parents actually made their kids remain inside and be quiet in observation of the Lord's Day. I nearly had to stay home myself, but my parents had relented and let me go, though they didn't come with me to the rink because Sunday was a busy day in our house, with church in the morning and company for lunch afterwards.

So my dad wasn't around to say no when the coach surveyed the dressing room and made the offer: "Who wants to suit up in goal?"

I was usually shy about jumping for things. I let a lot of opportunities get past me that way, but this day, I spoke up right away. "I can do it. I play on the street. I have my own gloves, pads and mask." My mom had brought me back a pair of "DR HT65" goalie gloves from a business trip as a gift. (Of course I still have them. Thanks for asking.) So on the street, I really was official, though the pads I'd fought so hard to get some years earlier were looking pretty small on my 13-year-old legs.

"We have the stuff right here," my coach replied, thinking that I meant that I had to have my own equipment.

"I know, Coach. I meant that I can do it," I assured him.

In fact, I needed a good deal of help to get into the full set of equipment. The goalie pads were far heavier than the ones I was used to, and the system of straps was complicated. The first time I tried to do them up, I got them all too tight. I could barely stand up afterwards. But I hid this from the coach for fear that he'd tell me this wasn't going to work out.

I guess if I'd had more time to think about it, I would have been scared. Or, more likely, my head would have been filled with fantasy images of who I was out there. This was in the winter of 1976, so Dryden had come out of retirement to play for the Habs again, but I wasn't crazy about him anymore and hadn't been since the 1972 Summit Series. His new mask, a big plastic one with red and blue circular paint accents, completely bugged me.

In my fantasies I could have been Bernie Parent, who had done a great job in the playoffs for Philly the couple of years prior. We all liked him at my school, but nobody could quite digest the idea yet that there was a team out there with orange sweaters wearing Stanley Cup rings. Another option was Rogie Vachon, who was holding fort for the far-off L.A. Kings, and he was cool. So was Eddie Giacomin. I probably would have been one of them in my head. But I didn't have time for either fantasy or fear. I was suddenly a real-life goalie.

I went out onto the ice at the Kinsmen Civic Centre in Peterborough and took my place in the crease. Like I'd seen goalies do a million times, I tried to rough up the ice, which was difficult considering I hadn't been able to put on goalie skates. The kid who normally played the position had taken them home, so here I was in my regular forward's skates. Still, I did a credible imitation of a guy who knew what he was doing, and I squared to the shooters for the warm-up.

There was only one kid on our team who had a really good slapshot. Chris Walker was a "bad boy," long-haired in that '70s rocker way, and with an older brother who everybody knew was trouble. He was one of the only kids I ever remember getting the strap at our school, and he was proud of it. I was surprised, actually, that Chris was playing hockey now that we had all moved on to grade seven. It was such a mainstream thing to do that it seemed like his rebellion in all other things would have kept him out of it. But here he was lining up on the blue line to take a shot at me. It boomed off my pads. I was glad he had observed the unwritten code and not moved in any closer. The other shooters were far easier to handle, and so the game started with the guys seeming somewhat surprised at my skills.

For me, the only memorable thing about the game itself was that I let in a really soft goal. The player came in on a breakaway but started to fall as he got close to the net. A defenseman must have been locked up with him. Meanwhile, I got ready for the shot, and I went down. Then, as I was lying on the ice, instead of a shot, I saw the offensive player and another body gliding toward me. The puck was out in front of them. I stretched my arms for it, but it slid right past me and into the far side of the net on my left. I can still see the goal in slow motion, which was how it looked to me then. I knew I should do something else—stand up, slide farther over, shove out my stick—but I couldn't make myself move at all.

Even though it was a bad goal, it was the only one St. James scored, and as we walked back into the dressing room the coach looked at me with surprise. "Hey, you're pretty good. You want to play some more?" he asked.

Truthfully, I had scared myself. I was better than I had thought I would be, those years of imitating Dryden and Esposito on my kitchen floor and in my imagination having taught me moves that actually worked on the ice. But I had no idea if I wanted to play in goal again. Although I had enjoyed it, I wasn't actually used to being good at hockey. I was a hard-working player. I knew my position when I played on right wing, and I did pretty well in the assist department. But I never started games, and I was more used to blending into the group on the bench than being the first kid the coach pointed at to get out there. Facing the pressure of being the goalie wasn't something I wanted to grab at too quickly.

I just smiled at the coach and walked past him, hoping to buy some time to think this over. I was calculating the chances of repeating my success. What if I got out there again and was a disaster? This had been only a scrimmage, after all. Why not quit while I was ahead? My record was perfect.

In the end, it was my teammates who talked me into playing again. Even I had to admit that I had been better than the regular goalie, so the next game, I was suited up. My dad wasn't at all surprised by this, so I guess the coach had OK'd it with him. As one of the assistant coaches, maybe Dad had been consulted anyway.

I played a couple of games, and again, I was good, all those moves I'd practiced on the streets of my neighborhoods in Montréal and Peterborough somehow translating into game-saving ability. I was so good in fact, that the coach from the team we'd played in our practice, St. James United, asked my dad if I could fill in a couple of games for his team. Now the stakes were raised, and the moment of choice was coming.

Our regular All Saints goalie had reclaimed his spot in net, but here was my chance to keep playing the position.

Dad left the decision up to me, and I agreed to do it, confident by this point that my success was not a fluke. I didn't worry too much about stopping the puck, but I did start to worry a little more about my safety than I had when I had jumped into that first practice. The padding, I reasoned, was pretty good. The helmet, which had a full cage on the front of it, was good, too. I had taken a hard shot to the ribs in one of my team's games, but generally the players were still not skilled enough to really launch any rockets, so the felt armpads and stitched canvas-covered chest protector were enough to keep me from serious damage. What I was worried about was my neck.

I tried to play a stand-up style. Although I no longer worshipped Ken Dryden, my style had been formed on the streets during the period when he was everything to me, and to the Montréal Canadiens. Back then, Tony Esposito was playing butterfly, but he was one of the only ones. The reign of Patrick Roy and the floppers was a decade in the future. Goalies mostly stayed on their feet, probably because the only place they really wanted to get hit, in the days before the equipment was so huge that netminders looked like Hulks, was in the leg pads. But what would happen, I wondered, if I went down on a shot, or was scrambling for a rebound, and someone shot a puck that hit me in the throat?

Even with no neck guard, I played on, though I never felt all that assured of my safety. This was reinforced one night when a guy came in on a two-on-one and slapped one from near the blue line that came straight for my face. I put my trapper out and blocked it, and the puck fell at my feet. I should have cleared it to the corner to keep the play going, but I flopped on it, forcing a faceoff in my own end. It was a minor mistake that came out of surprise at the height of the shot. I shook it off and continued, my newfound career progressing in a way that amazed even me.

The irony is that being good at the game was an odd feeling for me. Along with a couple of wins came a feeling of pressure. Could I keep doing this? I hadn't even told the kids at school what was going on, though the boys on my All Saints team knew. A couple of them went to school with me at Queen Mary, so the word was starting to get around. The situation was getting a little too big for me to handle.

Then my dad told me that he'd had a phone call from the coach on the team I was playing with as a borrowed player. League rules said that if I played more than four games for another team, I would be assigned to that team for the rest of the season. Continuing in net meant that my days as an All Saint and right-winger would be over and that I was accepting the pressure of playing goalie as a full-time thing. I had a few days to decide, but they needed to know. If I didn't want to play, St. James needed to call up another kid in time for their next game.

The decision seemed monumental. I had read about the lives of goalies, and I knew what pressure did to them. Glenn Hall threw up before every game. Terry Sawchuck's nerves got the better of him. Dryden had taken a year off in his prime. Thinking about these great men and how they had succumbed to the pressure, I knew that I couldn't continue to play in net. What if I was on a lucky streak, and it ended? I would be sitting in the St. James United locker room with no friends. I couldn't bear the thought that I'd be left without a team, without a position.

In the end, hockey meant more to me than my own success at it, and so I stepped back from my glory days and played out the season, and the next, on my regular team, in my regular spot. I did get a few more games in goal, and I was still pretty good, but I never again was asked to play for a team aside from mine. Even at that age and level, I guess the coaches knew who had the killer instinct.

chapter thirty-two

Sudden
Death

D oug Jarvis, one of the Petes' all-time greats, was a hero
during my Peterborough years. But where I lived, any
Pete was an object of worship in a way that resembled how the
Canadiens were mythologized in Montréal. So when our pastor announced that one of the Petes defensemen was coming
to our church to speak, there was a buzz.

That Sunday, I begged my parents to get to church
early. It had been promised that everyone in attendance would
get to meet the Petes player, and then he would be interviewed
as part of our morning service. It may seem absurd that we
were all, kids and adults alike, induced to crawl over each
other to meet a high school kid, but such was the power of
hockey. I think a lot of our motivation was the hope that he
would make it to the NHL. Not for his own sake, but so that

we could spot him on TV and turn to the guys next to us and mention that we'd met him, gotten his autograph even.

As it turned out, there was such a crowd that the pastor decided to just get the service underway and deal with the handshaking and autograph signing afterwards, so I took my seat midway back in the group of about 275 people and waited. We sang the usual songs, and because it was a Baptist church, men passed gold trays around, taking up the collection. Then our pastor got up, microphone in hand, and stood next to the day's hero. He was a big guy, dressed in a suit too tight for him, especially in the arms and chest. He told the story of how he had become a Christian and how he lived his life despite the pressures of worldliness that came with playing hockey. It was a story we'd all heard before from celebrities who'd been to our church, or who gave a similar "testimony," as we called it, on TV.

When asked how he could justify the fighting that was part of the game, given his faith and the supposed pacifism of Jesus, he just shrugged. "It's my job to do all I do out there heartily for the Lord. If my coach wants me to play rough, I play rough. If it comes to fighting, I can't back down. My teammates count on me," he replied. The pastor spun back his response into a Christian value somehow linked to faith and commitment and thus created an apology for whatever was necessary to win hockey games.

As the defenseman stood there talking, I tried to figure out what I would say in my grade eight class the next morning. I wanted to tell the kids that I'd seen a Pete, up close, but I knew that I couldn't really go into details. Church was something that nobody ever talked about in my school, a vast difference from my later experience in the U.S., where religion is a much more mainstream thing. I decided to tell only one person, Johnny Walsh, my friend who had introduced me to the Memorial Centre a couple of years earlier. This kid was a year younger than I was, also a big hockey fan, but not in my grade. He wouldn't leak out the word, and I'd still get to tell the story that was bursting inside me.

The next morning, I walked with Johnny to the bus stop as always, but this time with my secret at the ready. The thing was, he had a secret of his own. He had Petes tickets, right behind the bench, for a game later in the week. Two tickets, and his dad had told him that he could take anyone he wanted to. He chose me.

I was beside myself. Although the arena the Petes played in was small, relatively speaking, even the best seats I'd ever had had been a dozen rows off the ice, in the corner. To sit right behind the bench would put us in touch with the game like I'd never been. I could hardly wait to get to school now. This was a story that I could share openly. The other guys in my class would talk about it off and on for days. In my excitement, I stuffed my secret about meeting the Petes player to the back of my mind, thinking that there was plenty of time for me to spell it all out to Johnny before we went to our game.

That week was the same as every other, my grade eight teacher coming down on us with the usual spelling tests, math homework and the rest. But game night came at last, and Johnny's dad, as he had done before, dropped us off at the rink.

We insisted on getting there for the warm-up, but instead of standing behind the net like we did the last time, we decided to go to our premium seats right away. When the trainer came out to put the extra sticks in the rack, we were close enough to touch him. The players came out, and in the course of their drills, a couple came over to replace the lumber they carried. We were within spitting distance of them, and their faces were masks of concentration. Or maybe they were just unsure about what to make of two kids standing in their seats, leaning over to gawk at their every move.

The game began, and we split our time between watching the ice and watching the bench. The flurry that came with on-the-fly changes amazed us. Things didn't happen nearly this fast in the leagues we played in. As we sat there, I decided to unburden myself of the secret I'd kept all week. I had to tell Johnny that I'd seen number 12 (or whatever the number was) at my church last Sunday. I figured that mentioning church at this moment was OK. Johnny couldn't hurt me with the information, at least not here.

"See number 12?" I said. "He spoke at my church last Sunday. I got his autograph." Johnny didn't seem to know whether to say something about the autograph or about the church thing. He chose the latter.

"He goes to church?" he said. It was almost inconceivable, because we didn't quite believe hockey players did anything human, let alone go to church.

"Sure. He grew up in Toronto. His parents are Alliance," I said, naming another denomination of the Christian church. "He said he was 'saved' as a kid," I added. I knew Johnny would understand what I was talking about. In the summertime he had gone to a kids' group at the church directly across the road from his house, and their beliefs were similar to those at my church. To be "saved" meant to accept the teachings of Christ, which our church wanted everyone in the world to do. Even the Petes, improbable as it seemed to our kid brains.

As Johnny was about to register his surprise, number 12 came back to the bench for a change. He'd let a guy go around him for a shot on goal while we watched, and now he had a decidedly unchristian look on his face.

"Damn!" he yelled, just that single word, and not to anybody in particular. He spit it out into the boards in front of him as he swung around to sit.

I was mortified. This was the last thing he was supposed to say. Just days ago, he'd been standing in front of everyone

I knew and telling them how he got his strength from the Lord, how he remained calm during the hard times by relying on God's peace. I looked at Johnny, not knowing what to do, but feeling like I ought to apologize. He wasn't as startled as I was, apparently not understanding the weight of number 12's offense against the faith. I was relieved. Maybe we could just concentrate on the game, instead of what I feared, which was having to explain this behavior to Johnny.

Luckily, Johnny didn't bring up the swear word again. Maybe in the excitement of telling his dad after the game about our premium seats, he forgot. Maybe it just didn't matter to him like it did to me.

Instead, we talked about the speed and sounds of the game, which from our vantage point behind the bench had been unlike anything we'd ever experienced before. As we were talking, though, I couldn't help but flash back to the moment of anger when the defenseman had, in my mind, betrayed everything he had smilingly avowed just a few days earlier. I had no answer as to why he had reacted that way. All I knew was that it was a secret I had to keep. Nobody would believe me at church, so convincing was the defenseman's testimony. I was left to process my hero's fall from grace on my own.

chapter thirty-three

First
Intermission

H ockey is a rough game. But when you're a kid, at least up to a certain age, it's pretty safe. Nobody is fast enough or balanced enough to really deliver a decent hit, not on purpose anyway. I wasn't ever scared in my first six years of organized play. I had stayed with the game up through the Bantam division, playing for All Saints Anglican since I had moved from Montréal to Peterborough as a Pee Wee player.

Now here I was in grade eight, and I had played some in goal, but mostly I was still out on the forward lines as a right-winger. But there was a moment when that all changed and church league hockey got to be too rough for me. We were playing a team sponsored by a Catholic church, Immaculate Conception, though I had no idea what an "Immaculate Conception" was. I thought it was some kind of nuts and bolts company, and the thing they had wonderfully conceived was some invention. It didn't make any sense to me why the team was in the church league with the rest of us. But so be it.

Immaculate Conception was remarkable for how they played. They were rough and intimidating, way more so than any of the other teams in our league. They had a couple of big guys, too, much bigger than ours, even our defensemen, and they would really hit you.

The game started with me on the bench, as usual. I was due to go out on the third line. My dad was the assistant coach, in charge of the forward lines, and he played us fair and square, every kid getting equal ice time, though by this point in our careers, the league rules allowed the coaches flexibility in the use of players. We weren't playing by a three-minute buzzer any longer, as we had done all the years before.

Our first shift center, a kid I'd played with for years, sat beside me on the bench when he came back after starting the game. Mike was one of the first players on our team to wear a full shield combined with a piece that covered his jaw, and when he came through the door, he ripped his helmet off in frustration. He was so angry that he had to wipe tears off the inside of his visor.

"That number seven is dirty," he said. "That kid's tryin' to hurt me."

We'd been warned about that guy before the game. Our head coach was a man who took the game pretty seriously.

He always tried to scout the opposing teams, sometimes by word of mouth at the arena, sometimes by watching teams playing before or after us, knowing we'd meet them in a game or two. This night, he had told us to watch out for three players. Two of them were huge defensemen. There was no mistaking them. The third was this number seven, who was the only player on their team wearing a black helmet. The rest of them had white to match their blue and white jerseys. We wore black and red jerseys, and an array of helmets, black, white and red.

Now here was Mike, our captain, sitting on the bench complaining that it hadn't even taken one shift for that little number seven to get under his skin.

"What'd he do?" I asked in an almost pleading voice. I was one of those kids to whom fairness meant a lot. If an injustice had taken place, I wanted to know about it.

"He hit me hard, with his elbow," Mike said, stifling more sobs. I was shocked and sickened. My shift was next. I didn't want to go out and get "hammered," which was the word Mike used in describing what had happened to him.

Number seven played quite a bit of that game, and Mike wasn't the only one of us he frightened. By the end of the game, we were all shaken up. As I went through the line in the post-game "handshake"—actually, for anyone who remembers playing at this level, more of a hand-slap—I saw number seven grinning underneath his '70s hairstyle, his hair sticking out from the sides of his helmet like spikes. He had gotten the better of us, and he seemed devilishly happy about it. I felt a sort of strange sick feeling, and I couldn't understand why he would be proud of himself for having been violent. Where was his conscience?

Immaculate Conception players were dirty and rough. That's why they had won, and if they won the season's championship, it would be "no fair." We all agreed to this as we griped about it in the dressing room afterward. But we hadn't done anything about it on the ice, and there wasn't much we could do now. We weren't going to play their game. We couldn't. We had been coached to be polite, to play fair and to win with skill if and when we did get a victory. Intimidation was nowhere in our battle plan. Up until that point, it had never needed to be. That wasn't what hockey had been about.

A couple of weeks later, my family was at the Walters' house for dinner. Jamie Walter, their son, was a fellow All Saints player. My sister and Jamie's were good friends, too. Jamie's dad was a skilled tradesman, a guy who got his hands dirty doing hard work for a living.

While we passed around the roast beef, we talked hockey, and my dad said that he had heard that the house league was thinking about banning checking for the next season and letting us play no-contact. Jamie's dad reacted to this by saying, "I don't think that's a good idea. I don't mind seeing

Jamie get knocked around a little bit. It will teach him to stand up for himself."

Jamie was what we called a "decent" player—not a star, but not the last guy you'd pick, either. He wasn't big, though, and he had been just as scared as the rest of us during the Immaculate Conception game. Now here was his dad, saying that it was OK for a team to play like those guys had. This baffled me. I still hadn't processed the idea that as I matured, hockey wasn't going to stay the same game I had always known it to be.

Then Jamie's dad said words that spelled the beginning of the end for my hockey career: "The game from now on is going to be a lot more like playing Immaculate Conception than it has been before. That's just the way it's played when you get older."

While I tried to make sense of what seemed to be a betrayal of something I loved, my dad kind of shrugged. "I think they still need time to focus on their skating," he said. As a coach, he was more interested in us developing our skills than developing toughness. Maybe he thought we weren't ready. Maybe he didn't think that at the house league level, there was any need for us to be banging and crashing and getting hurt. Could be he was out of his element when it came to coaching that kind of game. Whatever the case, it was clear that for him, a game where kids got hurt, or had the potential to, wasn't fun anymore. But he didn't argue with Jamie's dad.

Maybe, I thought, *Mr. Walter is right about the future of hockey.*

As I was thinking about this, I was aware of a sinking feeling in my gut. I knew I hadn't done anything in that Immaculate Conception game except try to keep safe. I had passed or tipped the puck away from me whenever it came close. Every shift had been scary to me, not fun, and not glorious the way I had always pictured playing hockey. I couldn't imagine myself ever scoring a goal again if I had to worry all the time about getting my head taken off every time I touched the puck.

I carried these thoughts with me as we left the Walters' house that day, and all through the summer. When it came time to register for hockey again in the fall, I decided that I'd had enough. Like I'd seen some of my favorite pros do, I decided to end my playing days. It was my first retirement from the game, at 14.

chapter thirty-four

The Playoff Face

'm not sure how it was in other schools, but where I grew up, there was nothing more glamorous than getting stitches. In the face if possible. A black eye might come close, and a broken bone with a cast would also gain a guy considerable attention, but a cut could not be topped. Even today, when I see NHL players on TV with scars and current sutures holding together gashes, I'm reminded of the glory that came to any kid lucky enough to get cut.

Toothlessness was another mark of hard play. Remember the photo of Bobby Hull with the Stanley Cup, or Brad Park's interview after game eight in Moscow? Or any photo or video of Bobby Clarke playing? None of them had any front teeth. They were warriors.

I started playing league hockey in the days when there was no requirement to wear face protection other than a mouthguard, which was attached to the straps on your helmet and formed a tiny cage over your teeth, on the outside. Later on we had to put on visors or cages to cover our whole faces. Still, in minor league hockey, it wasn't all that likely that a player would get a puck in the face. Nobody could shoot it that hard. But the occasional stick came up and clipped some-one, who would then wear his injury proudly to school, the other kids asking a million times what had happened.

Unfortunately, this never happened to me. I never got hurt playing until I was older, and then not glorious injuries, just painful ones. But that didn't stop me from giving myself what the TV commentators call a "playoff face" when I was in grade 10—a year after my first retirement from organized hockey, ironically.

The episode started during a basketball game in gym class. I was under the basket, looking for a rebound, but I was completely surprised when the ball bounced straight down from the rim into my arms. I had to bend my knees to grab it—it got down to me before I quite realized what was hap-pening. As I did, some kid playing opposite me raised his arms, probably because the teacher was standing there yelling instructions—"Raise your arms on defense!"—he said to us over and over.

I came up with the ball and went to shoot it back at the basket, which was almost directly above me, and as I did, I flexed my knees, sprang upwards and drove my face right into the kid's elbow. Bang! I got that feeling of a fist pounding into sand that comes with a blow to the head. I grabbed my cheek, sure that it was already gushing blood. Visions of grade school glory danced in my head. But my hand came away dry.

I went to the locker room anyway, and there in the mirror was a tiny but visible purple welt, about a half an inch long, raised up on a bump that had formed under the skin. With any luck, I'd have a black eye in minutes.

I got home an hour or so later and ran upstairs to the mirror behind my mom's dresser to check my face, but I saw nothing more than what I'd already seen. The images of a hockey player's injury sticking out to show the world how tough I was were fading fast. I decided to take matters into my own hands.

I picked up one of my mother's safety pins, opened it, and gently creased the welt with the sharp end. It reddened. I did it again, this time digging a little harder. The skin broke ever so slightly. I went over it several more times, and then for good measure, I made a loose fist and gave myself a couple of whaps with my knuckles to bring up the swelling.

Voila! I had magnified a bump that probably would have been gone in a day or two into something that turned me into Tiger Williams, at the time the tough-guy left-winger for the Toronto Maple Leafs. Not that I wanted to be a Leaf, but to the people in my Ontario town, he would be the immediate association with a cut, bruise, black eye or whatever it was that I had given myself.

Later that day, my parents, who hadn't been home when I was working my wonder, asked me what had happened. "I got it in gym," was all I had to say. It was a secret code that said, "I'm a man now; this stuff happens in the course of my day."

When I got to gym class the next day, my teacher's eyes searched my face suspiciously. "You get that from yesterday afternoon?" he asked. His wording of the question allowed me to answer without lying. Technically, he hadn't asked me about the collision, and what I had *had* resulted from all that had happened yesterday afternoon, so I didn't hesitate to build the myth again. I shrugged out a yes.

He wasn't buying it. He had looked at the injury at the end of class the prior afternoon and determined that it was a minor bump. Now, he looked puzzled, like he was wondering what had caused it to grow into a cut. But all he said was, "Better be careful on those rebounds today." I turned and ran to join my team.

My classmates asked me what had happened, and to them I explained the dangers of gym class basketball. But none of these were my moment of glory. That came when I was walking down the corridor of my school, alone out there during the middle of a class period. As I took a quick left turn to the water fountain, the grade 11 physics teacher popped out of a doorway, himself headed for a drink.

I straightened up from the fountain and turned in his direction. His eyes immediately went to my face. "High stick?" he asked. It was a natural question, this being the middle of winter.

"Yeah," I said, not even hesitating. My hand brushed my cheek self-consciously, but I held his gaze.

"That looks nasty. I didn't know you played. Be careful out there," he offered, then bent to the fountain as I went on my way, afraid to say more lest he probe me for details.

Delight at my grand moment crept through me. In my imagination, as I hoped in his, I was crashing into the corner after the puck, Gordie Howe's power and Guy Lafleur's speed rolled into one, oblivious to the dangers of the game I played so well. I made a mental note to avoid physics at all costs in case that teacher asked me more about my playing career.

Today, if you look really closely, you can still see the fine scar under my left eye, though time and age have conspired to give me other lines that make it almost disappear. And if you ask me what happened, I'll only shrug and say, "Who knows? I played hockey for years. And in those days, we didn't wear a cage."

chapter thirty-five

Wearing the Zebra Stripes

The people who promote amateur hockey in Canada spend their money on TV ads to try to curb parents' anger at their children and at hockey officials. One such commercial shows kids sitting in the back seat of a car while a cop tries to give their dad a ticket. One kid pipes up and yells, "Hey, you're not going to take that, are you? Don't let him do that to you!" Or something like that.

Apparently, parents these days act in a way that makes these ads necessary. From what I've gathered, the problem is two-fold. On the one hand, the country panicked after losing a number of important international tournaments in the late 1990s. Canadians want their players to be the best in the world, and rightly so, as the inventors of the game. So there's a lot of pressure on the kids to be good. On the other hand, there's a lot of money in hockey at the professional level.

Parents know that, and they know too that their kid needs to show his skills early to make the NHL. Everyone wants a prodigy. Sometimes that pressure spills over to victimize coaches and referees.

This phenomenon is at least a few decades old. I know this firsthand. It's not what you think, though. My dad is a civil, decent man who went to almost every one of my hockey games. He even coached my team for several years. I never heard him yell except when it fit into the flow of the game. He was not one of the people those ads target.

I know about crazed parents because during high school, as a way to stay involved with hockey after I "retired," I started refereeing minor hockey games. The rule was that you could work one division lower than the one you played in. Thus, by the time I was in grade 12, I was officiating 15- and 16-year-olds. That was tricky, especially since some of them went to my high school and weren't, let's just say, the kind of guys to forget a bad call. But even that was not the greatest threat to my days as a "zebra."

Refereeing the Pee Wees was. These 11- and 12-year-old kids had started to get a feel for the game. They were good enough that they could play as a team. When they took a shot from inside the blue line, the puck sailed in on net, maybe wobbling a little, but most of the time it was pretty much on course. Their skating was decent, and the defensemen did a credible job of skating backwards. So what they played at the house league level was more or less a recognizable version of hockey, not some kind of mad scramble or comedy of errors where they fanned on the shots, went headfirst into their own goalie or scored on the wrong end.

The good thing about the Pee Wees, at least when I was working their games, was that they were still considerably smaller than most high school students, me included. And they hadn't yet learned that adults really aren't all-powerful. In the late '70s, kids could still be given the strap at school when they misbe-haved, and I as the authority figure was accorded some of the same fearful respect that they had for the vice principal, the chief disciplinarian at their schools. So generally, they took my direc-tion and didn't put up much fuss.

Too bad not all of their parents felt the same way. In that respect, maybe not much has changed, though I have heard stories of spitting, hitting and suing that were not a part of my career highlight reel as a ref. I did, however, have one incident that has become a favorite story of my dad's, one he trots out for company sometimes.

I was working a game on a Saturday afternoon at an arena in Peterborough. The place was a two-pad set-up, with a heated and glass-enclosed lounge upstairs where spectators could look out over each side. It was the same arena where I had made my debut as a goalie for All Saints Anglican several years before.

One coach had the strange method of pulling his players aside during the course of play if they made a mistake. He would make them stand in front of the bench and watch the play while he talked to them about their error. Until I realized what was going on, it seemed bizarre to me. I kept noticing a deficiency of players in the attacking zone, my instincts always being to keep a count in case a team accidentally had too many.

Early on in the game, the parents were thankfully invisible, that being the preferred state. As things progressed, though, I noticed a voice out of synch with the rest. "Come on seventeen! Get the hell in there!"

Shortly after, I noticed that number 17 was standing in front of his team's bench getting a talking-to. As I stood on the blue line (my partner referee in the two-person system was working in deep in this end), I could hear the coach explaining how 17 should stay at the blue line when the puck was in the attacking zone. It was all very polite. I didn't think the voice I heard teaching the kid his position matched the one yelling a second earlier.

The shifts changed, new players taking to the ice. The voice disappeared. Then a few minutes later it was back. "Move it, seventeen! Move, move! Damn it, move!" I looked over, and there was one face behind the bench that was not like the others. It was red, exasperated, defiant—it was the face of the voice. It hadn't been the coach.

The puck was now in 17's attacking zone. While the players scrambled in the corner, I looked for 17. He was halfway between the blue line and the faceoff circle, creeping in to join the frenzy of the offense, but tentative. His defense partner was stationed just inside the blue line, exactly where the coach had told 17 to be. "Go, go! Dig it out! Diiiiig it!" The voice was crazed now.

Seventeen's father had no interest in his son playing the glorious position of Larry Robinson or Brad Park. He wanted a Bobby Orr. He didn't care what the coach wanted. He had to see his son score a goal. If it happened every time the kid was on the ice, so much the better. But he was urging his son to do what I and the kid knew was directly against the wishes of the coach. The boy's hesitancy was obvious, which only made his old man more insane.

During the next stoppage of play, which brought about another change of players, I went over to the bench. The coach moved in front of his players to greet me.

"The voice, there, yelling. It's going to cost you a bench minor soon," I said to the coach. I thought a warning might give him a chance to run interference, quiet things down so that the game could go on. I had been calling games for a while, and I knew that one irate parent usually led to a second and third, and that the anger would quickly be taken out on the officials or the opposing parents.

The game resumed, and eerie quiet ensued. Seventeen, sitting on the bench, was waiting his turn on the ice. When he retook the ice, there it was again. "Stupid, stupid, STUUUPID!" Each word was louder than the last. "Doesn't anyone know how to PAAAASSS?" This time it was directed at more than the man's son. He was angry because the centerman, a decent little player with a helmet that didn't quite fit and a dipsy-doodle style that allowed him to fake out the opposition, wouldn't drop it back to the kid on the blue line for a shot. As I realized this, I told myself that it was enough. This was changing from child abuse to team abuse. I had to stop it.

I raised my arm for a penalty, then immediately blew the play dead, since 17's squad had the puck. I skated to the bench and motioned for a bench minor for unsportsmanlike conduct. "Two minutes unsportsmanlike—spectator yelling after the coach was warned." I made my voice as convincing as I could, then started to skate backwards toward the penalty bench to inform the timekeeper of the call. The coach looked at the irate parent, who in turn glared at me. I stopped at mid-ice. It was clear that this guy was used to getting his own way. I wondered how many Saturdays this poor coach had stood there, trying to teach these boys the game, and listened to this maniac curse him, his players and his methods. What were the practices like, or worse yet, the moments after practice, when this guy probably harangued the coach about every drill, insisting that his son shouldn't be confined to the rigidity of the traditional defenseman's role?

"YOU'RE NUTS!" the dad yelled. At least he hadn't called me a, well, you think it out for yourself. But his face said even more than his words. It declared, "War's on, kid."

My fellow referee was, during all of this, standing in the offensive zone where the play had been called dead, holding the puck in the circle so he could hand it off to me. Each ref dropped the puck in the zone where he was the deep man. I looked over at him and motioned him to meet me on the opposite side of the ice, in the referee's crease. It was an imagined safety zone, a place where I'd be more than an arm's length from the kook that I was confronting. Before I skated to meet the other ref, I stopped and looked at the coach, and with all my might I repeated, "Two minutes. Send over a player. And before we drop the puck, he goes upstairs." I pointed at the man with the voice, as if that were necessary.

I skated backwards toward the scoring table and my safe semi-circular haven, as I'd been taught to do. When I got there, I waited. The coach started to send a player over. Seventeen's dad, extremely angry, was beginning the slow blush of embarrassment. Yet instead of the tirade that I'd been expecting, he leaned over to argue with the coach, but softly. I couldn't hear the words. It was like a baseball-style meeting at the mound. Then when the player got to me, and I motioned him into the box, the dad suddenly stepped back from the bench. The two-minute indication went up on the score clock. That pushed his vitriol button again.

"Come on! This is NUTS!" the dad said. But he didn't stop there. "You're ruining this game!" he yelled across at me. With that, I decided that he'd crossed a line. He'd insulted me twice, and the next two minutes were sure to bring a torrent of more nasty words. With over a period left in the game, I had no choice but to follow up on my words to the coach.

I reached into my partner referee's hand and grabbed the puck. I slammed it down on the top of the boards in front of the scorer. She was one of the moms, and it made her jump. I turned around and raised my voice, though I needn't have. The place was deathly quiet. Players just stood in front of their benches. We were in uncharted waters for sure.

"He goes upstairs before we drop the puck," I said across the ice to the coach. It was too bad that he had to be the one, because from the look on his face moments before, I could tell that he had had all he wanted of this parent. "Upstairs." I repeated it and pointed to the lobby. The windows would enable him to look down, but they didn't open. He could yell all he wanted to. We would hear nothing.

I turned around to the timekeeper's bench and picked up the puck once again, then set it back down on the boards, but gently this time. Everyone needed to understand that I was going to stand there until the hour allotted for this game ran out, but I was not going to resume the play until 17's father had disappeared. What never occurred to me, of course, was that this could get extremely ugly. I guess I just figured the referee's jersey and shield-shaped "Ontario Minor Hockey Association" patch that I wore were strong enough to protect me and the others there from complete chaos.

Maybe I was crazy. All I knew was that it was my job to keep order, and I was going to do it, at the expense of the game if need be. And it worked.

The dad looked at me, then at the coach. But what must have persuaded him was the players. There they sat, their coaches having motioned them onto the benches in the interim. Their faces, for this was the era before the cage, were a mixture of pleading and confusion. This was their only game this week. No matter that it was mid-season. They likely weren't thinking about the season's standings. Nor would they have been thinking ahead to how they'd ever explain this at school on Monday. All they knew was that because of this man, *nobody* was playing.

The dad shrugged. No final curse came out. He just gave up, wrapped his jacket tighter around him and walked out. His posture didn't seem particularly defiant. Surprising, since I was a 140-pound teenager.

The game went on. The coach resumed his method of pulling his players out of the action to analyze the play. The kids learned something about hockey that day, not because of me, but in spite of the situation. Peace reigned. And by the luck of the draw, I never ended up doing another game with that team that year. Nor did I see 17's father again.

Thinking back to this incident, I wonder: Does 17 remember that day? I hope he does, both because he learned something about playing defense and because he's old enough to have kids of his own now. I hope he's not behind some bench taking refs' heads off every time they do anything that's against his perception of how hockey should be played. But even if he's out there somewhere behaving himself, there are too many others who aren't. Perhaps there's no better proof than a recent newspaper cartoon that shows a rink with kids playing on it. Posted alongside is a sign thanking parents for not having a fit and beating up the referee. If it wasn't happening, there'd be no need to satirize it.

chapter thirty-six

Double
Minor

After grade eight, at the end of my Bantam year, the league I played in didn't change to no-contact as had been hinted, and so instead of facing the terrors of midget hockey, I quit. The game was just too rough for me, and I'd had enough of being fearful of getting hit. Refereeing was some consolation for missing the game, and I did a good enough job at it that I was nominated to work the playoffs every year of my four-year career.

But in truth, wearing the stripes wasn't enough for me, and so when I was in grade 12 and the league changed its rules once more, to disallow contact, I decided to play again despite my layoff. I went to All Saints Anglican Church to sign up and was surprised to see crowds of guys there, all of whom must have decided that this new, kinder game was to their liking.

We had our first mass practice, with 30 players turning out for the Juvenile team. The coach didn't know what to do with us all. He suggested that we might even split to form two teams, if the league allowed it. That idea never got off the ground, though, and All Saints decided to go with the boys who had played with them all along. I got traded for the first time in my career. Well, "traded" is the nice way to say it. I was told I'd be assigned to another team to play the season. Imagine my surprise when my new coach told me that I would be wearing the blue and white sweater of Immaculate Conception, our old archrival and the team that had convinced me by their savage style three years earlier that playing league hockey wasn't for me anymore.

I showed up at an arena in the north end of Peterborough and suited up for my first game, not knowing any of my teammates. The coach stuck me on the third line, and I played my typical conservative, passing-based game. I did the same thing the next game and the next. My teammates, most of whom had played together for years, pretty much ignored me in the dressing room as well as on the bench. I tried to get noticed by hustling as hard as I could on the ice. Once or twice they gave me a nod of acknowledgment, but most of the time I was invisible. The one thing I noticed was an intensity to them that I hadn't felt when playing for All Saints. I just put it down to the players being several years older than when I'd last played competitively. I decided to make the most of this, my last season of league hockey.

Then I got hurt.

It was during practice, and I was cruising down on the off-wing, back-checking for a defenseman who was caught in the attacking zone. I had just reached the guy with the puck when he reared back to shoot. I was in full stride, digging to get in front of him, and he caught me on the instep of my right foot with his slapshot. The puck glanced off my skate and into the corner. I couldn't feel my foot as I chased the puck, but I played out the shift and went to the bench.

I sat down and took off my skate. Seeing that the foot was purple and swelling, the coach told me to put my skate back on if I had any thought of getting back on the ice. His gritty attitude surprised me. It was no wonder he could demand toughness out of his players. As practice ended, I noticed a tightness to the fit of my skate that hadn't been there before. When I got to the dressing room, I took the skate off gingerly. Immediately, my foot began to swell, and there was a bruise the size of a quarter on the spot where the puck had hit.

The next morning, which was Sunday, my dad took me to the hospital after church, which I got to skip for one of the only times I could remember. I was told that the foot wasn't broken, but that it was bruised to the point that I needed crutches for a couple of weeks and would walk with a cane for a month after that. Hockey, including refereeing, was over for me. My career with Immaculate Conception had lasted only a few games.

However, feeling better a few months later, I decided to go back to playing, rather than just let the season end without me, which I was tempted to do. When I entered the dressing room for the first time, the faces that looked at me registered only a faint light of recognition. I reported to the coach, telling him that I'd had a broken foot, just for dramatic effect, but that I'd recovered. He only half listened. "You'll play right wing then," was all he said. As I dressed, I decided that if I was going to salvage this season, which meant a lot to me after my layoff, I had to do something to get myself noticed.

I went out tentative, feeling awkward being on skates again. Dutifully, I policed my lane, as I had done all my hockey life, until sometime in the second period. I was nearing center ice on a play coming out of our end when an opposing defenseman got directly in my way. We collided, and he went down. The referee whistled play dead. I looked around, wondering what the call could be. We hadn't been anywhere near creating an offside. "Seven blue. Two minutes for body contact," he called out. *Hey, that's my number.* I looked at him in disbelief.

I had been a referee for three seasons myself, and I knew that the guy who protests the loudest is the guy who knows the least about the game. But this I couldn't believe. I hadn't checked the guy. It was just an accidental bump. Without thinking, I turned to face the ref squarely, slamming my stick blade on the ice. "What..." But before I could say any more,

I was given an additional two minutes for unsportsmanlike conduct.

Sitting in the penalty box, I was aware of a personal streak having ended. In my whole career, I had never had a penalty. Not ever. And now here I was, a double minor on my record. I wondered what my new teammates thought of me, the guy who'd been shipped over to them by a team with too many players, a team they'd probably been bullying ever since I had quit the game three years earlier. After sitting out my four minutes, I hustled back to the bench. At least the other team hadn't scored.

To my surprise, when I sat down, I wasn't reprimanded. Instead, the coach came up behind me. "Nice job, seven. Don't take any crap out there. Not even from the ref," he said. I was shocked at his tone. He wasn't angry. To him, I had done the right thing. It planted a seed of aggression in my mind as I sat there, awaiting my turn on the ice.

On my next shift I went out and followed a play right to the opposing net. One of our players had shot it in, and the goalie was covering the puck with his left pad. I reached out my stick and poked it, hard. A defenseman from the other side came over to move me out of the way, but as he did, the puck squirted underneath the goalie and went in. I had scored, and it was because of my coach's motivating push.

My teammates actually didn't realize it had been me. They thought the goal had gone in on the initial shot, but after our celebratory huddle, I skated past the referee. "You got seven on that goal, right?" I asked him. He nodded, and the truth exists in the tiny clipping from the *Peterborough Examiner* that I still have in my scrapbook. I had played with an intensity bordering on anger for the first time in my life, and it had worked.

That goal changed me as a player. I loosened up, stopped fearing failure so much. I didn't immediately become a star, but I enjoyed the game like I hadn't in a while, because I played to win, rather than not to lose. Immaculate Conception went all the way to the finals that year. I wish I could say we won, or that we beat All Saints, but we didn't.

Because of my injury, I never really got to know my teammates all that well, but I would like to think that if they have any memories of me at all, they aren't of a timid third-liner but of a kid who finally learned to play with some spirit.

chapter thirty-seven

Seeing the Tiger

When my family left Montréal, we had to say goodbye to my grandmother, who lived on in her grand apartment, Canadiens games beaming in whenever the team was playing. Every couple of months, we'd make a journey back to visit her, or she'd arrive in Toronto on the train to see us. Picking her up was a moment of great excitement for me and my sister, Sandra.

When we'd go back to Québec, we'd always relive our childhood days, sometimes doing things to put us back in touch with the place, like going to an Expos game or riding the subway by ourselves.

In the spring of 1981, I had committed to going to school in the U.S. when I finished high school, and so we went to Montréal for a visit that felt like it might be the last one for a while, since I'd be away most of the next year. Figuring it might be my only chance to see the Habs for a long time, I suggested to my dad that we get tickets to see them play, no matter who their opponent was.

"But they're always sold out—remember how hard it was to get seats when you were a kid," he replied.

"Standing room" was all I said to him.

I had heard somewhere that on the day of the game, it was possible to buy a ticket into the Forum so that you could stand along the top railing and watch the play a mile below. It wasn't the same as having a seat, but I reasoned that at least we'd be there, soaking up the atmosphere of that great place. Even then, I was keen on preserving memories of the past, and I thought about how going to the game would be just like when I was little and we'd seen Cheevers play, then later the New York Rangers. My dad agreed to do it, and early on a Saturday morning we headed to the Forum to get in line.

When we arrived there, he said what I'd heard in various other contexts a million times: "I'll circle the block and pick you up back here. Don't try to find me. I'll be *here*. You come back to this spot." I stepped out of the car, $20 in my pocket to buy two $8 tickets.

As I walked toward the line, a man intercepted me. "You want a ticket?" he said in a French accent. "You want to stand?" I nodded yes to both. I didn't really want to stand, but what I thought he meant was, did I intend to buy standing room tickets? "Standing make you tired," he added. I assented yet again. But didn't he get it? There were no tickets available otherwise. I made as if to go beyond him, needing to secure my place in the line. "I get you a good ticket. Two ticket."

I looked at him, understanding the game now. I'd bought scalper tickets in the past to see the Blue Jays play, not because the game was sold out, but to get a cheaper deal on extras that people showed up with and sold to the guys standing around outside the game. So my first question was a natural one. "How much? I need a pair." I was hoping that my $20 would secure me a couple of seats, rather than the standing-room spots. My dad wouldn't mind paying the extra few dollars if I burned the $20 for seats. I knew he'd much rather sit than stand.

"You give me forty. Sit right behind de net," the scalper said. Forty dollars seemed like a fortune to me. I was earning $2.35 an hour working for my dad in his warehouse, packing book orders for shipment via UPS. I must have looked pretty doubtful, because the guy tried to seal the deal with his next statement. "You never get de standing room, eh? Dey sell out like dat," he said, snapping his fingers to emphasize the point. I didn't know whether to believe him or not, but the line behind him leading to the ticket window was long, and I knew that there wasn't an endless supply of standing-room tickets. I decided I'd try to convince my dad to go for it.

I told the guy that I had to ask my dad and that he should wait right where he was. He nodded OK, and I walked to the corner where I'd been told to find our 1981 Chevy Caprice station wagon. Sure enough, Dad came around the block a second later. Instead of getting into the car, I tapped on the window, motioning him to roll it down.

"There's a guy here who says he has a couple of seats," I said. "He says they're right behind the net." Even as I said the words, I was doubtful, and it probably showed in my voice. My dad wasn't the type to go for a deal like this. Not that he was cheap. This was just so extravagant.

"How much?" he asked. I was surprised by the question. I figured he'd shut the door from the get-go. Now I saw a glimmer of hope.

"They're twenty apiece," I replied, thinking that it sounded better that way.

"Forty dollars?" he said, surprised. It doesn't sound like much money, but if it had been today, the price would have been more like $125. "Do you really want to do it?" he said as he studied my face. He must have seen that I did. "OK, here's twenty more," he said as he pulled out his wallet and grabbed the only $20 left in there. I reached in the window and took it, thanking him as I did so. "Hurry, he might be gone. Is he waiting for you?" He wanted to get this done, so he wouldn't have a moment for a second thought. "Don't you dare tell your mother we did this," he cautioned me as I started to head the other way, looking for the guy.

I approached the scalper again, wondering how this would go. I hadn't actually seen the tickets yet, so I wanted to have a look at them before I flashed my cash. I asked him to show me what my fortune was about to buy. He didn't let me get another word out of my mouth before he said, "We 'ave to go dere—where dey 'ave de ticket." He motioned around the corner and started to walk.

I was a high school kid, but no dummy. My first instinct was to say, "No thanks—this isn't the way this is supposed to work." I didn't think it was a good idea to follow the guy anywhere, let alone around a corner to who knows where with $40 in my pocket just waiting to be stolen. But then my lifelong love of the Habs took over, and I asked him where we were going. "Dere—the bartender 'ave it." He pointed to a small bar tucked into an alleyway. I clutched the $40 in my pocket more tightly. If I went inside that place, my money might be gone, and there might not be any tickets anyway. But I was halfway there now, and it was a Saturday morning. What could happen?

Nothing, as it turned out, except that I was mildly disappointed when I saw the tickets. Instead of the seats being side by side, they were one in front of the other, 25 rows above the net and right behind it. But standing there in that bar with the guy grinning at me and waiting for his $40, I realized that I was too far into this now to say no. It was these seats or no game. "OK," I said, "but only if you come back outside and give me the tickets in front of the Forum." I was determined not to hand him the money while standing in the darkness with early morning drinkers. We went back outside, and I held out the two twenties at the same time he held out our tickets.

That day, the papers were full of the coming match-up. Tiger Williams, who the season before had been traded from Toronto to Montréal's opponent, Vancouver, had said something unkind about the Québec fans and Canadiens players. So everyone was out for blood, including me and my dad. During the game, we screamed with the other people in the Forum as if we'd been to every game for years. I was in front of my dad for the first couple of periods, and in the intermission for the third we switched seats. Whoever was behind leaned forward to comment on the game to the other. It was as good as those Bruins and Rangers games we'd been to years before.

And that $40? We did tell my mom about it, and she said we were crazy. However, from the perspective of time, whatever we would have bought with that money would be long gone by now. But our memories of watching the greatest team in history are as alive as if we had just seen the game played yesterday.

chapter thirty-eight

Hockey as Tonic

S ometimes, hockey is more than a game. It's medicine, a remedy for what makes you feel out of sorts. I discovered this during a lonely winter spent in upstate New York, at a time when I thought that the game had been lost to me.

Eighteen years old, I had gone to the U.S. for a year at a private college. The fall semester, my first ever away from home, had been fine. I'd been so busy I hadn't even phoned home. I used to get messages passed through the college secretary that read, "Please call home. Everything is fine. No emergency. But we haven't heard from you in weeks." One time I got a postcard that read simply, "One letter wanted, any length. What's new?" Of course, I always resolved to get back to my lonely Canadian parents later. For now, I was living big in the U.S. of A.

Christmas vacation came, and I was home in Ontario. It was the December when Bob and Doug McKenzie hit with their version of "The Twelve Days of Christmas." I heard the song everywhere and felt like I had missed something; everyone but me seemed to know who these "hosers" were. The foggy feeling of being a tourist in my own hometown didn't last for long, however, because I had a crazy schedule that meant packing on Christmas night to go back to New York. On Boxing Day, a holiday not observed in my newfound country, I had to attend meetings in preparation for hosting a winter camp from the 27th until New Year's Day. It was a part of the learning experience, so the college administration said. I could feel a cloud of depression settle over me as my dad dropped me off in upstate New York on the 26th. I had never missed a holiday season at home before.

The college I attended was 40 miles from Lake Placid, where the Olympic "Miracle On Ice" had happened a couple of winters previous. The school was, literally, in a village. The only business close by was a deli, our refuge for pizza and candy to supplement the cafeteria diet. We didn't even have a grocery store. It was a big adjustment for a kid who had spent much of his growing up in Montréal.

As I walked back to my dormitory on Boxing Day evening with the pine trees towering above me and several feet of snow on the ground, the darkness and silence of the campus mirrored what was in my soul. Earlier in the day, I had found out that my assignment for the week wasn't going to involve working with the teenage guests at the camp. Instead, I was going to be a part of the maintenance crew, a fun job in 10°F.

My tasks might be anything from unclogging drains to clearing snow from the driveways.

The next morning, I showed up at the maintenance shed to get my assignment. The man in charge looked like one of those guys depicted as a plumber in TV ads. Sporting a big gut and a dark blue shirt stained with grease, he seemed like he ought to have a cigar stump permanently planted between his teeth. I told him my name, and he looked at me and said, "You want to shovel?" I thought about the walk I had just taken to get to this building from my dorm. The snow had crunched underneath my feet. Everyone born in a northern climate knows what that means. Cold.

I looked the guy in the eye. I'd shown up early, and no one else was there. I was hoping, by being eager, to get a good job. I had heard through the student grapevine that if you were lucky, you could pull duty hanging around in one of the lounges to keep the fireplaces stoked. Being inside meant warmth, and girls nearby. Now here he was suggesting that I go out into the cold and stay there for the day. I quickly calculated the wisdom of asking whether I had any other choices. Doing so might ensure that I got something worse. I had a feeling that maybe, somehow, what he was offering me was a perk, though I couldn't read anything from his expression.

"OK," I replied, searching his face for any signs. He didn't seem to take any pleasure in my response one way or the other. If he had done me a favor by not sending me out to one of the hated jobs, he wasn't letting on. "Where do I go?" I asked.

"Report to the outdoor ice. You'll find the equipment there," he said. It sounded like it was the military and he was sending me to take some hill in the name of the country.

"Equipment?" I asked. What if he expected me to operate some kind of snowplow?

"A shovel, a shovel," he replied. He waved me away as if I had been a kid asking for more Kool-Aid at summer camp. "Keep the ice clean. Keep checking it all day. What you do otherwise is up to you."

Doesn't this guy know I'm Canadian? Keep the ice clean? It was something I had done practically every day of winter all my life on one rink or another. I sailed back to my dorm to let the guys know what I'd drawn. More importantly, I wanted to grab my skates. I'd be faster clearing the ice that way than on boots.

When I got to the rink, I realized what the guy had been suggesting—that this job wasn't going to take me long. There wasn't enough ice surface to keep me busy for more than a half hour. With any luck it wouldn't snow, and I'd have to clear only the scrapings made by skate blades. I would have to spend the day there, but I could occupy myself however I saw fit as long as my job was done. Most of the Americans at the school would probably have shoveled and then headed indoors, but for me, the natural thing to do was to play hockey all day.

The kids staying the week, the "campers," came and went. There were several Canadians, and they played hockey. Some of the Americans did, too, but others just skated in circles, even the boys. It was something that I would never dream of doing, but while they were at it, I used the break from our pick-up games to plow the ice. Once or twice, the maintenance guy drove past in his college truck. He squinted out the window at the ice, making sure I'd done my bit, then nodded his approval at me. He registered no surprise to see me on skates. It occurred to me that he'd known what he was doing when he gave me this duty.

As the days went by, I thought of my family. We always extended the Christmas festivities over the week until New Year's. Mom made dinners that were traditional in our house. We played games together, not for their own sake, but to keep the world away and prolong the holiday. I felt the loss of it, and I wasn't just away; I was in a whole different country. Looking up at the pine trees around the rink each day, I felt small and lonely. I vowed to keep in touch with my parents more than I had in the fall semester.

At night, after the campers retired to their cabins, I would go back to the rink to clear it one more time, piling the scrapings up on the sides. Several nights, a light snow would fall, silhouetting against the rink lights. I'd take my stick from the place where I'd left it earlier in the day and drop a puck from my pocket onto the ice. With my ears freezing in the night air, I'd skate around alone, handling the puck like I was Bobby Orr breaking through the St. Louis defense to score that famous flying goal. At those moments, I'd be lost, my heart light, my distance from my family and country erased.

Sometimes, hockey is all you have, and it's enough.

chapter thirty-nine

Glorious Scoring Opportunity

After my first year of college in the U.S., I volunteered to stay on as a summer camp counselor at a place in upstate New York run by the school where I was studying. My assignment was to work with teenagers on an island surrounded by one of the Adirondack Mountains' huge lakes. Six days a week, I got up at 7:00 AM and spent the day doing activities, from attending meetings to supervising swimming, and at 11:00 PM I went to bed in one of the cabins set among the woods. I had just one day off to go into town on the mainland to get whatever I needed, but overall, camp was great, except for the activities program.

How do you keep hundreds of teenagers from either killing each other or making out with each other while marooned on an island for a seven-day stay? The answer the camp directors arrived at was to divide everyone into teams and have them compete for points. The winning team would get a steak cookout at the end of the week while the losers ate "tube steaks," known to most people as hot dogs.

It was a great idea, except that teenagers, even at that time, were more sophisticated than that. The idea of being either a "Miner" or a "Panner" for seven days and playing games like "Gold Nugget Dodge"—dodge ball renamed to fit in with the week's theme—made them roll their eyes. Thing was, it didn't matter if they liked it or not—my job was to make sure every one of my campers participated. The ever-present threat was that counselors would lose their day off if their campers had poor attendance. The thought of that happening and being stuck on the island for nearly two weeks straight was enough to keep most of us in line, most of the time, so I tried to get my campers into it. I'd yell at the sidelines, encouraging them, or talk it up the night before we were to play a softball game. But much of my enthusiasm was forced, and I was resentful that the activities directors—the "ADs"—two guys who were students as I was, didn't do more to make the games seem relevant to the weekly themes, or to make the whole thing somehow more sophisticated, something that would appeal to the age group.

Then one day, something close to miraculous happened—floor hockey sticks and two nets materialized. They were brand new, and nobody knew who had ordered them. The best speculation was that they had been requested during the winter camp, for use in the gym, but had gotten waylaid somewhere. I didn't care. I saw a chance to play a game that was fun, no matter what stupid name the activities guys gave it. I quickly lobbied to have floor hockey, played on a tennis court, included in the activities roster. They agreed.

I was in my glory. This was my game, and even though counselors weren't allowed to play along with their cabins, I could get my campers to the court early and warm them up, teaching them some skills and developing a crude sense in them of how to play positions. My enthusiasm didn't hurt, either. They sensed how important this was to me and responded by going willingly to the games, rather than having to be dragged. My days off were no longer in jeopardy.

Around the second or third week, though, things caved in on me a little bit. The other counselors resented that my team won most of its games, and I was called out because I'd spend an extra hour now and again at the courts when my cabin had no activities scheduled, normally my free time. I was running practices for my cabin and attending games played by other teams. It was more fun than sitting on the beach for hours.

One afternoon, I was warming up my group for floor hockey when one of the activities directors, a guy from Philadelphia, showed up to start the day's game. "Hey, you're here a lot," Tom said to me. Normally, he wouldn't have gotten off his pedestal to say anything unless he was telling you to round up your group of campers so that play could commence.

"Yeah, well, it's hockey," I replied. I had been in the U.S. for nearly a year, and I had learned two things: Most Americans love to know that you're Canadian, and most of them make the immediate association of your nationality with hockey. My reply to him was supposed to be all the answer I needed to explain my willingness to spend so much afternoon time at the tennis courts.

"We like hockey, too, where I come from," he said, reminding me that he grew up in Philly. "Flyers won a couple of championships, you know," he added. Of course I knew. I further knew that he couldn't think of the name of that "championship," or he would have said "Stanley Cups." I was getting a pretty good fix on his hockey knowledge.

"You're pretty good at this?" he asked, motioning with his head in the direction of the players I'd just been helping.

"Sure. You know, we play all our lives," I responded, surprised that our conversation continued. This guy was the type who normally wouldn't give me the time of day. He was the AD, after all, holding a vaunted position at the camp with the singular advantage of being a day job. He didn't have campers to worry about like the rest of us did. After dinner, which concluded with "challenges" (contests in which campers competed to see who could eat the most raw eggs or do the most pushups), his job was done for the day. He and the other AD even had their own cabin to sleep in. So I was surprised that he was taking time to talk to me, and I wondered what was up.

"Why don't you play here, then?" Tom asked. It was a stupid question, and he knew it. Counselors did not participate in campers' activities. We were there to supervise, to make sure the kids had fun but stayed safe.

"You know we aren't allowed. But I'd love to," I replied. I was telling the truth. I missed the game tremendously. It was the first year of my life that I hadn't seen the playoffs, and that was only part of my sense of loss. Being on that tennis court, even just for the warm-ups, made me feel like a kid again, playing on the streets of my neighborhood.

"Today, we'll say that there aren't enough players. You and me, we'll both play," he suggested, smiling at me. I could tell that he'd been wanting to do this, too.

"To referee...?" I got the question only partway out when he interrupted. "Carl will do it," he said. Carl was his AD partner. "I told him to come down," he added. Normally, Carl would be supervising another game somewhere else on the grounds.

"Sure, if you say it's OK," I said. Excitement filled me as I went back to my group and announced that I would be playing, not just watching.

I hate to say it, but getting in the game was a bit of a disappointment. I was really a lot better than most of the campers, and so it was more of a challenge to discipline myself not to dominate the game than it was to beat them to the ball. I could stickhandle; most of them could not. So I moved through the opposite team's defense with ease. It was probably something like what a young

Wayne Gretzky felt before his dad moved him up to play with kids older and bigger than he was.

But whenever I decided to score instead of passing, there was Tom, chasing me down and trying to grab the ball off my stick. Sometimes he would do it, but most of the time I could elude him. His moves were so obvious and exaggerated that I had little trouble deking him almost out of his pants.

He played hockey like a lot of people do if they don't have much experience. Holding his stick with his hands much too close together, he golfed at the ball, bending way too far over at the waist. To me, it was comical. To my campers, it was obvious that he didn't have much of a clue what he was doing, and that raised a problem. After I'd beaten Tom a few times, the players on my side started to snicker when he came after me. I tried to ease up on him, passing the ball even more than I had before, but all that did was make it clear to everyone that I was purposely dumbing down my game. Tom grew irate, and before the game was finished, he took over the refereeing duties with the excuse that Carl couldn't stay around to see things through.

Naturally, with him off the court, I had to quit, too. But I did so almost with a sense of relief. I hated to see him make an idiot of himself, though I should have been glad of my chance to show my skills, even if they only looked good because of my competitor's lack of any. Goodness knows he'd taken every chance to act superior in front of me and my lowly fellow counselors all summer.

At the end of the game, Tom came over once more. "Kind of a drag playing with a bunch of kids, huh?" he said. He acted as if it had been him versus me, and that we were equally matched.

I just looked at him, trying to penetrate the layers of arrogance that made it impossible for him to see what had just happened. He really believed the crap that was coming out of his mouth. I couldn't say much in the face of this kind of blindness, so instead I asked him who he had favored for the Stanley Cup in the year just past. His preoccupied stare tried to cover the fact that he had no idea the Islanders were in the middle of their dynasty run, having defeated Vancouver in four games. I couldn't resist one more jab: "Well, after they kicked Philadelphia's butt two years ago, you had to know they'd be good for a while, eh?" I excused myself to gather the sticks and stow the nets.

As it turned out, that was the last week we played floor hockey. The game was shut down for the rest of the summer, with the justification being that it didn't fit in with the themes of the subsequent weeks of camp—Yankees versus Red Sox, skaters versus surfers and Army versus Navy. Of course, I was the only one to really care, but no one believed how lame that excuse was.

And the equipment? It disappeared as mysteriously as it had come. When I asked about it, I was told the director of the winter camp wanted it stored in his facility on the mainland, fearing that it would get lost or damaged if it stayed on the island for the summer. I never saw it again.

chapter forty

The Day the Hockey Gods Had My Number

I went to college at three different schools. I started and ended in the U.S., but in between I spent two years at a small Baptist college in London, Ontario. One of the fortunate side effects of this was that I had the chance to play hockey again. It wasn't something I had considered when I enrolled, but when it was announced that new players were welcome to try out for the team, I went.

The school budget only allowed for one on-ice practice a week, every Thursday afternoon. It was more a scrimmage than anything else. Our coach was an American who looked like Columbo in his trademark trench coat, so that's what we called him. His strategies mainly consisted of telling us to "check those guys right through the boards," though the games we played were gentlemanly rather than rough and tumble. Still, we were the Flames, and I wore the blue and white sweater proudly in the photos that were used in college publicity.

One of our toughest games of the season was against our college's alumni. I know that sounds suspicious, if you think of the alums as old guys who played a dozen years ago and are now well on their way to a paunch. In fact, these guys had graduated from college just a few years earlier and were now attending the graduate school seminary that was also part of the institution. So they were men, bigger than we were, and they hadn't lost any of their skills.

The alumni game was held in our practice rink, and to cover the cost of the ice time, each player had to pitch in a few bucks. I had a job selling men's suits at a department store, so I didn't think twice about the money, but another player on our team was planning not to play because of the cost. There was a recession in Canada, 1983, and the guy was doing all he could to keep ahead of his tuition bill so that he wouldn't be sent home.

I slipped his fee and a note into our captain's mailbox at school a couple of days before the game, but didn't identify myself. My teammate was one of our better players, but it wasn't for that reason that I secretly paid his fees. It just seemed like the right thing to do.

As we gathered at center ice before the game, the guy looked around the group and said, "One of you guys paid my dues so I could play today. Whoever it was, thank you." I averted my gaze, glad that the cage I was wearing covered my face. I was determined not to let him or anyone else know that it had been my good deed that put him onto the ice that day. Call it the example of my father coming to life in me—it was what he would do under the circumstances, but he'd never let on to anyone.

The game started with me on the bench, but I was soon taking my regular turn as right-winger. And before the first period ended, I scored. I was in front of the net when a puck came dribbling out from the scrum, and I flipped a backhand toward the pile. Somehow it got through. This was great! My game was made. In a lot of ways, I still had the mentality of a kid playing hockey. I cared about the team, but what I really cared about was being able to go to school on Monday to tell my friends that I had gotten a goal. Now, no matter if we won or lost, I had a story to tell.

The game meant more than that, though. Our team normally played in front of a few dozen family members and girlfriends, but because the alumni game was attached to the weekend's festivities gathering the graduates of both college and seminary, there were at least 200 people in attendance. As I sat on the bench after my goal, I could feel the excitement of the fans for the first time. The game was now tied at 2. And then the hockey gods smiled on me.

It was the second period. I was ending a shift, tired, but I was pursuing an opposing left defenseman as he stood at his own blue line ready to clear the puck. As he gathered it onto his stick, I knew where he was going with it, and so I moved slightly to my right toward the boards, my stick stretched out in my left hand in order to keep him from passing into the center of the ice. He flipped his clearing pass up ice, but I squeezed my shin pads together and blocked it. At that instant I thought I should clear it down into their end and go to the bench for a change of players, making the safe play, the one I usually made. But something urged me forward.

The puck fell at my feet off my pads, and I kicked it forward with my right skate, then took it onto my stick, shoveling it ahead of me. My momentum had carried me to the blue line and right into the defenseman's teeth, but I swooped around him toward my left, quickly switching the puck to my forehand, and then once inside the zone, back to my backhand. He was behind me now, but his buddy was coming from my left. I set the puck onto my forehand side once more and raised my stick for a slapshot. I wasn't looking at the net but playing with a gut instinct that told me where it was and where the holes were. It was as if everyone else on the ice was frozen in space, waiting while I wound up.

I let fly with the shot and beat the goalie cleanly. I raised my arms like every goal scorer everywhere has done for a hundred years. As my teammates mobbed me, I replayed the goal in my mind for the first of what has been probably a million times.

I was the hockey hero I'd been dreaming of being since I had first put on my cheese cutters. I couldn't quite imagine how I had done it. It hadn't been a practiced move or one I'd seen on TV and imitated on the streets in front of my house as a kid. But it was the greatest goal of my life, almost like someone else was wearing my number seven sweater.

The game continued, but not for me. Visions of the goal just kept showing on the newsreel in my head. Even after the hundredth time, it didn't diminish, though I did pot another goal, adding to my triumph with the only hat trick of my playing career.

That goal happened toward the end of the game, off a pass from the faceoff circle. I was standing in the slot—just like Phil Esposito used to when he played for the Bruins and Rangers—and my centerman, who had drifted to the boards, picked up the puck. He rifled it cross-ice to me, and I redirected in with a one-timer that went straight to the net and between the goalie's pads. *Hat Trick!* The words flashed in my mind as they would appear in a headline in the local paper. I would have been beside myself if I'd been able to believe it.

I was congratulated for the goal, but nobody's words stick in my head. My feat must have been mentioned in the school newspaper, but despite being an ardent scrapbooker, I have no record of it. However, a couple of days after the game, a fellow resident of my dorm caught me in the hallway. He was a big guy, the kind you'd label an athlete without knowing anything else about him. For some reason, he didn't play hockey. He had been at the game, though. Before this moment, we had spoken only a few times. He was one of those people you just didn't approach. If a conversation was in order with a normal mortal like me, he would initiate it. Now, he took me by surprise by doing just that.

"Hey, that goal you scored?" It came out kind of more question than statement, and his eyebrows arched as he said it.

The words "Hat Trick" once again flashed on the neon sign in my brain, but I didn't have to ask him which goal he meant. The look on his face told me. "Yeah?" I replied, trying to act like it was no big deal.

"All I saw was you raising your stick in the air to shoot, then the back of the net bulging. The shot was so fast, I didn't even see the puck. I had no idea you could do that," he said. Neither had I, but I didn't say that. It had been the best moment of my playing career. Ever. It defied commentary.

"Yeah, thanks." I didn't have any more to say, so I just continued past him, down the hallway.

My dorm-mate's words confirmed what I had thought about the goal. It was my moment of singular brilliance. That puck was mine. It went where I told it to, from my skate to my stick to the net. I was beyond my usual abilities by a mile. I wondered why this hadn't happened in a hundred games before, or even in one of them. How I would have loved to go to Preville Elementary School on a Monday morning and talk about this while the other boys, with Johnny Modell at the center of the group, told about their weekend's triumphs! I would have been the hero of my class, far eclipsing other guys with their mediocre wrist shots and deflections, for my goal was truly glorious.

My theory on it now is that it wasn't me at all. It was the hockey gods working their mysteries. And what prompted them to action was my silent generosity in covering that guy's fees and then not saying anything about it. I can't prove it, but I can't explain that day any other way.

If I'm right and it was them, then the hockey gods know a thing or two about timing. The goal and the hat trick came near the end of my playing days, not a bad time for the greatest achievement of my hockey career. And the goals also came when I was old enough to treasure and remember them in every detail, and that counts for a lot.

PART THREE

Loving the Game

chapter forty-one

Some Games You Run, Others You Skate

After putting in my two years at college in Canada, I decided to go back to the U.S. rather than finish my BA in Ontario, so I again left my home and, though I didn't think that much about it at the time, hockey. This was my second retirement from the game, but at least this time I was not quitting out of fear, and I had my hat trick to remember as the crowning moment of my playing days.

My first fall back in the States, I made a decision. If I was going to live here, I was going to get into American football. Four downs, small end zone, the whole business. The gridiron would become my passion. Dutifully, I spent Sunday afternoons watching the games on the 12-inch TV my grandmother had left me as part of my inheritance two years earlier, the same TV that had shown her all those great Montréal Canadiens Stanley Cup victories in the waning years of her life.

In many respects, being a football fanatic was the only option in the Ohio town where I lived. The sport was what everyone talked about on Monday morning, and people would be evenly divided between supporting the Cincinnati Bengals and the Cleveland Browns. Among the students I hung out with, there was one hockey fan, but her knowledge was confined to whatever Wayne Gretzky, playing with the Oilers thousands of miles away, was doing. To the rest of my comrades, hockey was about as familiar, and as interesting, as cricket.

Football, however, was part of the fabric of life. At a Thanksgiving Day assembly held at my college, the president of the school gave a speech in which he mentioned that the next day, the holiday Thursday, we'd all be eating turkey and gathering around our TV sets to watch the games—both the Cowboys and the Lions traditionally played on Thanksgiving (and still do). He left the impression that no one anywhere in the country would miss the action.

As the season progressed to its playoffs, I found myself more and more intrigued with the game. I couldn't appreciate it from the point of view of someone who had played, but then, I reasoned, my Gran had never played hockey, and she had loved the Canadiens. Learning about the game and its complexities from a fan's perspective was good enough.

That year, the Cleveland Browns were pretty good, and though I was living closer to Cincinnati, home of the Bengals,

I decided to make the Brownies my team. Playoff time came, Christmas being over, and the games became more intense. Super Bowl Sunday, perhaps as important as any other holiday in my adopted country, was approaching. It would mean the world to me for my newly loved team to play in the big game, especially in my first season as a fan.

As the Browns continued to win, excitement built. When it came time for the conference championship game, which would determine one half of the Super Bowl equation, a friend asked me over to his house to watch it on his giant screen TV. It would be just like having a ticket to sit in the stadium—minus the freezing weather and the expensive snacks.

Of course I went, realizing that there was more than football happening here. I was being accepted as part of the tribe. I had passed some kind of test that I didn't even know I was taking and had been allowed into the inner circle. The people gathering at his house to watch were all hardcore fans. I had become like them. I was now American, at least symbolically. All the while, the hockey season was going on, but I had no idea how it was progressing.

That day, I abandoned myself to the intensity of the football game, like the people around me. When the Browns scored, I cheered. And when the opponents kicked a field goal, I, like the others, turned my back on the set in disrespect.

Then, as halftime approached, the two-minute warning sounded. The break allowed the TV people to sneak in a bunch of commercials, at which time the host grabbed the remote for a quick surf of the channels. He flipped past the usual assortment of other shows, old movies, MTV. Then he arrived at a hockey game. It caught me by surprise. I didn't have cable, which was the only way to view hockey at that time in the U.S. unless you lived in a market with a team. I was in Dayton, Ohio, so I hadn't seen a game all season. Now here it was, January, and I was reminded that a world that I had removed myself from was going on without me—not just hockey, but Canada itself.

When the hockey game appeared on the screen, all eyes darted to me. Their glance was a reflex that I've since learned all Americans possess when it comes to hockey. They equate Canadians with it, as if everybody who grew up North of the 49th parallel had played in the NHL. I didn't know quite what to do, so I smiled as if to say, "Yes, that's hockey. But honest, I'm here to cheer for the Browns. I really am one of you." They smiled back; surprisingly, nobody asked the usual "Did you play?" We were all here to watch the Browns. I took their silence as a sign of acceptance. Still, the pause was uncomfortable. I wished that the host would go back to the football channel.

My anxiety wasn't just because of the awkwardness of the situation, with me being the center of interest. It was also because, in my heart, I felt guilty. Seeing the players on the ice, I realized that I had abandoned the game that was the real love of my life, trading it for something foreign while trying to convince myself that this was OK.

The clincher was seeing the players skating around in those few minutes, the action smooth and flowing, their strides powerful and fast—then the abrupt change when the TV went back to football. The first play had just finished, and the players were walking back to the huddle. I remember the linemen particularly, huge fat guys sweating in their tight T-shirts despite the weather. Football just didn't have anything to offer next to the grace of the hockey game.

The football game carried on, the Browns lost, and there was no Super Bowl appearance. I was sad about that. I had enjoyed being a fan. But I gave it up after that season, because I decided that having something to say at school or work on Monday morning was not as important as being connected to a game that you grew up on.

So what if I was weird, the Canadian, a perpetual loser in the office NFL pool? I would never care all that much who had been great at football in the 1970s. But I would always care that, as a seven-year-old kid, I had seen Gump Worsley play on TV.

He hadn't worn a mask, and to me, having seen him was as important a memory as my dad and I watching Apollo 11 land, and then going outside to look up at the moon, wondering where the guys were who we'd just seen on the TV in our living room. Those guys may have been brave; they may have been crazy. But they were no more a bunch of heroes than Gump Worsley, Ken Dryden and Tony Esposito. American things, such as football, were fine for Americans; I would stick to hockey.

chapter forty-two

There's More Than One "Mr. Hockey"

Despite the relative absence of hockey in Ohio in the mid-1980s, I tried to keep the game in some form or other alive in my life, though sometimes only by the thinnest of margins. At Miami University in Ohio, where I went to graduate school, I was the faculty mentor to a hallway of guys, one of whom was in my freshman English class. We attended movies with their sister hall, had dinner now and again in one of the campus cafeterias and bowled a couple of times at the lanes in town. Then winter came, and I saw a notice for intramural broomball. I'd been in the U.S. for three years, and as a poor graduate student, I had no cable TV. Hockey had thus disappeared for me, except for the odd university game I attended. *Why not?* I thought as I looked at the poster. *It's got some resemblance to the game I miss so much.*

Don't laugh. Broomball was the closest I could get to the game itself, and after all, it's played on a regulation rink with hockey nets. The only difference is that instead of a puck, you play with a giant rubber ball, and instead of a stick, you whack that ball with a broom-like object. I figured that I'd be doing my university service by leading the team, plus I reasoned that even though it was kind of a laughable game, it was enough like hockey that I'd be pretty good at it. I was right.

Running around on the ice in your sneakers is not a ton of fun, but I had my hockey shin pads, and so I figured I'd put them on over a pair of sweatpants. Instantly, I was immune to falling, so I started to move like crazy all over the ice, smacking that rubber ball as hard as I could every time I got anywhere near it. And I started scoring.

Before I knew it, we'd played several games, and I was being looked to as the captain of our team. I scored at least half the team's goals, so it seemed natural, but actually I was surprised at my success given that the students I was playing with on this co-ed team were 18 and 19 and fit as people that age tend to be. Several looked like real athletes, so to have them coming back to the bench to consult me on strategy was flattering. I was supposed to be the nerdy, skinny English professor just doing his best to get his dorm into university life.

Halfway through our season's 12-game schedule, I was on the ice one Saturday morning right when the Zamboni left it. Like everyone else, I had a helmet-and-cage combo on, but mine was my own, a Cooper drawn from my hockey bag, not the university-issued CCM the other players donned. Plus, I was wearing my secret weapon shin pads and my hockey gloves, which made it a lot easier to get close to the net without getting hacked to pieces.

Play started, and I took the ball right off the faceoff, but was surprised to feel a stick between my feet. I landed hard on my face with a guy crashing down on top of me. The other team's center had chased and dumped me, and would now serve a penalty for his trouble. I thought nothing much of it and went on to score on the power play. This was my game.

As I was sitting back on the bench recuperating afterward, a guy from the other team ran by me, turned his head and said in a sing-song voice, "Miiiister Hockey." I looked around, surprised, and the girl who sat next to me, from our sister hall, shrugged her shoulders. I was a faculty member, after all, and I wasn't used to being insulted in front of my students, or any students, if that's what he'd meant by his taunt.

The game continued, and soon our players started coming back to the bench complaining. The other team was playing them rough, not body-checking, since it wasn't allowed, but checking in the sense that they were right on top of us all the time. I put it down to good defense, but when I went out for another shift, I noticed that I had two guys on me. Getting close to the net, I could feel their brooms overlapping mine. One guy reached out and poked me in the pads with the end of his stick, saying "Miiiister Hockey" as he did it. They were all in on it, it looked like.

By the second of the two 15-minute periods, players were refusing their shifts. Todd, the Resident Assistant student who had signed me up as the dorm partner in the first place, sat next to me on the bench. "What should we do? The guys are scared to go out there," he said, motioning to our players. "They're hacking the hell out of us, and nobody else has gloves and pads." It was almost an accusation, like I'd somehow drawn out the aggression of the other squad.

I had no idea what to say in response. I felt just as I had when I was a Bantam All Saints right-winger and our team had played Immaculate Conception. I was both scared and puzzled. I didn't understand not taking the game as just good fun. Was it so bad that we were winning? Was it any fun to win by beating the crap out of the other side, intimidating them into submission? I have never been comfortable playing in that sort of environment.

I realize I sound as though I didn't get the point of the Bobby Clarke slash on Valeri Kharlamov in the Summit Series at all, but come on—this was an intramural match, with members of both genders playing. Did it have to turn into a Junior B hockey game where everyone has to fight just to prove his worth?

Instead of giving Todd an answer, I went out to take a final, very long shift, figuring I'd show my team that I had gotten them into this and I would see it through.

I was nowhere near the ball when a guy from the other side came over and cross-checked me with both hands thrust out as far as he could. I stumbled and fell down, but jumped back up again. As I started toward him, trying to figure out what he thought he was doing, I saw his face under his cage. He was a former student of mine, and I started to soften in recognition, when I realized that he wasn't doing the same. My face froze, and my insides tightened.

I remembered this kid from the previous semester. He was one of those students who was completely wrapped up in fraternity life, a slacker and a partier who had done the least possible in the class. I never remember students' grades, but I'm sure he'd earned himself a C. Now here he was, punch-drunk with the opportunity for revenge. It was a perfect chance for him. When else could you take a stick and use it against your professor?

I had no idea what to do, so I did what came naturally to the kid who always takes his share of the tougher boys' bullying in school. I tried to be conciliatory. "Is that you, Jason?" I asked. "You remember me, right?" What an inane question. Of course I knew it as I said it, but I figured on diffusing his violence this way. He looked at me like I was crazy and raised his shoulders just a fraction, as if to indicate that he'd hit me again if I moved a muscle. "Miiiister Hockey" he said, and turned to walk away.

Despite the other side's efforts to hinder us, my early goals stood up, and we made it through that game and won. We played out our season, too, but it wasn't the same afterward. I felt responsible for getting these really great students involved in something that had turned ugly, and they probably felt as though I'd created the problems in the first place by showing up in my gear and acting like there was something real at stake.

Maybe I should have explained to them that to me, broomball was like playing hockey, and that winning some games made me feel that our team was in our own tiny way playing out a quest for glory like the one that NHL players take in an attempt to win the Stanley Cup. But they wouldn't have understood that Canadian fantasy, so I just went back to being the English professor, half a generation older and not quite interested in what they were passionate about. Maybe I am Mister Hockey after all—with all due respect to the great Gordie Howe.

chapter forty-three

Like Swimming Through Jell-O

In 1989, a year or two after I moved back to Dayton, Ohio, from Oxford, Ohio, to take a teaching job, I found out that the college had an intramural floor hockey league that played Friday and Saturday nights, and I decided to get involved. I figured it would be nice to play again, to reawaken a little piece of the game in my life. So I got onto a team with some of my students after being reassured that the refereeing was professional and things would not devolve into thuggery the way broomball had in my last intramural experience.

We played a game or two, and I found myself having fun and contributing, but not scoring. I reverted to my game from years before, acting as playmaking right-winger, feeding ball after ball into the center to set up what I hoped would be great scoring chances. Still nobody scored. One particular Saturday night, I decided to switch roles and do some coaching while

I played. We were up against a team with some guys who looked really into it, especially their goalie. He was from Toronto, and he had the full set of street hockey pads, gloves, stick and mask.

I took one of my guys aside. "See what I've been doing? Getting into the corners, finding the ball, doing anything to get it in front?" I said to Robbie. And I really meant "anything"—I had shot it, kicked it, whacked it, hacked it. "You take my position and try to do that. I'll watch and tell you how it's going," I added.

I stood on the sideline, roving up and down the right wing, yelling encouragement. The guy was athletic, and pretty soon he figured out that he could shield the ball with his body, keeping the defenseman away, and make a backhand pass out from the corner to the sweet spot in front of the net. And he did it quite successfully. I had cloned myself. Now if only someone would do something with these centering passes.

I pulled aside the kid who was playing center. "You sit down for a while. Watch what I do. Robbie is going to feed those balls out from the corner. Watch where I stand, how I get the ball and how I shoot it," I instructed him.

It seemed apparent to me that the guy just didn't know how to get himself in a good spot to take the shot. Balls had been going behind him, off the heel of his stick, into his feet. He was no Phil Esposito, but I would make him king of the slot. I was feeling pretty good about myself. It wasn't like I was the dominant player, though I clearly understood the game at a level not many of these Americans did. But with my coaching on superior strategy, we would become unbeatable. I had the same visions of glory in my head as a kid standing on his street but mentally being galaxies away in an imaginary quest for the Stanley Cup.

I took up the spot in the center, and play resumed. First drive, I shot the ball into the corner, and Robbie raced in after it. Meanwhile, I parked high, about where the top of the faceoff circles would have been if this court wasn't painted up with lines for volleyball, and I waited. I circled a little bit to throw off the back-checker who was covering me. A second later, Robbie squirted the ball out to me. I couldn't get a handle on it, and it sailed past to the left wing.

I resisted my long-obeyed winger's urge to chase it, reminding myself that playing center meant it was OK to stand in the slot and wait. But my left-winger couldn't retrieve the ball, and back on defense we went.

A few minutes later, we were back in their end, and once again, I waited. This time, Robbie did it exactly like I'd modeled it. He shielded the ball with his body, took it on his forehand, then wheeled around on his backhand and fed it right into the slot. I was just about to whack it hard at that kid from Toronto with his official equipment (or with "all that junk" as the Camerons would have said years before) that made the net so tiny, when I felt the shaft of a stick pushed hard over mine. I couldn't move my arms at all, and the ball eluded me again.

I turned to see where the referee was and caught a glimpse of the guy who had impeded me. He was in the classic obstruct-from-behind position, with his hands far apart on his stick in a way that had enabled him to practically wrap the stick around me. I was in a cage. There was no way I could go anywhere. This was holding. I had been a referee, and I knew it should have been called.

I went over to the ref and asked him what was up. "How could you let that go?" I said politely. "The guy had me tied up completely."

"That's allowed," he said, with a distinctive Pennsylvania twang. "He can do that if he thinks you'll get off a shot."

Now, I knew that wasn't right. In fact, what he said was the very definition of holding as it's called out in the *National Hockey League Official Rules*, which I had read over dozens of times years before. "What are you talking about?" I asked him. I had had faith in the system of rules and officiating in this floor hockey league, so this non-call seemed crazy to me. Did the guy have any training at all? He had a referee's shirt on, just like the kids who officiated the intramural basketball games, but looking the part and playing the part of referee were apparently two different things. I just stared at him, not sure what else to say.

He realized that he owed me some kind of an explanation. "That's the way the game is played," he said. "I see it every time I watch a Pens game at home." It confirmed what

I had thought about the accent. "Have you watched the NHL lately?" he added.

Normally, this would be an insulting question. I'm Canadian, after all. But in fact, I hadn't. This was in the middle of my worst hockey dry spell of all time. There was no hockey on non-cable TV in Ohio, and the only games I could count on seeing were on my twice-yearly trips home to Ontario. Unable to give him an answer, I turned and went back to the game. I would take this up with the director of the intramural league on Monday, on a faculty member to faculty member level. Playing like this wasn't much fun at all, NHL or no NHL as the model. I also decided that I would study the games on TV when I got home for Christmas a few weeks later. Our game continued with me trying despite the obstacles to teach my guys how to score, but having no success. Whenever we did get a good shot off, the opposing goalie nabbed it.

In the weeks to follow, the season moved toward its end, and my team played out its string without making the playoffs. I tried to devise new strategies to spring players free but didn't get far with the effort. About the only way to escape the hooks and grabs seemed to be by sheer force of will or by lucky timing. The skill and finesse that I felt could be showcased, even playing on the floor and with a ball, just didn't have a chance against this form of defense.

Good to my vow, when I got home to Ontario for Christmas, I turned on the tube to check out the ref's story.

What I saw, as every fan who remembers the clutch-and-grab era knows, was that the guy was right. Watching the game on TV gave me the feeling of trying to run in sand. Every bit of momentum was lost as players held each other up on back-checks, grabbed sticks poised for shots and generally did all they could to clog up the ice, making speed and finesse impossible. It was like they were all swimming through Jell-O or something. I could almost feel myself pushing them along, trying to override the anchors that held them back. My arms and legs got tired just sitting there in front of the TV set. I didn't get it. What had happened to the quickness of Lafleur and Cournoyer flying down the ice? How could the league think that this style of play was a good thing?

Maybe my memories were just of an era that was faster because of the players who'd been out there then, I reasoned. There was now no Bobby Orr streaking up and down, and no "Flying Frenchmen," as the Montréal Canadiens had been called when I was a kid. Or maybe it was true that the guys were getting bigger and the equipment larger, and so the ice surface wasn't big enough anymore. That's what the papers said to explain it. I didn't buy any of it. This style of hockey wasn't fun to watch, and it wasn't fun to play, at least in the floor hockey version of it.

I wished with all my might that they'd do something to get hockey back to the way it had been, not so much for my sake as for that of the kids whose memories were being formed by this style of play. They might have Gretzky and Lemieux to create their dreams of hockey greatness, but aside from those guys, the game had devolved into something barely resembling the exciting free-for-all it had been during the heyday I remembered.

What was the remedy? It would take Gary Bettman a few years to come up with a decent answer to that question, and years more to put it into effect.

chapter forty-four

The Night Hockey Came Back to Me

When I moved to the U.S. in the mid-1980s, hockey essentially disappeared for me. Living on a student's budget, then later on a graduate school stipend, I had to do without cable for years. I tried to follow the game as best I could on friends' TVs. *USA Network* carried the playoffs for several years, so I saw bits of Patrick Roy leading the Canadiens to the Stanley Cup in 1986 and losing it in 1989 to Calgary. But except for the rare times that I was home in Ontario, I didn't see any more hockey on TV until the Canadiens won again in 1993. I think that's because there wasn't any, unless you lived in a place with a team, which I did not. So Mario, I'm sorry, but your Cup wins don't resonate in my memory. I regret that.

The loss of the game bugged me enough that when the NHL decided to make some changes in leadership in 1992 with the departure of John Zeigler, I did something to bring the game back to me. I sent a letter to the league office, addressed "To Whom it May Concern." I was hoping to catch the ear of the new president (soon to be called "Commissioner" with Gil Stein's departure in February 1993), who ended up being Gary Bettman. I suggested that there be some kind of regional game of the week for people in markets with no team. My games, in southern Ohio, could be Chicago or Detroit, or even Pittsburgh contests, I reasoned. At the time I could not have imagined them putting the NHL in Columbus. That's like having a team in Kansas City or Cleveland. Oh, yeah, they tried that, too, in the 1970s.

No one responded to my letter, but shortly after Bettman took over in 1993, a TV contract with *ESPN* emerged. Finally the game was back, which coordinated nicely with the timing of my finishing the graduate degree I'd been working on for five years. Although I was teaching full time, I was suddenly sprung free from the burden of finishing my doctoral dissertation. As a reward for getting my PhD, I decided to give myself a couple of months doing whatever I wanted to. So I started watching hockey. What would turn out to be a league record for playoff overtimes began on April 18th with a win by Buffalo over Boston.

The overtime contests continued almost night after night. In fact, by the time the Kings and Canadiens faced off in the finals in this Centennial year of the Cup, there had been 25 overtime games, far eclipsing the former record. Montréal was on a record streak as well, with seven overtime wins, one better than the earlier record of six set by the Islanders in 1980. I was in heaven. And so I watched, never in bed before midnight, always going to work the next day with the taste of overtime excitement still on my tongue, though no one at my college followed the games as I did, so I couldn't share the feeling with anyone.

And that wasn't the best of it. Even more remarkable was Montréal's journey. After a decent season, they started turning themselves into a Cinderella team. They'd been sixth in the league but third in the Adams Division, with 102 points. Pittsburgh, by contrast, coming off two straight Cup wins, had 119 points, plus the momentum of Mario Lemieux having recovered from cancer to win the scoring title despite playing only 60 games. That, in my opinion, will always rank as the single greatest achievement in sports history, ahead of the great Maurice Richard and his first-ever 50-goal season, even ahead of Gretzky's many fantastic accomplishments.

But when the finals rolled around, the Pens were out, and the somewhat oddball match-up of Gretzky versus the Habs was on. What luck for me! I started wearing my Canadiens jersey to work a couple of days a week, as if to prove that my loyalties were with the game and that the rest of life was just stuff I had to do while waiting for the drop of the puck later in the day.

The series started out with Montréal losing at home. I, along with a lot of other people I'm sure, feared the worst. The Kings had beaten us 4–1. The next game, though, the Habs came back with a win in overtime. It was the continuation of their streak, making it eight overtime wins in a row. This was the famous Marty McSorley stick game—the one where the Habs took the chance of calling for a measurement on his lumber and got him for having too big a curve. There was magic here, and I could feel it. How I would have loved to be in Montréal, reading the reports of the games in the *Gazette* the mornings after. Sometimes, the *Dayton Daily News* had little more than a summary of the game.

The next two games were played in L.A., at that time a far-off place of mystery to me. (I could have never imagined I'd be living there within three years.) Again, the Canadiens won, twice in overtime, and came back to Montréal with a lead of 3–1. I was beginning to hope for the improbable, another Stanley Cup, and the team had extended the overtime record to 10.

The fifth game was at the Forum, and the Canadiens reversed the score of the first game, prevailing 4–1. They won the series by the same score, though now when I think back on it, it was much harder fought than that sounds. It seems like it went to six games, if not seven.

Anyway, the feeling was the same and I, like many other people, had been there for the whole thing. In total, there were 28 overtime games during the playoffs, most of which had been on TV. The hockey records state that the month of May had an overtime game nearly every other night, so my memories of being very sleepy at work that whole month are not far off.

Exciting playoffs are one thing. Exciting playoffs in which your team takes an improbable victory are another, and as that fifth game ended, I was beside myself. Eight hundred miles away, the Canadiens could not have known it, but I felt that they had won it just for me, as a gift for my having achieved my own greatest dream, the PhD. I went out into the backyard of my suburban home, shook up a can of Coke and opened it so that it sprayed everywhere. Then I dumped what was left over my head, just like Patrick Roy, Guy Carbonneau, Kirk Muller and all the others had just done with $100 bottles of champagne.

They had not won. *We* had won, and I was a part of it as surely as if I had been there. It was like 1971 all over again for Canadiens fans, because the win was something we hadn't expected. Maybe it wasn't as dramatic as beating Chicago in seven after being down 2–0 to start the series, but it was a Stanley Cup win in an era when they were statistically going to come but once in a couple of decades or more, and it had been done in a series of miraculous overtime victories.

That night as I stood there in my backyard in an American city and celebrated alone, hockey was alive for me as it hadn't been since I'd been a kid. Despite living hundreds of miles from the nearest team and not having gone to a game for more than a decade, I had my game back. I vowed to myself that I would never lose it again.

chapter forty-five

The Night Brett Hull Disappeared

When I was a kid, there was a mystery shrouding the Montréal Forum that made the place seem unapproachable, less an arena than the home of the gods. From time to time, my dad and I would drive by there on the way to my grandmother's, and I'd read the marquee outside. It would tell me that some concert or other was coming to town. Or the circus. I never quite believed they allowed elephants into the place where the Canadiens played their games. I thought the real Forum was sealed off from such indignities, in a giant plastic bubble, and this place I was looking at on Saint Catherine Street was just a false version put there so nobody would realize that the original had been removed for its own protection.

When we had tickets to a game, the world became a different place. I wasn't the only one who experienced the feeling. Any kid in my school who knew he was going to see the Habs play would start talking about it weeks before. The week of the game, he'd have nothing else to say except to speculate on what each of the great players would do at the game. I did this myself, knowing I was going to see the Boston Bruins and later the New York Rangers come to town, the two games I saw live when I was a boy.

My dad wasn't much of a watcher of sports, so I was lucky that some kid in my class gave me some advice before my first-ever NHL game, the Boston one: Get there early enough for the warm-up and stay until you see who the three stars are. It's advice that I still follow today, and it was on my mind one time in 1994 when I found out that I'd be able to take in a Blues game while at a conference in Illinois at a university near the Missouri border.

I had a friend who worked at the university get me a single Blues ticket. It was going to be my first game since 1981, when my dad and I had paid $40 for two tickets to see the Canadiens play Vancouver and Tiger Williams. I was beside myself, thinking that the NHL game would be a part of my conference weekend. Hockey had come alive for me again the spring before with the Canadiens' unlikely win of the Cup, and I was craving it like I hadn't for years. St. Louis versus San Jose wasn't exactly an original six match-up, but the Blues had some decent history, and they had Brett Hull.

Thinking of my old grade-school buddy's advice, I naturally got to the arena early. In fact, I was standing there when the doors opened, so eager to see the warm-up that I'd practically run from the parking lot. I presented my ticket to the old man at the turnstile and walked in, the third person through. The lobby was empty, but I didn't pause at the snack bar. I was going to have to circle the place to get to the section where my seat was, and I wasn't going to take a chance on missing the players when they came out onto the ice.

As I walked, I noticed that at each door there were a couple of people dressed in sport coats with Blues emblems on the pockets. As each fan came through the gates, they handed him or her a small towel with the Blues logo on it. I approached one of them and asked how a person could get such a prize. It was like the old days of being in the Forum, hoping my dad would let me buy one of those tiny hockey sticks with all the Canadiens' autographs lithographed onto its shaft. "You get one as you come in. One per guest," was the sport coat's reply.

"I wasn't given one at my door. Could I have one, please?" I said as politely as a kid asking a teacher for a favor.

"You get one when you come in the door," was his bureaucratic reply.

"But I was the third person in, and they didn't have them at my door," I said. "You can see that I don't have one."

I spun around, arms out, as if to show that I was disarmed. All the guy did was glance at me while he kept handing a towel to each person going by him.

"You get it at the door when you come in," he repeated. *What a goofball.* This robot wasn't listening to me. I felt a lump of frustration and anger rise in my throat.

I could see that my only recourse was to dash to the door I'd come in, hoping the warm-up wouldn't start without me. I sprinted. When I got to my door, sure enough, there they were, two more uniformed representatives of the St. Louis Blues, just barely into the supply in their boxes. They must have gotten to this spot a little late. I approached them, that sick-scary feeling in my stomach, hoping against hope I could pry a towel from them. I felt as though I was on the playground again, inches away from the card trade I'd dreamed about, not sure if the other kid would go through with the exchange right as it was about to happen.

I started talking almost before I got to the guy. "I came though this door earlier. I was the third person. I just wanted to get here in time for the warm-up. Please, can I have one of the towels? I didn't get one when I came in." I looked into the guy's face; he looked into mine. This time, I was talking to a human being, a hockey fan who knew the importance of something like this, an NHL souvenir. He handed me a towel, and I started the mad dash to my section behind the net in the end the Blues would twice defend. Luckily, the warm-up was just commencing.

One thing about the game itself struck me immediately— it was fast. Perhaps it was where I sat, or maybe it was because I hadn't seen a live NHL game—or any hockey game—for so long, but I couldn't believe how quickly the shots came in on goal. More than that, I was surprised at how fast the deflections happened. The goalies had to be amazing to track the puck from the blue line in, and when it was tipped, they shifted their stance and focus just as quickly. It was almost as if they knew ahead of time what was going to happen. I was once again astounded at the game.

Of course, I stayed until the end, and as many of the other fans filed out, I waited for the three stars to be announced and to take their little spins on the ice. I don't recall the other two stars, but the first one was Brett Hull.

I had watched him carefully during the game, especially when he didn't have the puck. He was in the middle of his tenure with the Blues, and the word I'd heard on TV was that he was a great scorer but lazy with his defense. Pretty much all I'd seen this game proved that. I was disappointed. I felt he should have done more to justify his fans' obvious adoration of him. All over the arena, people had expensive replica jerseys with Hull's name and number on them. They had cheered his every touch of the puck, and he had rewarded them with two goals.

It was those people with the Hull jerseys on who were still standing around as the arena emptied, as I was, waiting for the last ritualistic moment before admitting that the game was over. We were the true lovers of hockey, I told myself as I waited for his name to be announced, sure that he'd come out and skate around, helmet off, golden hair flying like his father's had when he was the "Golden Jet." The fans would give him a huge cheer. In that moment, I felt a tinge of sadness that they'd never yet won a Stanley Cup in St. Louis. They deserved it.

"And the first star, Brett Hull!" the announcer said. The crowning moment of my game had come. I watched the bench where Hull would appear, but nothing happened. I looked around me, curious about what everyone else thought of this. They all just stared at the spot where the other two stars had appeared, expectant.

Brett Hull never appeared for his star. He left his fans standing there, looking as I was at the place where he was supposed to be, dumbfounded. After a minute, we all realized that this was it. He wasn't coming out. The fans shrugged and filed out as the less faithful had done a few minutes before.

Maybe Hull was hurt. Maybe he was being disciplined by the coach. Who knows what happened. But the net effect, at least to me, was a feeling of great disappointment. What if this had been Montréal, and I had been the eight-year-old kid I walked behind as we left the arena? I don't think I would have told my friends at school about great saves and glorious

goals. I think I would have told them that Brett Hull had disappeared before the game was over, because to me, and maybe
to that kid, the game wasn't over until the three stars had
taken their moment in the sun. It was as important a ritual as
a team skating the Cup around the ice after winning game
seven.

As I left the arena and drove past the famous arch back
to my hotel in Illinois, I contemplated the experience. The
game had proven itself to me, being better than I had expected,
yet the ambiance had been just a little bit off. I briefly thought
that maybe I shouldn't take the whole thing as seriously as I had
learned to do growing up where hockey was a religion. This,
after all, was not Montréal, but St. Louis. But I knew no other
way to approach the game. It was all or nothing. I'd learned
that every moment of every NHL game is sacred and was to be
savored. I only hoped for the sake of St. Louis that someone
would stumble onto this truth for themselves, and I still do.

chapter forty-six

You Played, Right?

Americans always ask the same two questions when they find out you're Canadian: "Do you speak French?" and "Did you play hockey?"

How do you explain that it's not just about playing hockey, it's about living it? What's interesting is that they seldom think to ask the second question in the present tense. Not even in places in the States where they have a lot of artificial ice and a pretty large hockey subculture. They always want to know what you did as a kid, assuming, I guess, that these are things you leave behind when you grow up.

I'm always tempted to answer their question with a swagger. How are they to know that everyone played, that not playing during my growing-up was a sign of some kind of pathology, a secret to be hidden like the fact that your parents were health food nuts? We tormented one kid in our school mercilessly because he never, ever had a bologna sandwich in his lunch. It just wasn't natural, and we made sure he knew it.

For a moment after the question comes, I feel as if I should invent a past far grander than mine ever was. Maybe reach down and rub my knee as I throw out offhandedly, "Yeah, sure I played. Might have gone somewhere if it hadn't been for this thing." What would they know? They have no idea of the selection process that started when we were small, sorting kids into two piles, the "maybe he has a faint shot somehow" and the rest. Sure, I played. But that was just what everyone did.

More pressing to me is the question asked in the present—do I play? The guys my brother-in-law works with in Ontario still play at 40. I suppose if I lived there still, I would too. But I quit the game—again—thanks to an injury that occurred long after my competitive playing days had ended, and though I hate to point fingers, the reason was that the guys on the ice with me were just not experienced enough. It was my third retirement from the game, and at the time, I thought the final one.

I was teaching college in Ohio, and it came up that there were some students with hockey experience who had decided to form a club team. They asked if I'd like to join them for some practices, helping them get organized and doing some coaching. Sure, I figured, why not? Why not get on the ice and feel the thrill of the puck on my own stick, instead of just watching others play?

The first practice took place on a Friday at 11:00 PM, the pressure for ice time in Dayton apparently being almost like what it was when I was growing up in Canada. I showed up to the arena with my gear sorted. I was missing my helmet, it having been stolen from a storage locker in my old apartment, but what did it matter? The worst we'd be doing was scrimmaging, and I had a mouthguard.

Players took shots on the one goalie and at the opposite, empty net as I went onto the ice. I could see that we had the usual mix of American talent. Some of the guys were pretty good. The rest played at about the level of Bantam players back home. Their skating was wobbly in places, their shots weak, or if hard, unpredictable in their direction and velocity. I realized I had a lot of work ahead of me if I was to turn this group into a team.

I organized a scrimmage in order to evaluate the potential to get these guys playing as a unit, dividing the group in half. I decided I would play as well as watch and assigned myself to a side to begin.

Play started with me on the right wing, and I had taken a couple of shifts when I found myself back-checking on the wrong side. I was about at the faceoff dot on the right side of my defensive zone when I caught up with the player with the puck. Being one of the less experienced guys, he fumbled with it as I caught him and ended up kicking it toward the boards. I started after it, expecting him to do the same. It was a play

I'd seen a thousand times, and I started to cut around behind him to beat him to the puck. As I did, I knew he'd turn clockwise, out of my way.

Only he didn't. Instead, he turned counter-clockwise, shoving his stick out just as I accelerated toward the boards. I went right over the stick and headfirst into the wall, sticking my arms out as I flew. I hit with the crown of my head first, then my momentum carried me forward, my neck bending and my right ear smashing flat against the boards. I landed in a heap, quickly jumped up and collapsed again.

One of the guys said to me later that he had looked at me in that moment and thought, *The guy's paralyzed.* I got up again, though, and skated to the bench, woozy. The practice went on without me, and though I managed to drive myself home, I was pretty miserable by the time I got there.

I had a whiplash injury so severe that my doctor told me it looked on my x-ray like I'd been rear-ended by a car going 70 miles an hour. Both my thumbnails were completely black, despite my having worn hockey gloves—I'd thrust my hands out to slow my momentum and smashed both hands into the boards. I had a slight separation of the right shoulder. My arm hurt so much I couldn't iron a shirt for two months. The doctor further said that I'd hit just off the center of my head. If I'd been slightly to my right when I hit, my neck wouldn't have flexed. It would have broken. That was enough damage for my early-30s body to take, and so I announced, once more, my retirement from hockey.

For a while, I didn't regret the decision at all. Even now, I think about that night and what would have happened if my head had been positioned an inch the other way. I might be in a wheelchair today. Maybe that's a little dramatic, and maybe now that it's happened once it would never happen again, but the thought alone gives me a creepy feeling.

But do hockey players ever say "enough"? I saw in the *Los Angeles Times* a while ago that Canadian actor Alan Thicke had lost a bunch of teeth practicing for a charity game. He'll live with that forever, just as I sometimes have a week at a time when I can't get the nagging pain out of my neck and back. It makes me wonder at our folly. Yet cartoonist Charles Schulz played hockey all the way up until he died, in his 70s. Maybe he provides the lesson that it's never too late to lace up the skates and enjoy the grandeur of flying across the ice, pretending you're Beliveau, Dionne or Peter Forsberg, living the dream that first started when your mom took you to a school-yard rink to while away a winter's afternoon on your cheese cutters. Maybe that urge to play is just a part of us if we love the game. And indeed, as time went on, hockey pulled me back onto the ice. But not before I'd changed locales to a place that would have seemed to me the least likely to foster my ongoing dreams of hockey glory.

chapter forty-seven

Bringing the Game Home

At one point in my working life, I had the fortune to move to Los Angeles from Ohio. The first Sunday I was there, I turned on the TV and saw the Kings playing. What a window this opened for me—I realized that quite by accident, I was back in a land of hockey. I don't think it was my fault, but that same week, Gretzky was traded to St. Louis. I hadn't even had a chance to give him a call to say that I was in town. Still, Gretzky or no Gretzky, being in L.A., as far away as it seems from the center of the hockey world, allowed me to reconnect with the game in ways that being in Ohio did not in those days before the Columbus Blue Jackets.

I figured I would find some hockey fanatics in my new city, people who had some of the same memories as I did about other parts of the subculture, because for me growing up, hockey wasn't just what I played; it was also hockey cards, Esso Power Players albums, autographs, and on and on. And for me, like for every other Canadian kid of my generation, table hockey had been crucial in creating Christmas day memories and providing a diversion during those early spring days when it was too warm to have ice anymore and too rainy to play on the street. Living in a city with an NHL team again, I expected to find some compatriots who shared these memories and might want to revisit them.

My job in advertising had me working in an ultra-hip, design-studio office. We had a pool table and leather couch in the middle of the floor, and the California work style was big enough to include everything from James Dean shrines to puppies that came to work with my colleagues and spent the day whimpering under their desks. Surely a table hockey set wouldn't be out of place, I reasoned. I went home to Canada that Christmas determined to bring a game back with me, confident that I would start a new sensation at the office. Pretty soon we'd be having tournaments, setting up real seasons and playing for our own version of the Stanley Cup. Of course, no matter what teams other people wanted to be, I would represent the Montréal Canadiens.

Back in Toronto, I got a table hockey game at Canadian Tire and took it out of the box to check it out. My brother-in-law and I played a few games. I took the red players and he the blue, even though he's crazy about the Red Wings. I forgive him for his fanaticism because he inherited it from his dad, rather than picking it up in the late '90s like a lot of other people I know. Anyway, he knew it was out of the question for me to take the Toronto-looking team.

New Year's Day came, and I had to pack to return by air to L.A. My dad helped me box up the game. We created an extra-reinforced carton to cover the box the game came in, just in case Air Canada did a number on it. And to be safe, I cut a picture from the Canadian Tire catalog to show the guy at U.S. Customs so that he wouldn't make me undo the carefully wrapped box. It was typical Canadian over-compensation, and I'm sure the agent could smell my innocence as he asked me what was in the box, then waved me through.

First day back, I took the game to work. With my colleagues looking on, I carefully cut away the carton my dad and I had assembled. The picture of the game drew some interest. Then I took the set itself out and started to install the plastic players on the tiny pegs. As I did, I reminisced out loud about the version I'd had as a kid. It had been like this one, only the players had been made of metal and the wingers hadn't been able to go behind the nets so far, like now. "That's a nod to the Gretzky era for sure," I informed the people gathered to watch. I raised my eyes to look at the faces around me, but nobody seemed to have much of an idea what I was talking about.

I got the players and the nets installed, then set the game in the middle of the conference table where I thought we would play. I told the guy who sat opposite to get ready for the faceoff. I dropped the puck and tried to move my centerman back with it and pass it off to the wing. My opponent just slammed the rod of his centerman into the set as hard as he could, trying to jar the puck to his side. I swooped it back out of his grasp, then played it up to my wing. A shot from the blue line missed, and his defense got it. He slapped it as hard as he could toward my goal. So it went, my finesse and strategy matched by his aggression.

To him, the game wasn't about memories or the chance to reenact a season of the pursuit of the greatest trophy in the history of sports. It was about being rough and tumble—football on ice. His last comment to me before we went back to work told the tale. "Do they fight?" he asked. "It's not real hockey if they don't fight."

What was I to say? I just looked at him, wondering whether to ask if he'd ever seen Wayne Gretzky fight. I stayed silent.

Over the next few weeks, everyone had a turn. I even came back from lunch one day and found a couple of people playing by themselves. I thought for a moment that I was getting somewhere, helping these Americans to love the game. I watched them, then took on the winner, but such a spontaneous game happened only that once. My idea for a tournament never did get off the ground. There were too many other things to do, like have a birthday party in January for the long-dead Elvis.

I quit that job to go back into teaching a few months later. When I did, I decided to leave the game behind as a legacy. I still had hope that someone would draw up a schedule that went from preseason to Stanley Cup finals. A while later, I found out through a friend at the company that the hockey set was sitting under the pool table. I told her that I was glad to know that they had found a place to keep it safe. But what she meant was that it was gathering dust there. I never did go back to pick it up.

chapter forty-eight

The Great One
Returns to Town

I moved to L.A. in 1996, a few days before the Great One left town for St. Louis. I never got the chance to see him play live as a King. But in February 1998, I found out that he would be returning to town for what some people thought might be the last time. The NHL was about to take its break for the Olympics, and Wayne and the Rangers were going to play the Kings at the Great Western Forum, where the Kings played from 1967 until 1999. I decided that I had to go. I didn't want to have to explain to my grandchildren some day that I had lived through the Gretzky era and never seen him with my own eyes.

I'd heard the old joke about Kings games that went something like this: A guy calls the box office and asks, "What time is the game tonight?" The operator answers, "What time can you show up?" During the Gretzky era, of course, everything had changed. It became fashionable to attend the games, so everyone from Goldie and Kurt to Mr. T might be seen there, whether they had any idea what hockey was about or not. It was just the L.A. thing to do, a competition to see whether your press agent could get you a better seat than someone else's. But after the Great One left, things calmed down. I had been to a game in the fall of 1996 to see the Canadiens play and had sat among a relative handful of fans in a mostly empty upper deck. So I figured on going to the Rangers game and walking up to buy a ticket. It was on a weeknight, to boot.

When I got to the Forum, I realized the folly of my calculation. Not only was this the Gretzky game, but there were a lot of bandwagon Rangers fans wanting to see what had become "their" team in 1994, after the victory over Vancouver for the Cup. I got to the box office window to find that the tickets were sold out.

I started back to my car, wandering through the maze of people, including ticket scalpers. As I did, a guy walking with a couple of friends bumped me on the shoulder. He was talking and gesturing excitedly, oblivious to someone going the other way. I turned to him, about to say something, when I saw something work the final inch out of his back pocket and flutter to the ground. It was one of the bigger, nicely printed tickets. A season ticket. I picked it up. I was holding in my hand the key to a seat far better than what I could have bought, even had I had the money. I was in!

It didn't occur to me that once I got in, I'd be seated right next to his friends, who would want to know how I'd come by the ticket. All I felt was the anxiety of knowing that I'd have to give it back. I couldn't bear the guilt of crushing this guy's hope to see the Great One play. I just assumed that his dream was the same as mine. I ran after him, tapped him on the shoulder and handed him the ticket. "This fell, back there," I said to him. He looked at me, trying to put it together, then grabbed the ticket and left me standing there. He called out a half-hearted thank you over his shoulder as he kept on walking. I wished in that instant that I had just kept his ticket, but I turned to leave again.

When I got to the sidewalk leading to the parking lot, a guy approached me. "Hey, couldn't get in?" he said to me. I nodded. "I got a ticket," he said.

Sure you do, I thought. *So do those fifty other guys over there. That doesn't mean I'm going to pay you what you want for it.* I started to open my mouth to say it when he spoke again.

"Look, I work for the Forum. I'm not supposed to sell this ticket. But I don't care about hockey. So here's what you do. You go to that car over there," he said, pointing to a green mid-1980s Toyota. "Open the driver's door. There's a ticket on the seat. You put whatever you think it's worth on the seat and take it. I only got one."

I'd been in L.A. two years, and I'd learned not to trust anyone. What if someone was hiding in the car, ready to relieve

me of my cash, and no ticket in sight? I started to back away. He
read my hesitation. "Look, here's my badge," he said as he pulled
a plastic workplace ID tag out of his jacket. "Great Western
Forum" it said at the top, along with an icon of the building.
Below it was his picture. He held his fingers over his name.

If this guy was a crook, he was a way-too-clever one,
I decided. There was no way he would have gone to all the
trouble to fake the badge if this were a rip-off. Petty criminals
just aren't that thorough. I decided to take him at his word
and nodded again. "OK," I said.

I walked over to his car and opened the door, trying not
to look too conspicuous. Around me, people were moving in
waves toward the game. There on the front seat was a ticket, all
right. It was small, printed with a dot-matrix script. I recognized
it as a seat in the peanut gallery, far from the ice. The price on it
said $15. I reached into my pocket and grabbed the $20 I had plus
the $2 I'd received in change from the parking attendant, which
I left as a tip. I grabbed the ticket and shut the door. As I went past
the guy, I said a thank you that dwarfed the one that jerk whose
game I'd saved had given me. He was startled at my enthusiasm
but smiled back and told me to enjoy the game. His lack of interest
was my luck.

Inside the Forum, I climbed to my seat. It was at center
ice, but way up, so high that I could reach out and touch the
back wall a couple of rows behind me. In this outdated arena,
the roof sloped low over my head. The whole section, in fact,

was like a forgotten land. The peanut sellers didn't even come up this far.

Way below me, the Great One did his magic. He was in the late stages of his career and not a huge factor in the game, but he still had the knack of appearing and disappearing on the ice. Even though I watched him rather than the puck, he could elude my eye, shifting and darting in and out, going where it made no sense to go, but always ending up where he needed to be when it counted. I sat there in awe at his skill, sure that I wouldn't have enjoyed the game any more had I been seated 50 rows closer to the ice.

This was hockey, and it was beautiful.

chapter forty-nine

Hope in the Wasteland

I guess most people "back East," like in hockey towns Toronto or New York, think of L.A. as a hockey wasteland. In some respects, it is, but the longer I live there, the more I discover the game just under the surface of things. There's the fan support for the Kings, upheld by a loyal band, if somewhat small by Toronto or Montréal standards. And there have been moments when the Kings have created some great memories. The irony of it is, sometimes the greatest moments have happened almost by accident.

It's like there's some kind of strange magic going on, giving the fans in L.A. things to cheer about, but constantly keeping them off guard. For instance, the Kings barely made the playoffs in 2001. During the final run at the end of the regular season, I was in Florida, having convinced my family to meet me there for a spring vacation. My brother-in-law, Phil, and I stayed up until the wee hours one morning as the Kings beat Phoenix to assure themselves a place at the playoff table. A week or two later, the first home playoff game came, L.A. versus Detroit, the Wings having won the first two back in Michigan. It looked like it would be a repeat of playoffs past, with the Kings bowing out to the stronger team.

I managed to get tickets to the game, which was scheduled for a Sunday night. The trouble was, the L.A. Lakers had played that afternoon, so Staples Center, where the Kings had been playing since 1999, was booked. Nobody had expected the Kings to get into the playoffs. Because it was impossible to schedule the hockey game for the next day, it was decided that it would take place late Sunday night, starting at 8:30 PM. That's where the surprise came in.

Fans were used to 7:30 PM start times, so people just showed up when they normally did, which was 7:45 PM. Whether by anticipating this or by lucky accident, the Kings' management had set up a number of booths and attractions on the streets surrounding the arena to keep people entertained while the workers inside converted the arena for hockey. The crowd, all 18,000 of us it seemed like, was gathered together. Pretty soon, somebody started yelling "Go Kings Go!" It echoed from one side of the building to the other. "Let's Go Kings!" was next. "Deee-Troit Sucks" came after. And so it went until the doors opened, just before game time.

When we went in, ushers handed us shakers resembling plastic wigs on the end of a little paddle, and the normally bored and aloof crowd, still living on the juice of the excitement outside, stayed pumped up. The game was deafening. I bet even the famous people sitting in the good seats 100 rows below mine were cheering. I know my section was crazed with Cup frenzy.

The jaded and successful Detroit players probably thought it silly. Maybe you would, too, if you're from a city where hockey success comes more easily than it has here over the years since the Kings lost the finals to Montréal. Here was a first-round game in a city that would probably watch as its team got swept. Why get all excited?

But the Kings didn't lose. They won. When Luc Robitaille, interviewed after the game, was asked what it felt like to win the historic first playoff game since 1993, he shrugged it off. "We're not interested in history. We're interested in winning the series," he replied.

The Kings pulled their improbable victory called the "Stunner at Staples" in the next game, winning 4–3 in overtime after being down by three with less than five minutes to go. Then they went to Detroit and won again, taking a 3–2 lead in the series. They came back to L.A. and won the series in game six in overtime. Improbable in a city where success breeds fan interest and therefore makes tickets impossible to get, I was there, too. A friend who worked with a local doctor offered me a ticket that had me sitting in the corner near the

Detroit net during the second period and the eventual over-time frame. With the others in the full house that was Staples that night, I watched as Adam Deadmarsh swept in on goal and deflected a shot into the net to give the Kings the series win.

After the goal was scored, Chris Osgood just lay in Detroit's net for a long time, stunned. I don't think any of us quite believed it, either. It's unexpected moments like these that suggest that the hockey gods haven't forgotten L.A.

chapter fifty

Hockey Mojo

Ever since I was little, I have believed that what I do influences the outcome of NHL games. When I was a kid watching the Canadiens during one of their playoff wins in the 1976–79 Cup run, I sat in front of the TV with a stopwatch, timing the action. Every once in a while I'd let the clock run past the moment when play was stopped by the whistle. I reasoned that if the game went by a little quicker, the Canadiens would have a greater chance of winning. I only realized near the end of the game that my timekeeping had no bearing on the official time of the game.

Even now, I always wear my replica jersey on the day of my team's playoff games, whether I go to the game or not. I have other magic that I work, too. For example, the year the Kings upset Detroit in the first round, things looked like they were going L.A.'s way. I allowed myself the hope that this could be a big year for the team, and so for the second series, against Colorado, I knew I had to get involved. I went online to get tickets, but as is usual in L.A. with big events, I had no luck. Instead, I decided to participate from home. The rituals I practiced were spontaneous in their invention, but when they worked, I realized that I had to continue them.

My first ritual was to help the Kings' goalie, Felix Potvin. He'd been streaky in his career at times, but great for L.A. since they'd grabbed him from Vancouver in mid-season. I tapped the underside of an antique table that sat beside the chair I watched the games in every time he made a save. It was a combination of the old knock-on-wood routine and a connection to my grandmother, whose table it had been before she passed away many years prior. I figured she'd been good luck for the Habs all those years, so why not?

If Felix was good, Patrick Roy had to be bad, so I figured out a way to curse him. Between periods, I would take a walk up and down my street, stepping on the sidewalk cracks and saying with every step, "Patrick Roy, Patrick Roy." Except that instead of pronouncing his name properly, like "Rrrroooi," or saying it as Americans do, "Wa," I'd say his name like it looks, "Roy," as in "Roy Rogers." I could think of no higher insult. This ritual developed into my taking long walks on the days of the games. "Patrick walks," I started to call them, and I'd say his name a thousand times, literally, as I stepped on all the cracks in the sidewalk. I figured that if "step on a crack, break your mother's back" was true when we were kids, then my ritual would surely help.

My final ritual evolved during my long walks in my neighborhood, which was mostly Chinese. I knew that there are a lot of superstitions in Chinese culture, so I figured I'd get in on them by tossing two coins into a fountain at a small shopping plaza near where I lived.

The Kings won game one in Colorado, then lost three straight. It was at this point that I developed my coin ritual, and it worked. They came back to win games five and six, and the final contest was set for Colorado on Wednesday, May 9, 2001.

Trouble was, I was teaching an evening class, and the final game landed on the one night of the week when I had to work. What choice did I have? I taped it, and I hoped that somehow the hockey gods would understand that my mojo would come after the fact in my universe but maybe coincide with the game in theirs.

I watched the game into the wee hours of the night after I got home, diligently tapping for saves and taking walks between the periods. And the Kings were doing fine until they lost the game in the final period, and with it the series. I hung my head in regret, my dreams of a Stanley Cup having disappeared, and I knew that it was partly my fault.

The Kings lost because I had left it up to them to win. It's not that I could have rearranged my work schedule to see the game live, and I'm sure the hockey gods understood my sense of duty and would have rewarded it if they could, but I blew it. I had made a calculated decision not to go to the fountain that day, thinking that the other charms would work and that I'd save the coin toss for the next playoff round, when the Kings would need it even more. I had hoped that the players' skill and determination would override my mojo. When I was wrong, I disappointed a whole city. And worst of all, I left the Avalanche, our hated rivals, alone to march to a Stanley Cup.

chapter fifty-one

Now That's a Wicked Curve

H aving been in the U.S. for more than 15 years, I finally decided to apply for citizenship in 2002. It wasn't that I wanted to be rid of my Canadian roots. In fact, since I'd moved to L.A., I'd treasured them more than ever due to a combination of feeling that Canada was now very far away and knowing that there was a large expatriate Canadian community in California. I seemed to run into Canucks everywhere. But I was feeling at home in L.A., tenured in my teaching job, and I decided that rather than be a guest in the U.S., I should make the arrangement more permanent.

In the course of filling in the paperwork, I consulted a friend who had married a Canadian woman. He in turn steered me toward his lawyer, Paul, a fellow with an office in downtown L.A. So on a Monday afternoon, I found myself sitting there, on the 31st floor of one of the city's handful of skyscrapers. My mind was preoccupied with two things. The first was the likelihood of an earthquake happening at this moment, and the other was the amazing vista out his office window, which faced south.

I had stood up and was scoping out the view of the ocean 20 miles away from behind his desk when the lawyer walked in. As if to explain myself, I said, "Hey, you have a great view of Staples Center." And he did—the distinctive arched roof of the building stood out from what was around it.

"Yeah, I remember when my dad used to take me to hockey games at the Forum. It was nothing like that place," Paul said as he gestured to the three-year-old art-deco wonder. I had my own visions of being inside that place and good memories of watching the Kings, but his words made me wonder. Why had he immediately interpreted the thread of the conversation to be about hockey, since the more famous Lakers played in the arena also?

"You went to games as a kid?" I asked, trying to calculate how old he was. He seemed about my age, which meant that he'd seen the likes of Rogie Vachon and Marcel Dionne play in the old Kings yellow and purple.

"Sure, we're from Winnipeg," he offered. "Moved here when I was 10. Back then, my dad and I would be at the concession stand and we'd see one Winnipegger after another. It got to be funny after a while. It was like we hadn't left home."

I could now hear his accent, which was stronger than mine. Sure, he was Canadian.

I could feel the bond of countrymen that you read about in old British novels, two Brits finding each other in some far-off corner of the Empire and sharing tea. I couldn't help but ask him the question I'm asked all the time. "So you played hockey?"

"Oh yeah. My whole life. My dad was a goalie, too. Pretty good in his day. Probably would have played in the NHL if he'd been younger. But you know, the old six-team league..."

I interrupted his sentence, excited by the flow of the conversation. "Sure, then there was expansion, and you had teams like the California Golden Seals," I said. I searched my mind for other hockey trivia from the early '70s. Finding none, I asked instead, "What year did you come down here, anyway?"

"1974," he replied.

"So you remember the Winnipeg Jets? I mean, the WHA version?" I asked. I had recently seen a *Fox Sports West* television network program called "Beyond the Glory: Brett Hull." It was part of an ongoing series profiling the real lives of sports celebrities. One of the things that struck me the most about Hull's life was the trauma on his family of moving to Winnipeg in 1972 when his dad signed with the WHA for a million bucks. It was what kept Bobby Hull out of the Summit Series, though the show hadn't mentioned that. They had focused instead on the hype surrounding the move.

Winnipeg had been turned upside down, even having a welcoming parade for their new dignitary.

"Sure, I remember when Hull moved up there. The whole town went crazy. I was in grade two," he said.

"Did you see any games?" I asked. If he answered yes, he would be the only person I'd ever met who had actually been to a WHA game, live. I mean, I'm sure they're out there, but it doesn't come up very often in conversation.

"I don't remember, but I do have Bobby Hull's hockey stick," he said. I did a double take. This was an adult version of the greatest of playground boasts, and I needed some verification. He continued. "Some kid at my school had a father that worked for the team. Our school raffled off two sticks. My friend won one—I won the other." I looked at him, incredulous. "I still have it. It's autographed by every member of the Jets from Hull right on down," he added. Neither of us could remember any of those other players right then. He finished up by saying, "It's a piece of history all right. Has a pretty good hook on it, too." Everyone knows that Hull was famous for that.

"Maybe you could lend it to the Hall of Fame?" I offered. I could see it there, behind glass, accompanied by a small plaque with Paul's name engraved on it as the benefactor. But as I said it, I must admit that I wasn't thinking of what the stick might mean to some young kid taking a tour of the Hall, where it was just as likely as anything to get lost among the amazing sights that overwhelm the visitors there.

What I couldn't get over was that here I was, in the middle of a desert city at the edge of the Pacific Ocean, thousands of miles from Canada and decades from the end of the WHA. Yet I was only one step removed from the great Bobby Hull, who had, at one moment in his life, had his hands on the stick that was now in Paul's San Fernando Valley basement.

I realized in that instant that I had not lost hockey in moving to the U.S., and even less in my migration to L.A. It was all around me still. I just had to look a little harder to find it than I would have had I stayed in Canada. But sometimes I'm lucky, like in talking to this lawyer, and hockey just seems to find me.

chapter fifty-two

A Hero Says Hello

The NFL plays its all-star game, the Pro Bowl, in Hawaii the week after the season ends. It's the same every year: Commentators in colorful shirts stand in the sunshine while players in the background toss and catch the ball, warming up. They play a game featuring simple run-it-up-the-middle type offense in front of a half-full stadium. If hockey used that template, its All-Star game would be played somewhere cold, the guys with the microphones barely able to keep from shivering as they did their introductions and called the game. The atmosphere would be matched to the sport's origins that way.

But that's not how it is. The NHL moves its All-Star game from city to city, which is how L.A. came to get the perk in 2002. I was lucky enough to get a ticket to that game, something I suspect would not have been possible in hockey-mad Canada.

My all-weekend pass allowed me entrance to three things. The first, the "YoungStars" game on Friday evening, was paired with the skills competition. This was fun, but it featured a lot more standing around and waiting by players than I had imagined. It was like being at a taping of a TV show. Come to think of it, it *was* the taping of a TV show.

At the All-Star game Saturday afternoon, I tried to memorize the face of every player on the ice and to remember something about how each one skated, what he did away from the puck or anything else that would help me bring those guys back to life for my future grandchildren, who I expect to love the game, no matter where they're born.

The two games weren't the whole of it, though. My ticket also included the "NHL Experience," an indoor theme park with hockey games, displays, hardest shot clocking booths and other attractions. I debated whether to get up early on Saturday morning to go; it all seemed too silly. The venue had been open all week, and I hadn't bothered. But at the last minute, I decided to at least take a tour of it, since it was included in the ticket package I had.

I got there with hours to spare before Saturday afternoon's game and was greeted with a display of all the league's trophies, including the glorious Stanley Cup. I'd seen the Cup before, but I wanted to get a picture taken with it, since I had my Kings jersey on this time. Defying tradition, I touched it for the photo. I will have to wait to see whether I've cursed the hopes of my new team winning it someday.

Then I noticed the autograph tables, where there were two people signing. One was a former Kings player from the 1980s, Jay Wells. He looked like one of those golf-shirted insurance guys who visit you when something has gone wrong in your house. He pleasantly chatted with each person as he signed programs.

The other face was recognizable to me, as it would have been anywhere. It was Frank Mahovlich. I checked out the length of the lineup to see the two of them. It was barely 20 people long. I couldn't believe my luck, but then my heart sank. I didn't have so much as a scrap of paper to get him to sign.

I did a quick scramble to the other side of the L.A. Convention Center, where there were sports memorabilia venders set up for the weekend. I combed through hockey cards, trying to find a Mahovlich. Any one, new, old, WHA, I didn't care. I found nothing.

I went from vendor to vendor and asked if they had a Mahovlich. Each time, I got the same blank stare. "Mahovlich? No, nothing of his. When was his era?"

"Come on," I wanted to shout, "I mean, the guy only scored 533 NHL goals!" It's times like these that I long to be back in Canada.

I changed my tactics and started to ask vendors if they had any Montréal Canadiens memorabilia. Finally, I came up with a crest, the "CH" that adorns the center of the Habs jersey. It was made of felt, looking like something from the '50s or '60s. I paid the guy five bucks for it. Perfect. I went back and got in line.

Twenty minutes later, I got Wells' autograph and then waited for Frank. While standing there, I heard the guy in front of me say something to him. "Did you ever win a Stanley Cup?" the guy asked.

The Big M tried to be polite. "I won several. This is the ring from one of them." He stretched out his hand. The ring was large, gold with a diamond in the center, and it said "Toronto 1967." That surprised me. Why not one of the ones from the Montréal era?

The guy looked at it like he had no clue at all who he was talking to. "That must have been the highlight of your life," he said. I'm sure Mahovlich's mind flashed to winning four Cups with the Leafs, two with Montréal, playing the Russians, getting into the Hockey Hall of Fame, and on and on, but maybe he wondered what the point was of listing these accomplishments, resumé-style, to someone who didn't have a clue who he was.

"It was a thrill," said Frank politely, and signed the guy's program. I practically shoved the dude out of the way then, moving closer to pressure him to give me my chance. He'd had his 15 seconds of contact, and in my books, that was enough.

As I approached Frank, I looked at his teeth. I'd seen a grinning, toothless Mahovlich in dozens of pictures, and I had to see what they'd done to repair the gaps. Checking the teeth of hockey players is kind of a morbid fascination of mine. Sure enough, Frank had new pearly whites, though not quite the same color as the natural teeth that surrounded them. I saw the teeth as a badge, a symbol of games played and Cups won, almost like the ring that he wore.

Holding out my crest, I blurted out, "I grew up in Montréal." I felt that I had to apologize for the Montréal crest, because for some reason he had his Toronto ring on, as if he were there to represent the Leafs. Actually, I was caught in a moment of confusion. To me, his Toronto era didn't exist; I'd only ever known him as a Canadien. Thinking of him as a Leaf, or a Red Wing for that matter, was like finding out your dad has an ex-wife from before you were born. You can't quite see that person as part of his history, or him as having been connected with her, but you know it's true. As it turned out, no explanation was necessary. Mahovlich grabbed the crest. "Montréal, eh?" That was all he said. I'm sure he gets that kind of thing a lot.

But I had more to say. "And I remember you in the 1972 Summit Series. My brother-in-law and I watch the final game on tape every Christmas," I said. Now he looked right at me. I had become a person with a past that overlapped his, and who, I would like to think, was an oasis in a desert of fans approaching him for an autograph but having no idea of the breadth of his accomplishments.

The Big M smiled at me with those shiny teeth and said, "You know, the prime minister and I are going over in June to commemorate the series. We're having a big dinner there on the site where the goal was scored." He leaned back in his chair as an invite for me to respond, oblivious to the lineup behind me. "I'm really looking forward to the trip, though I'm not sure yet who else can go. From the team, I mean."

"That sounds like a great thing. I'll bet there will be lots of goings-on in Canada this fall, with this being the 30th anniversary. I'm going to be sorry to miss it, being here," I replied. As I was saying this, I congratulated myself for not sounding like a complete idiot.

He smiled again, seeming to understand, and spoke words that I think now might have been offered as consolation: "My brother Peter is going to be here later on today." I didn't quite know how to say that I wouldn't be able to stay, since I was about to head to Staples Center for the game. I felt as though I was turning down an invitation to dinner.

He looked down then, almost surprised that the crest was still in his hand. With a flourish, he signed it "Frank Mahovlich #27" and gave it back. When I said thank you, I meant more than for the autograph. I meant it for the Cups and the Summit Series too. I hope he understood.

chapter fifty-three

The Million-Dollar Question

It's not hard to run into a hockey fan in L.A. It happens to me all the time. But it's not like being in Canada. Instead of just taking it on faith that the person really knows the game, I have to double-check his or her hockey savvy. In a way, it's unfair of me, but I often lead with the question I've been asked so many times, "Did you play?" Who says you can't be a fan if you've never been on the ice? My Gran is a perfect example. But somewhere inside me, I want to reserve the title "true fan" for someone who knows what it feels like to skate with the puck, to go into a corner, to block a shot and break a bone in the process.

To ask the American fan if he (assuming most are guys) ever played is like him asking me if I did—we're both working on a stereotype that assumes the other's identity before the fact. But when the answer is no, I must admit that he has to prove himself a little more heartily before we can really have a conversation where I think of him as part of the brotherhood, unfair as it may be, or not.

I was sitting in a coffee shop right down the street from my house when the NBA All-Star game came on TV in the spring of 2003. Most people at the counter were paying at least passing attention to the TV screen mounted in the corner. I turned to the guy next to me when Michael Jordan was introduced, and shrugged. "It's not hockey," I said, "so it really doesn't matter that much to me whether he starts or not." It was Jordan's last year, and there was some controversy over the matter, which had been endlessly discussed in the papers and on sports talk radio.

"I'm something of a hockey historian," the guy replied, picking up on the cue I'd given him.

I jumped to an unfair conclusion right away. *Here we go. The guy doesn't know the difference between offside and an offside pass, but he's been to one Kings game in his life on free tickets his company gave him, so he's an expert.*

Then he surprised me. "I remember the 1972 Bruins. They won the Cup," he said. Now, this was getting interesting. I didn't even bother to ask him if he'd played. I wanted to relive the old days too badly to disqualify him on a technicality.

"Phil Esposito was still with them then?" I said it as a question, but only to form a test. Everyone who knows anything about hockey in that era can picture Phil, greased-back hair, standing in a Boston uniform shoving in rebounds or hanging back in the slot and powering wrist shots past terrified goalies.

"Sure, and Bobby Orr," he offered.

OK, but that's still pretty basic knowledge, I thought to myself.

He didn't give me the chance to respond. Instead, he went on. "Johnny Bucyk, Carol Vadnais, Derek Sanderson, Gerry Cheevers, Don Awrey, Wayne Cashman..." He may have named a couple of others in addition. It didn't matter. I was convinced. I didn't think I could name that many of the Habs from the 1971 roster when they'd beaten Chicago and my world had come alive to hockey. And so we talked hockey and the good old days.

Because he remembered the 1972 Bruins so well, I had to ask: "Where were you on September 28, 1972?" He just looked at me. "When Paul Henderson scored for Canada?" I added. He thought about this for a while and came up with nothing. I explained a little bit more, and when he heard me mention the Russian team, he turned the conversation to the "Miracle On Ice" of 1980. He even knew that the U.S. game against Russia in those Olympics was not the final one. That was impressive, but it still wasn't quite enough. We talked a while longer, then I paid my check and bid him good day.

My hunger to find a fan with memories that stretch past one team and to the game and its great moments as a whole remained unsatisfied. I left wishing that someday I could meet up with an American who remembers the great Summit Series as I do. Someone who was in Canada on a business trip or who happens to have acquired a set of the DVDs of the game. Then we could really talk hockey.

chapter fifty-four

Penalty Box

As every hockey fan knows, the Ducks took New Jersey to a seventh game in the finals in 2003. I cringed at the thought of Anaheim winning a Cup before the Kings, but I enjoyed the playoffs anyway, their rhythm mirroring the rhythm of my life since 1993. Around that same time, though, I did something that proves that I have other dimensions to my life beyond the game. That June, I interviewed to spend the following spring semester teaching abroad, despite knowing that doing so would mean I would miss much of the 2004 playoffs. Why did I do this? Because my wife, Gaby, had it as her lifelong dream to live in England. When I was selected to go, I greeted the news with joy and dread. The playoffs! What if this was the Kings' year, or Montréal's?

We got to Oxford in February 2004, and I kept in touch with what was going on in the NHL by reading online magazines about the game. Then I realized by scanning the local TV listings that they actually did have NHL hockey on "telly," broadcast live. The games appeared in the middle of the night, since England is five hours ahead of the East Coast of Canada and the U.S.

What else could we do but go out and buy a TV? We headed to a local electronics retailer and picked out a nice cheap model. I felt compelled to explain to the salesman that the main reason for our purchase was so that we, or rather I, could keep my eye on the greatest sport on earth, hockey, and that we'd only be there a few months, so we really didn't need anything more expensive.

"And do you have your television license, Sir?" the salesman asked me. He didn't seem all that interested in knowing about the state of the NHL on British TV.

Television license? I had no idea what he meant, so I said the only thing I could think of. "We don't want cable," I replied. "I just want to watch some hockey games on regular TV." I didn't know if I had the lexicon right. Did they call free TV "broadcast" here? I looked at him for approval.

"No matter, Sir. Everyone needs a television license. If you don't have one, they will know. They'll come 'round and fine you," he said.

"Even if you don't want cable?" I couldn't understand this in the least. Why would they charge you for free TV? And who were "they," anyway? I imagined some sort of KGB-type operatives, the TV police, sneaking around listening through the walls of people's apartments to see what they were tuned in to.

"It's not about having SKY TV, Sir," he explained, naming the cable TV over there. "It's about the adverts. The license pays for the programs. That way, we have fewer adverts," he said. "I've seen telly in America. It's all adverts."

I gave up. OK, I'd get a TV license. "How much is it?" I asked. The price he named was high, and he didn't sell them anyway. I had to go to the post office to take care of that. For the time being, we decided to buy an FM radio with a CD player instead of the TV we'd picked out. At least we'd be able to listen to the BBC.

Later that day, I stopped in at the post office and found out that there were only two ways to get a television license—expensive, and super expensive. We could buy a yearly one, which was out of the question, since we'd be there just four months. Or we could buy a semi-yearly one, at a higher rate per month. Given our budget, I decided that telly wasn't that important. The play-offs would still be on when we got home, anyway.

Flipping through the newspaper a few days later in our TV-less apartment, I figured out a way to get a TV without the license. I would buy a used set, from the classifieds. That way, there'd be no record of the purchase. The following Sunday we took the bus to a town south of Oxford, Abingdon, lured there by the promise of a used TV for £10, at the time about $18 US.

The man selling it said it wasn't the greatest, but it would do for a spare set or to hook up to a video game console.

He showed us the TV, mentioning again that the remote wasn't the greatest but that it would make a good spare set. I was surprised, actually, that he was selling it so cheap. An equivalent new model would cost £60 or more, and this set looked as though it had some life left in it. In response to his explanation about the set's condition, I reassured him that we wouldn't be watching it much, just using it for hockey games, broadcast late at night. He looked at me like he had no idea the game even existed, then he asked us how we were going to get the TV home.

"On the bus," I said, the idea of lugging the TV to the bus stop and then sitting there with it not the most appealing thought. He offered to drive us back, and he dropped us off at the door of our apartment building.

Two nights later, on a Tuesday, I set our alarm clock for 12:30 AM, and woke up to watch Montréal play Boston. It was a thrilling game, more so since the Canadiens won it, though I did sleep through part of the second period and perhaps through a little bit of the class I taught the next day. No matter. I had seen hockey again, and it wouldn't be the last time. They showed a couple of games each week.

However, my grand scheme came crashing down with a letter addressed to the residents of the address where we lived. It was from a government agency in charge of enforcing the TV licensing rules, and it informed me that they knew that we did not have a TV license.

My first thought was, how do they know we have a TV? Of course, they didn't know. But their database told them that no one living in the apartment had recently paid for a license, and I suppose it was just logical to believe that nobody lived without a "box."

I ignored the letter, but instead of keeping the TV in the living room, where we'd had it, I moved it to the bedroom. Besides hockey, we watched other programs, mostly the quiz shows that the British are famous for loving, but always with a little bit of concern. Someone had told me that the TV licensing people drove around in vans, Orwell-type contraptions filled with equipment that allowed them to detect the presence of—what?—TV signals being pulled in by fugitive sets? Something like that. And that they would come to your door if they detected that you were watching without authorization. I am not making this up.

A couple of weeks later, one more late-night hockey game under my belt, I picked up the mail, and there it was again, the letter. This time, it was in a large white envelope, the kind that informs you that you've won a fabulous prize, but only if you show up at a car dealer's lot that very weekend to claim it. The return address told me that this was serious, and I opened it.

"Do you really want the shame of prosecution?" The letter started out. "Do you think we haven't heard every excuse before?" And then it went on to list the things that people had said to the TV police to convince them that the television in their living room is never used. The best excuse was something like, "I only keep it because the cat likes to sleep on it." We didn't have a cat.

I imagined myself furtively peeking out the curtains every so often to make sure the van wasn't on the street, or waiting for a knock on the door every time we watched TV. In a polite country like Britain, I was pretty sure they wouldn't just bust the door down. So I'd have at least a couple of minutes to stow the TV in the bedroom closet. (We'd started keeping it there when not in use anyway, unplugged, in case it gave off some kind of a signal even when not turned on.) Then I'd have to answer the door, book in hand, looking like I had been busy with my work for hours. My only choice would be to lie to them about the TV, hoping that they didn't have some kind of power that allowed them to search the premises without a warrant.

But was this what we'd come to England for? I felt like a criminal already, which I suppose in a sense I was, since I had watched TV without a license. I had even conspired to do it.

"The shame of prosecution." The words rang out in my head.

That wasn't going to do, but the license was outrageously expensive, especially since we didn't spend all that much time at home anyway. As an alternative, I called the cable people, but found out that that too was out of the question, since we wouldn't live in the apartment long enough to recoup the costs of installation.

I reluctantly admitted to myself that, as great as being in England was, it was going to cost me something—most of the NHL playoffs. I put the TV in the storage closet in the basement shortly after that and never bothered to clear it out when we left the apartment a few months later. By the time we got home, Tampa Bay was facing Calgary for the Stanley Cup. Of course, I watched all seven games.

chapter fifty-five

ENL,
not NHL

After giving up my scheme to watch hockey on British TV without buying the proper license, I decided that if I was going to see any hockey, I'd have to see it live.

Don't scoff. They actually have a league over there, playing in arenas around the country. The rules state that most of the players have to be British, but there are also some ringers brought in to fill out the rosters.

In Oxford, the arena was called the Oxford Ice Rink, and I found it quite by accident. The parking lot was the place where the Megabus to London picked up and let off passengers. The first time we walked over there, searching for the "Oxpens Coach Park," the sight of a large glass wall exposing what looked like a hockey rink caught me completely off guard. I walked away from where we were supposed to get on a 9:00 AM bus and approached the arena. Posters announced that the "Oxford City Stars" would be playing the "Invicta Dynamo" on Sunday night in an English National League match. I had found my place.

That Sunday evening, Gaby and I showed up early to make sure we got a ticket. A few pounds later, we had two seats. At the ticket window, the woman had asked us, "City Stars or Dynamo?" I wasn't sure what to say—was this some kind of a survey? Was she asking me to place a bet? I instinctively said, "City Stars." The seats she sold me were among the Oxford fans, as I shortly discovered. It was the first clue that the game over here was different from hockey as I knew it. What hockey arena in North America segregates its home fans from those for the visitors? Exactly.

As the game wore on, I was more than glad that I hadn't said "Dynamo." Their fans, smaller in number than those for the local team, were twice as vocal. And the pattern of their exuberance unnerved me, though it took me a while to figure out why. As I watched, I finally placed it: the soccer pitch. They sang, they chanted, they held up signs. They threatened the Oxford fans with leering slurs. Everything they did was exactly patterned after the behaviors I'd seen on TV. The ones that preceded a soccer riot.

I suppose it was all in good fun, a set of carnival-type behaviors that everyone knew had a code and that was confined to the boundaries of game-time. But all I could think of was those "football" games that ended with fans streaming out onto the field, beating each other senseless. I tried to maintain a low profile, studying the mechanics of the game rather than involving myself in rooting for either team. It was only slightly comforting to hear the announcer request that spectators refrain from the use of foul language.

On the ice, what I saw was hockey, but only in the loosest sense. Rather than playing positions, or working out offensive strategies like the "cycle" currently used by forwards in NHL games, the players just huffed it down to the opposing end in a wave, threw the puck on net and banged away until someone scored. Which they did, repeatedly.

The final score was 8–5, and not because the goaltending was particularly weak. Rather, it was because the game was all offense. Nobody played defense—not the forwards, who did no back-checking but instead waited near the blue lines for the puck to squirt free so that they could move it back up the ice to attack the other team's net—and not really even the defensemen. They stood around waiting to time a run at someone. The hits were hard, though perhaps by NHL standards not delivered with much grace. No one in the stands seemed to care, though. They were in love with the action.

As I sat there, I thought that maybe the game strategy, too, owed something to soccer. The game these blokes were playing was essentially an inverse version of their "football." In that game, play goes back and forth in the middle of the field. Fans yell and scream, but when it comes down to it, nothing much happens, at least if you measure it by the standard of hockey. The whole thing involves half a dozen or so shots on goal for each side, and one or two goals, if you're lucky.

Hockey, by contrast, especially the way these guys played it, was constant action. Pucks banged off the goalie, were flung wide, picked up and swung out to center again for a return rush that never quite got organized. Once the puck crossed the blue line, the pattern repeated itself until the defensive team could retrieve it and then start it out again in an attempt to crash in on the net at the other end. It was like they were making up for the lack of action in soccer by their constant frenzy of activity on the ice.

It was fun to watch, and seeing the game did make being away from the NHL playoffs a tiny bit more bearable, but it was more like watching an interpretation of the game I knew than the game itself.

When Gaby asked me what I thought of the game, I said, "It's nothing that a little coaching wouldn't improve." But maybe that wasn't right, either. This wasn't a flawed game; it was their game. The players were, most of them, fairly well skilled and tough to boot. Teaching them the North American version of the game wouldn't be an improvement on what they were doing. In fact, their fans seemed quite happy with play the way it was. I decided that the only fair thing for me to do was just to accept that.

The end of the game brought one more slightly bizarre revelation. Instead of the customary three stars, one player was selected as star of the game. For his trouble, he was given a case of beer, which he skated to the scorer's bench to retrieve. It made sense, in a beer-loving country, that this would be the prize. I thought back to Tim Trimper, Doug Jarvis and Greg Millen from the Peterborough Petes of my youth and the number of watches they had received for being the first star of the OHL games I'd seen. Surely, they might have liked a case of Labatt's Blue a lot better. Maybe these English did know a thing or two.

Immediately upon grabbing the beer from the guy behind the glass, the star, now helmet-less, ducked his head and started skating wildly. As he did, his teammates pursued him. I figured they were trying to get his beer. But when they caught up with him, they rained down punches as he kept ducking out of the way. The scrum looked good-natured, more or less, but hardly the treatment an NHL first star would expect.

He escaped eventually, both his body and his case of beer intact, and took a final skate around to acknowledge the fans. With the others, I clapped. If this wasn't hockey as I knew it, it was hockey as they knew it, and that, for the moment, would have to do.

chapter fifty-six

Line
Change

After I got hurt playing hockey with a bunch of college students when I was in my early 30s, I decided that it was time to give up the game. I would still love it, watch it, talk about it and count it as a major part of my life. I just wouldn't don skates, grab a stick and go out on the ice anymore. The decision was perhaps easier because, having moved to California shortly after the great injury, it was years before I met anyone who played. It wasn't like I was living in Canada or in the northeastern U.S., where many of the guys I knew would still spend an evening a week playing out their dreams of glory. On that account, I really didn't even miss the game, and I stayed active in other ways. Plus, I fell in love with the team in my new hometown, the Los Angeles Kings, and devoted myself to following them.

In 2004–05, some years after my decision to quit playing hockey, the NHL had its lockout season. Like many others,

I muttered the words, "Lockout. It's not a strike," over and over to myself the weekend when the last hope for a solution to salvage the season and playoffs dwindled. My incantations didn't help. Once the lockout announcement was made, I wasn't angry, though I should have been, because I'd missed most of the previous spring's playoffs while in England. And it wasn't betrayal I felt. That would presume too much. I was just hollow.

Over the next little while, I realized that I was missing hockey when I couldn't remember what month it was. My spring is dated by the start of the playoffs, which is usually preceded by the Kings squeaking in over the last few games as I keep my eye on that eighth conference spot. That brings us to about April 10 each year. Then it's the first round, when there are so many games they can't even put them all on TV. I tape and watch all that do come on. The second round usually has me seeing my team off, or watching them barely hold on, and then it's into the third, where I often have to pick another team to follow. Usually in the West, it's anybody but Colorado. I've always had a soft spot for the Blues, actually. It goes back to those days when as a kid in Montréal I was barely aware of a life beyond myself, and they lost in the finals the couple of times I watched snatches of games on TV.

By the third round, when there's a game every day, I know it's late May. I don't have to look outside. And even if I did, it wouldn't look much different than any other month in California. The games are my calendar. But during the lockout year, there I was, trying to figure out why it seemed so summer-like when there had been no grand disappointment of the Kings losing and no lost teeth or players knocked unconscious by the opposing team's hit men. There was no passion. Just the late spring. School was almost out, too. But it didn't seem like it to me. And so I looked forward to October and the hope that all would be right again.

To fill the time, I joined the NASCAR nation. Not by signing any roster or swearing allegiance to the spirit of Dale Earnhardt, but just by pledging to watch every race and all the pre-race hype each weekend as well. I lasted three weeks, then I rebelled. I couldn't stand the constant barrage of commercials in and around the races.

It was then that I made a crucial decision: Since hockey had not returned to me, I decided to return to hockey.

Actually, for a year or so, my friend John had been bugging me to play in his arena. Not his exactly, but an arena he runs, a giant place up in what people here call "the Valley," where you wouldn't think that hockey would thrive. Not with temperatures soaring to 100°F most of the summer and fall, and kids with other things on their minds than learning a game that requires expensive ice time just to practice. Hockey's not natural here like it is where I grew up.

I had treated John's invitations with a degree of skepticism. Why would I want to go all the way up there to play hockey again? Hockey has taken on new meaning for me. I don't play it.

I watch it. I theorize about it. I study its history. Finally, none of these arguments would do, and so I agreed to go to the arena one Saturday to watch his son's playoff game and take part in a free skate. I'd have hockey again. It just wouldn't be NHL hockey.

My expectations, I have to admit, were low. I figured that these kids would play like Canadian boys a division below them. Was I surprised! These kids, 9 and 10, played like pros. Their skating was solid; their shots rose from the ice. And the goalies—they didn't just flop around. They played the butterfly like a couple of miniature Patrick Roys. Maybe this had a lot to do with John being the coach. He's Canadian, and he knows the fundamentals of the game. Apparently, he has the skills to teach them, too. I was so excited to see the game thriving here that he caught me off guard after the free skate.

"So now that you're back on the ice, why not come out on Friday for 'Stick Time'?" he suggested. He knew that I had neither skated nor played since I'd come to California.

The vision of endless days until the lockout was settled flashed through my mind. Then, the night I'd hit the boards did, too. I had thought it had been the end of my playing days.

"It's no contact, just a bunch of guys, whoever shows up, playing pickup," he continued.

To my horror, I felt myself nodding yes. I was stuck.

"Come out early, and let me look at your equipment. Whatever you don't have, we have. People leave stuff behind. I'll take you into our closet and get you fixed up," he offered.

The next Friday, I kept my word, dragging my ancient Peterborough hockey bag out of the garage and heading to the Valley shortly after lunchtime. When I got to the arena, I found John in his office. He asked me to open my bag.

As I pulled out my equipment, he laughed like I was Rip Van Winkle in reverse—or like the equipment was. "You're not going to believe how much stuff has changed," he said. As he suited me up in used stuff, I was shocked to note now much bigger everything was, from shoulder pads to shin guards. But lighter. The gloves, especially, had transformed. Mine had solid cuffs that went halfway up my forearms. The new ones were short, and they had cutouts in them so that they moved around on the hands.

He took one look at my stick, a wooden Cooper TNT model, and handed me a Nike Ignite 5. I could barely feel it in my hands. What got a real laugh were my stockings, the kind that you wear a garter belt to hold up. It had been that way my whole career. "We don't do it that way anymore," he said. It was like I was wearing Granny panties or something.

All suited up, I followed him to the ice and stepped on. Aside from the laps I'd done the Saturday before, I hadn't been on a hockey rink for better than 10 years. I felt like I could fly, like I was reawakening some long-lost ability. This, not to mention the narrative running in my head, told me that at this moment, I was tapping into the primeval roots of my Canadianness, the very core of who I was.

But after we'd picked teams and started to play, a feeling that I hadn't had for decades crept up and grabbed me. Dread. Fear that I would make a mistake with the puck. I was on John's team with two other guys, and as I skated around, I tried to be out of position so they wouldn't pass to me. When they did, I dished the puck off as soon as I got it. The one time I decided to attack, I watched a wobbly wrist shot go right into the goalie's pad. And I was 10 again, but not a healthy, youthful 10. A scared, inadequate 10. The 10 I'd been when I'd played for the LNDB squad near my home in Brossard. The one that always watched other kids score and only rarely put the puck in himself.

What about the hat trick I scored in college? I thought. *What about the fact that I'm a grown-up now, and that if these guys laugh at how I play, it doesn't matter?* And I knew that I wasn't as bad as all that, anyway. *What about my love for this game?*

I played out the hour, surprised at how tiring hockey is, physically. But it took all my might to push the sense of uselessness down, to talk myself into doing this for fun. As we sat in the dressing room afterward, I wondered if playing had been a good idea. Sure, I'd gotten back to something I loved. But playing the game again also awoke a part of me that adult success had put to sleep, and now I would have to deal with it. Yet despite my doubts, I left the arena that day feeling more Canadian than I had in years and glad that John had shaken me from retirement once more.

chapter fifty-seven

My Only NHL Goal

The entry of the California Seals, later Oakland Seals, later California Golden Seals, into the NHL in 1967 might not have been hockey's most glorious moment. And in truth, since I was just a tot when it happened, I have only vague recollections of the team existing, and those date to sometime around 1972 or 1973. I had hockey cards of some of the players, though like the Vancouver or Minnesota ones, they were not something I or any boy in my school valued at all.

The team moved to Cleveland as the Barons in 1976, but by that time, my Montréal Canadiens were starting on their streak of winning the Stanley Cup every year, and Cleveland wasn't a city I could even locate on a map. I doubt I was the only one who forgot them once they were there. They merged with the North Stars in the late 1970s, and that team, as fans remember, went to Dallas and won the Cup in 1999. But what relationship the Stars squad had with the lowly Seals clubs is beyond the ability of even a metaphysical California type (which I am not) to answer.

Put it this way: The Seals were horrible, and very shortly after they were born, they died. Before they disappeared, however, they left one gaudy reminder of their existence on hockey history. That was when owner Charles Finley, who probably should have stuck to running his Oakland A's franchise, dressed them up in white skates.

The stark picture of the skates standing out against the background of, well, anything they stood next to, is burned into my mental photo album. Little did I know at the time I saw this monstrosity on TV that some years later, in 2005, I would be sitting in a hotel lobby talking to one of the players from that white-skated team, Morris Mott.

Looking up his stats a few days after meeting him, I learned that Mott had been drafted by the WHA's Calgary-Cleveland franchise in 1972, as a 26-year-old defenseman. He was signed by California that fall, a free agent, and played most of three seasons with the Golden Seals, 199 games in total, with 18 goals and 32 assists. His big-league career continued with a two-game stint for the WHA's Winnipeg Jets in 1976–77.

But I didn't know any of that the night I met him. All I knew was that Morris Mott, PhD, who was chairing the session of the "Hockey: Canada's Game?" conference at which I was delivering a paper, had just admitted that he was, in fact, an ex-California Golden Seal.

Someone else in our little huddle was grilling him about playing in the NHL. I listened in, having no question to ask since I had no recollection of having seen him play. But I did remember one thing. The skates. "Did you play during the era when that team wore the funny skates?" I asked, and right away I kicked myself for the choice of the word "funny." Why hadn't I just said "white"?

He smiled. I checked his teeth, just as I'd done with Frank Mahovlich. More by reflex than anything, actually. Some looked to have been replaced.

"Yes, and I've still got a pair, hanging around the house somewhere. But they're so old, they've hardened up, the leather. I couldn't get them on now if I tried," he said.

I suggested a donation to the Hall of Fame as an alternative. Mott just blinked and stared at me. I wasn't sure if it was because he hadn't thought of the idea before or because I had suggested that he desecrate a treasured icon of his past. I looked around for help. Luckily, someone prompted by my skates question started talking about the era when the Flyers had worn the one-piece pants. Or was it Vancouver? None of us could remember exactly. A few minutes later, we all loaded into a van to go to a nearby arena for a game of pond hockey.

Once there, the bunch of us, probably 20 or so, put on the jerseys that conference organizer Andy Holman, himself a former McGill football player, gave out. Mine was burgundy, with the number five on the back. I had brought my camera, and as

I got up to walk to the ice, I gave it to a guy who wasn't planning to play. He had agreed to record the event in snapshots for me.

"Hey, take a picture with Morris," he said to me. Mott was just exiting the dressing room, wearing a jersey the opposite of mine, gray. We each wore regulation CCM helmets issued by Andy. In addition, we had proper gloves, and I had a pair of shin pads on. I'd brought them as insurance against an injury. OK, I brought them because my wife had told me she thought it would be safer. As I've aged, I've developed an accident-prone personality. She says it's because I'm always thinking about too many things. Like the history of hockey.

We took the snapshot, me with my arm around my new NHL buddy, and headed out to the ice. Then Andy yelled, "Game on!"

Handling the puck and passing it around felt like the old days on the rink at the corner near my house. The whole purpose of this game was to play "shinny"—that's even what it had been called in the emails announcing the conference. I didn't feel the same as when I had donned the full set of pads on that Friday afternoon in L.A., which had brought back strange feelings of inadequacy the first time I took to the ice. Back then, I had done everything I could not to touch the puck.

Now I found myself wanting it, anxious to move it up, and determined not to make the mistake that had characterized my career in minor hockey—passing too much. I had never carried it from blue line to blue line, I had realized one day some years previous. I was always too scared. Now here I was, almost willing to rag it, and having a blast.

At one point, I got a pass just inside the other team's blue line, and in the instant when the puck came to me, I saw out the corner of my eye that the defenseman was a few steps away, between me and the goalie, and that the netminder was leaving a little bit of the top left corner open. I kept skating in the direction I was going, toward the boards to my right, and then I fired back across the grain, past the defenseman and over the goalie's right shoulder, to that spot where the net had an opening. I scored.

My celebration was muted. This was, after all, a scrimmage, but as I went back to the bench, I felt like I always had when I'd scored as a kid. It didn't matter what else happened in the game, I had my goal. And in truth, it didn't matter at all, because nobody was really keeping score, so maybe for once I was right.

I sat there with my oversized cheapie mouthguard—the kind you stick in boiling water and then form between your sizzling teeth and gums—sticking out in front like I was in some dental office horror movie. An instant later, the guy who was holding my camera came over to me. He'd been in the end where I'd scored the goal. "You know what you just did?" he asked me.

I looked at my inquisitor and removed my mouthguard. "What?" I replied. *I mean, aside from scoring that beautiful goal?* I fumbled with the mouthpiece, trying not to get it too dirty with the glove I was still wearing.

"You beat Morris," he replied. I must have looked unsure of what he meant, so he repeated himself. "That was Morris out there on defense."

Morris. Morris Mott. The realization hit me that I'd just scored a goal on a real live NHL defenseman. I mean, did it matter that he'd been retired from the game for decades and was now living the life of a scholar?

Not a bit. His skills were still there, as I'd noted to myself when we'd first started to play. At the time, my judgment on the matter was not clouded by selfish motives. I'd merely been trying to satisfy myself that he could still play, as if to know that the magic that leads a guy to the NHL never leaves him, despite his direction in life.

Sure, he was older than I was. Maybe by a good bit. But his size and confidence on his feet and his ability with the puck still put him above all but one or two of us, most much younger.

I beat Morris, I said to myself, trying like heck to recall the image of the goal. I had seen the defenseman, timed his movements to screen my shot. But I hadn't looked at his face or recognized who it was. "You get some pictures?" I asked the guy who had given me the revelation. He nodded.

After the game, I sat across from Mott in the dressing room, and I couldn't help but say something. "Hey, I guess I beat you," I offered. He looked at me and smiled. "That goal that I scored, the fadeaway shot," I said, wincing at the basketball term.

"Yeah, that goal. You lifted the puck," Mott said. I wasn't aware of any rule that said I shouldn't. "And I wasn't wearing any equipment out there," he added. He wasn't angry. He was just stating what apparently to him was the obvious.

I paused. Had I broken some special code? Did it negate the beauty of the goal? My doubt was only for an instant. Then I realized that it wouldn't have made any difference. I had read the play, timed his movement so that he would be moving toward me and screening the goaltender. My right-handed shot would be unreadable to the goalie because Morris was in the way. And with the goalie also skating from my left to right, more net would be exposed every nanosecond. And I had actually realized that and timed my shot to take advantage of it. Whether he'd had pads on or not, that shot would have beat Mott cleanly.

I didn't say anything else. The old pride, that quality that got Mott off the Prairies and into the best league in the world was still there, and I wasn't going to win anything by making a stronger plea for my case. So I shut up, smiled and went back to wiping off my skate blades. I had scored a goal against an NHLer. It wasn't an NHL goal, but it was the closest I would ever come, and I would treasure it forever.

Looking back on it, I'm still unconvinced by the argument that wearing equipment would have made it easier for Morris to stop me. But I do have an idea about what he meant. Maybe he just wasn't comfortable without his white skates.

chapter fifty-eight

Bacon Street West

For years after I moved to California, I felt displaced. Although there was hockey, it wasn't the same hockey I knew, because hockey here meant the NHL. There wasn't much of a hockey culture at the local level. At least, not that I was finding. This realization was brought home to me every time I went home to Canada for a visit.

My parents had moved to Oshawa in 2000 to be closer to my sister and her family, and on summer evenings there I would take a jog after the heat had gone away but before the sun went down. I'd see them everywhere in this newly constructed suburban neighborhood—nets standing in front of garages, sometimes with sticks carelessly thrown down in front of them after their owners, presumably kids, had been called in to dinner or perhaps for bed.

My California neighborhood, similarly middle class, also bore signs of kid life on its lawns and in its driveways. But the artifacts weren't hockey sticks, but basketball hoops, the kind with a water base that could be moved around, or tiny soccer nets, half-moon shaped, which stood on lawns. It just wasn't the same. I decided that, though Gaby and I didn't have kids yet, I would start to change things in my neighborhood, beginning at home. All politics, after all, are local, right?

I headed to Target. But not just any Target. The new one, out on the east end of Pasadena. I figured that if anyone had what I needed, they would. And what I needed was a hockey net. I had sticks around, old ones that I'd played with years before, wooden ones that would do just fine on the concrete of our back driveway.

Finding my way inside, I blinked at the freshness of the store. Along with the newness came unfamiliarity. Things weren't where I was used to them being. I started toward the back of the store, then stopped someone wearing the red vest signaling that she was an employee.

"Do you have hockey sticks?" I asked her.

"What are they for?" she replied. I could tell by her accent that she hadn't been born in the U.S. But it wasn't as if I was asking for lunar landing devices. It is in moments like this that the feeling of alienation in living here is most acute.

"Well..." I started, not being able to think of another way to say it, and I repressed my urge to say something smart.

"They're to play hockey with," I said. I could see by her expression that I had come no closer to expressing myself. "Sports equipment," I decided to try. "Where is that sort of thing?"

She took me back to a corner of the store where baseball gloves, bikes and tennis equipment of all sorts stood waiting for eager hands to grab them and begin new athletic pursuits. She wandered up and down an aisle, looking from side to side. I still wasn't convinced that she knew precisely what for, so I moved ahead of her, nodded to say thanks for getting me into the right general vicinity and started looking myself.

On an aisle end, next to golfing stuff, I found it. Street hockey equipment. Not much of it, but the essentials—nets, sticks, balls. And amazingly, it was all on clearance. Odd for a brand new store, but maybe someone knew that with the NHL on lockout, nobody in this part of the world was going to be taking up hockey anytime soon. I grabbed a net, some of those hard orange balls and five plastic pucks. I wasn't sure that I'd like playing with them, but they too were cheap, and I figured that if I didn't take them now, they'd be gone.

Marching to the front of the store, I started to formulate my plans. Earlier in the spring, at the same conference where I'd met Morris Mott, I had met Jack Falla, former *Sports Illustrated* feature writer and the author of *Home Ice*, a book that talks about the rink he has built in his backyard for the past couple of decades. The "Bacon Street Omni," he calls it.

He was more than nice to me, agreeing to read the manuscript of the book you're now reading. He also offered advice that helped me find a publisher, because he thought I had written something that other people would enjoy.

I decided right then to call my backyard rink the "Bacon Street West," forgetting the "Omni" part for no logical reason. It might not have the tradition of his rink just yet, and it wouldn't take near the effort that a full-on flooded rink would require, but it would be a sacred spot nonetheless. I planned to build boards, set up my net and start firing away with these pucks and balls. Someday, my kids would play on it. No roller blades allowed. Only sneakers and tennis balls— just like what we'd done when I was a kid, and what was done on every street in every town in hockey country, probably even at the very moment when I was paying for my net.

Once I got it home, the net took me 10 minutes to set up, and I realized that I didn't actually need boards. The fence between my house and next door, like most of those in suburban California, is six feet high. It would be rare that I would launch a puck over top. I could just blast away and let the misses hit the fence.

So there I was on a Friday afternoon, taking shots. The whack of the puck against the boards when I missed resonated against the quiet in the backyard. At one point, I heard my neighbor come out her back door. I thought for a minute that I ought to stand on my tiptoes and say something about what

I was doing. After all, I'm not a kid, and it's not that normal to see a grown man playing all alone in his backyard, is it?

Having a need to explain myself might have been the Canadian in me. Californians, by contrast, don't bother. They just live and let live. So I didn't justify myself, but instead I kept pounding out the shots, doing what I'd spent countless afternoons doing most of my childhood.

The fact that I didn't explain my actions to my neighbor might say that I've become a little bit more Californian than even I would like to admit. But as I raced back and forth after my official NHL street hockey pucks, I thought how absolutely right this felt. Hockey country, I had learned in a million ways over the 10 years since I'd come to the West Coast, is where you make it.

chapter fifty-nine

This is the NHL!

There's something weird about L.A. I mean, weirder than the normal weirdness you probably associate with the place if you don't live there. You can be just about anywhere, talking to anyone, and find out that that person won an Emmy, or has a cousin who is in the NBA, or her dad (in the case of one of my college colleagues) plays piano with the Smashing Pumpkins. No kidding. There's just a strange quality to this place that means that you're somehow never far from fame.

So it didn't seem all that odd to me when a student in my class, a woman of middle age, commented to me one night, "Oh, yeah, my brother-in-law is in hockey. He works for the L.A. Kings." But I still did a double take, wondering what she meant by "works for." It could have been anything from trainer to arena gopher.

"He's Mark Hardy—he's one of the coaches. He's a really nice guy," she said. Now I really gulped. Here I was, one Kevin Bacon degree of separation from an NHL coach and, I quickly realized, a former player to boot. What should I say? I said nothing. "He doesn't have much to do, what with that lockout and everything. He's teaching some hockey schools. I guess his wife, my sister, is starting to want him out of the house," she added.

I screwed up my courage and blasted away. "I write about sports, mostly car racing, but I'd love the chance to talk to him, maybe write a feature story on him, if you could put me in touch with him." My head scrambled around the idea. There was no way this could really happen. And I had no publication outlet for such a story. But I would find one if she said yes.

"I'll see him next week. I'll ask him then," she said. I wondered if anything would ever come of it. That's the other thing about people here. They always tell you they'll get back to you. They never do.

But this wasn't the average Californian I was dealing with. She understood follow-through. And pretty soon, I was in email contact with Mark Hardy, Assistant Coach of the L.A. Kings in charge of the defense. (Most of you know, of course, that he was let go later the following season, broomed out with Andy Murray.) I proposed a meeting. By this time, I had made contact with an online magazine based in New York, *Inside Hockey,* and talked the editor into running a feature story on Hardy. I couldn't believe my luck.

A few weeks after talking to the editor, I found myself at the Kings' practice facility near the L.A. airport, camera and tape recorder in hand, doing my interview. Since the team was on lockout recess, there was no pressure, no work that Hardy had to attend to. He showed me everything, from the weight room to the training devices that I'm sure didn't exist when he had played, from the late 1970s to the mid-1990s. I couldn't help but wonder what someone like Rocket Richard would have said had he seen some of these contraptions.

Hardy even took me outside to see and photograph his 1993 Toyota Land Cruiser, which he'd bought the spring the Kings went to the finals against Montréal. I didn't say too much about how happy I'd been to see the Habs grab that Cup, their 24th. Those finals, he said, still lived in his memory as a magical time, despite the final outcome of the series that saw his side lose.

In the time we spent together, I asked everything I could think of, everything I had wondered all my life as a fan of the game. What did players eat, where did they live, who watched over their equipment? He answered every question, deferentially, as a human being, not a former NHLer. I asked him at one point whether he felt, sometimes, like just shouting in a store, "I'm Mark Hardy! I played in the NHL!" He laughed like it hadn't ever occurred to him that it would matter to anyone, at least out here.

Before we parted, he took off the jersey he'd worn for the photos, signed it and gave it to me. It's what today's kids call "old school," the yellow and purple of the Marcel Dionne era, and authentic, with "Hardy" and "5" on the back. I told him that I would treasure it forever, and I will. I wore it home and didn't take it off for several days. Someday, I'll give it to my child, if Gaby and I have one. Failing that, I'll give it to my nephew, Daniel, or my niece, Sarah. I know that despite being groomed from birth to be Wings fans, they would preserve the jersey as an heirloom, the way I take care of the watch given to my grandfather when he left for World War I.

The story ran at InsideHockey.com a few days after I submitted it. I looked at it for many days afterward. It wasn't so surprising to me that I'd written it or had it accepted. I'd sold lots of writing in the past. It was that I, a kid from Montréal, a hockey worshipper, had talked to an NHLer. For an hour. Even better, when he had seen the story, Mark had told me on the phone, "You're what we need in this town. Someone writing about hockey who really knows the game." Are there too many words in that sentence to put on my tombstone?

But that wasn't the end of it.

In the ensuing months, I managed to convince the editor of *Inside Hockey* that I had the ability to cover a few games for him, and in that capacity, I saw Mark just after the second or third game in the fall of 2005, when I was waiting for the dressing room to open so us media types could hound the players for quotes.

"How you doing, Mr. Kennedy?" he said. I looked around, hoping some of the long-timers had seen that I wasn't just a nobody. I was known.

"Good," I replied. "Although it's a little hard to contain myself. I was just standing up in the press box before the game looking around, thinking to myself, this can't be happening. This is the friggin' N…H…L." I said it with emphasis on each letter. I didn't tell him that I had called my wife earlier, when nobody else was around, and screamed those same words into the phone in my absolute glee. But I know he understood the feeling because of what he said next: "I say the exact same thing. This is the N…H…L."

A second later, the doors to the Kings' locker room opened. I put my game face on and headed in with the herd. At least while I was working, I had to pretend that this wasn't otherworldly. I figured that if I acted like I belonged, no one would know the difference. Before the year was out, I had covered over 30 games.

chapter sixty

My First
Stanley Cup

M y growing-up years in Montréal corresponded to the run of Canadiens' Stanley Cup championships that started in 1971, continued in 1973 and culminated in 1976–79. In other words, the Stanley Cup finals were in my town practically every year.

But when the Habs won again in 1986 and 1993, I was living far away, and for the next decade the finals always took place somewhere other than where I was. During my period of intense love for the Los Angeles Kings, I wondered what it would feel like to have a final series in my city. I couldn't quite remember anymore.

It happened, sort of, in 2003, but not to L.A., where I settled. To Anaheim—the Mighty Ducks—the team I most hated at the time, mostly because of the preposterous idea of naming a team after a movie. Still, I took a day off from teaching to watch the seventh game on TV, just in case the Ducks won. I felt relieved when they didn't. I couldn't imagine them claiming the Stanley Cup before my team did, who I referred to at the time as "The Great Los Angeles Kings."

Four years later, though, the Ducks were playing for the Cup again. And since their last finals run, I had become a hockey writer. In that capacity, I made a few forays down to Anaheim during the 2005–06 season, mostly for Kings' away games. I went to every Anaheim Stanley Cup playoff home game in 2006, and when the Mighty Ducks lost in the Conference finals, I was disappointed. This should have been my first clue that something was changing in me.

June 22, 2006, was the day it started to make sense. As the uniform of what was now the "Anaheim Ducks" was showcased, I felt a shift—like cheering for the Ducks would somehow now be possible. I liked the new colors and was incredibly relieved that the "Mighty" and the duckbill logo were gone. *These Ducks*, I thought, *might just be worthy of some love.*

During the 2006–07 season, I split my time between L.A. and Anaheim, covering about a dozen Ducks' games and much of the playoffs through the first three rounds. It mattered to me suddenly whether Teemu Selanne scored or whether journeyman Brad May was in the lineup. I talked to the players, wrote features on them and speculated on their chances of winning the Cup. But I also speculated on my own chances of being able to see the finals. For the first three play-off rounds, the team issues the media credentials, and I was never denied. For the finals, however, it's the league itself that gives each writer the OK. This, I sensed, would be the real test of whether I was in or out—a hockey writer or just a guy with a hobby.

I asked the publisher of *Inside Hockey*, Kevin Green-stein, to apply on my behalf, but I thought that maybe I would be pushed aside by the big time, or full-time, writers. Kevin sent me an email that said, "I just heard from the NHL, and if the Ducks are in the finals, you're in." I was amazed.

Me, covering the Stanley Cup finals. A few years previous, I would have been ecstatic just to attend a game in the first round. In fact, I had been, seeing the Ducks' first playoff home game with Gaby in 2003. But now the Ducks were returning to the finals and taking me with them, though none of them could have realized that my dream was as big as theirs.

At the media day the Sunday before the series started, I asked players how they felt about the exciting events to come. My exact question was, "I didn't sleep last night thinking about what's going to happen. How do you feel?" In every case, I got a huge smile—from the young Corey Perry to the veteran Sean O'Donnell.

But around town, the atmosphere wasn't what I'd hoped. There wasn't much of a buzz. This disappointed me, until I realized that the feeling a hockey fan gets in Southern

California is more special than it would be elsewhere precisely because it's private. Nobody can accuse you of riding the bandwagon, because there really isn't one.

But no matter. I was going to see my first live Stanley Cup final series. During the Anaheim portion, I went to the arena early each day, determined to feel every moment, to remember them all and to write about the games with passion.

In truth, despite my recent conversion to an interest in the Ducks, I was more concerned about whether I would get to see the final game live than about who would win, because I wasn't planning to travel to Ottawa. Had it been a choice of the Ducks winning it in Ottawa or having Ottawa win it in Anaheim, I would have taken the latter, because seeing the trophy presented and skated was something that had been so important to me for so many springtimes.

In the end, the hockey gods made it perfect. Anaheim won, and they won the Cup at home. I doubt that very many fans or any of the hockey media would have guessed at the start that Anaheim would claim the trophy in five games, but that's how it went.

I watched from the press box as they brought the Cup from behind the bench and presented it to the waiting captain, Scott Niedermayer. And in that instant, I felt my throat tighten. Not because I was so happy that the Ducks had won it, though I was, but because of all the previous times this

ritual had been enacted and all the players who had raised it
above their heads—Jean Beliveau, Henri Richard, George
Armstrong, Ted Lindsay, and on and on back into the mythic
past of the NHL.

As I stood there, streamers fell from the ceiling, and
fans screamed and waved orange towels signaling support for
the team. I wondered whether they were thinking the same
thing I was, though I knew it was unlikely. For most of them,
hockey does not have a history that goes back 100 years, but
one that began in 1993. But it didn't matter. They would learn,
and there had to be at least one kid in the crowd for whom
this was as important as 1971 is to me, when the Canadiens
defeated the Black Hawks.

I went to the locker room and got sprayed with cham-
pagne as the players celebrated their win. Then I realized that
the Cup was not there, and I walked through the tunnel to the
ice. There it sat, at center, surrounded by a small throng of
people and guarded by Chris Pronger. I approached it, and as
someone in the group lifted up the Cup, I stuck up my hand
and measured its roundness with my palm. I felt the indents
of players' names underneath my fingertips.

Of course, I had touched the Cup once before, in 2002
in L.A. during the All-Star weekend, but this was different.
I was touching the Cup on the day it was won, on the ice it was
won on.

According to superstition, my having done this means that I will never win the Stanley Cup myself. But in my heart, I know I already have—in 1971 for the first time and then every time the Canadiens won it afterward, and now, in 2007, in California. But this win was different, because I had played a part in it by writing about the team and talking about them on their radio post-game show. This was my Stanley Cup.

chapter sixty-one

Aging Out of the Game

Sometimes, my brother-in-law Phil and I discuss how it is that we ever got to be 40. If you're our age, you've also had this conversation. Like us, you probably say it with a tinge of regret. Maybe it's prompted by a hockey commentator's words that a player is "old," a "veteran," or that it's "simply amazing that he's still playing in the NHL at his age." Turns out that age is 37, or 39, or 45. I'm thinking of guys like Adam Oates, Sergei Fedorov or Chris Chelios. When I look at them, especially Oates, whose face isn't criss-crossed with scars, they don't look old, or maybe I don't want them to seem that way, because if they're past their prime, then so am I.

What strikes me in that moment when Ron McLean, or one of the commentators on American TV like Bill Clement, says something about the player's age is that I never think about the guy as old. It's easy to forget that many of the players are in their

20s. Many of them, now, could be my kids without any great stretch of biology.

Thinking about it from the other way around, I realize that when I was idolizing Ken Dryden during the 1971 play-offs, he was just 23, though at the time, my nine-year-old brain made him as old as my dad or any other adult.

When I think about time and age, I'm reminded that despite never being all that good at hockey, I always held the dream most Canadian boys do—of playing for the Stanley Cup. Now that the players are almost all younger than I am, for the first time I'm realizing that I will never compete for that trophy.

In an odd way, when you're a little older it's easier to believe the fantasy that you could have been an NHL player. When you're 10 and not good enough to make the select team, or you see the 15-year-old kid in your high school head to Junior A and then, just maybe, to the pros, you understand that this is probably not something you could do. But as you age, you start telling yourself, "Hey, I was pretty good. I just didn't get the right coaching. If I had, I think I could have done something in hockey." Distance makes this illusion seem less ridiculous.

Then one day, you're older than every single player on your favorite NHL team, and despite the fact that you look pretty good, stay in shape and feel like you're the same as you were when you were 20, you realize something: There has never been a professional sports rookie as old as I am. Ever. And the absurd dream becomes just that, a dream.

But for me and Phil, there's a consolation prize to being our age. We experienced the goal. We were there. Not in Moscow, but living, breathing and agonizing while the Canadian team played the Russians in the Summit Series. These memories are so precious that I'm not sure either of us would give them up, even to be 10 years younger.

Americans younger than 50 don't have such a singular moment to look back on. Many think that they do, of course, from when the Americans won the Olympic medal in Lake Placid, but if you ask them how the American Olympic team won it, they'll say that it was by beating the Russians. The Russian game is famous, but those who really remember know that that wasn't the gold medal game. Those guys had to play again to secure the medal. So the "Miracle On Ice," though spectacular, doesn't quite have the one instant of sheer ecstasy that our moment has.

Every Christmas for the past 10 years or so, Phil and I have been able to relive the glory of 1972 via a videotaped copy of the game. No matter how hectic the holiday time is, we always manage to watch it together. Sometimes it's in the middle of the night before I have to get on the plane the next morning. Then we talk about the year past and the year to come, kids, parents, other issues. The game gives us an anchor. Maybe to some people it proves that we're getting old. To me, it proves that we're learning what's important. And it shows that what matters most in life, to us, will always be tied somehow to the game of hockey.

Will They Grow Up Hockey?

I wonder sometimes what will happen with my kids. They haven't been born yet, but when they are, what part will the game play in their lives? I tell myself that after an initial rebellion, they'll settle down to like what their father likes. After all, they'll see me devouring the playoffs year after year and know that there's magic in those two months when the taste of Lord Stanley's Cup is on my tongue.

But will they really get it? At the very least, hockey won't be the all-consuming passion for them that it is for me, because in all likelihood they won't live the game the way I did and the way most every Canadian does, as well as a lot of Americans who come from the colder parts of their country.

Recently I was in Oshawa, visiting my dad and my sister and her family. (My mom, who introduced me to a real hockey rink when I was about four, died in 2003.) We were driving to the store one winter afternoon when I had my dad take a detour into one of the neighborhoods filling up the countryside east of town. There, a pond had frozen, and kids played hockey with adults, whiling away their Christmas holidays. The ice was bumpy, and the players were of all ages, but the sounds and rhythm were the same as they've been for a hundred and some years. If I'd had my skates and stick, I would have joined their ragged game of pickup. Instead, I just stood there for 10 minutes absorbing what I saw and thinking to myself how lucky they were.

If they'd known I was having these thoughts, they would probably have called me nuts, especially since the next two months in Ontario would be an unending string of bitterly cold and miserable days. Meanwhile, California was having the most perfect winter ever, with hardly any rain and sunny 70°F days one after the other. But imagine trying to get a pickup hockey game going in my neighborhood, ice or no ice. People would think you're crazy. In fact, in the whole time I've been in L.A., I've seen only one street hockey game. One. Hockey exists here, and there are even what they call "ball hockey" leagues. But childhood the way I lived it does not.

In Montréal, every February, we had winter carnival. There was a parade, and every minor hockey team had a "float." Back then, that consisted of a flatbed trailer with a few balloons tied to it, pulled along while all of us stood on it freezing in our hockey jackets, waving at whichever parents were brave enough to line the route in the cold. One winter it was so cold that my mom made me put my snowsuit on under my hockey jacket, fearing that with the LNDB jacket on alone, I'd freeze to death. I looked like a snowman.

At school, we had a special outdoor activities day, with sports contests and a costume party on skates. One time, some kid named Ross came in with kitchen utensils hung all over his coat and a small horse's head mounted on a broom- stick pilfered from his sister's toy box. He skated around with the horse between his legs as if he were riding it. "The Galloping Gourmet" won some kind of prize for his trouble. After the skate, we were served hot chocolate from a giant vat. I took one taste and knew it wasn't like my mom's, which was made with milk. These are my memories of winter.

My kids won't share these if I'm still in California while they grow up. Their memories will be of warmth and sunshine mixed with the occasional two days of driving trop- ical rain. That's winter here. Where does hockey fit into that?

Sure, there are leagues for them to join. My friend John, who runs the giant ice complex out in Valencia, says that people of all ages play, day and night. Hockey schools go on year round, but especially in the summer. He's even told me that a few players from the Summit Series Soviet Red Army team go there, and that they get involved in some of the schools. Where else are you going to find that?

But it just doesn't seem the same to me, taking your kids into hockey practice wearing a golf shirt, while they are in short pants and Vans sneakers. As soon as the ice time is over, you're back out into the near-tropics, hockey forgotten. How is a kid going to hone skills when there's no encouragement to play hour upon hour, taking on all comers on a homemade rink and only quitting when you can't feel your toes anymore or the last kid's mom calls for dinner?

One Christmas, returning home to L.A. on Air Canada, I sat among a group of young players who had been to Toronto for a tournament. They were from Huntington Beach, which is down the coast in Orange County, not too far from the home of the Anaheim Ducks, and they all had trophies. The pilot introduced the team on the intercom, mentioning that they'd done well in their competition. I couldn't help but wonder whether they'd really won anything, or whether the trophies were for having come so far just to get their butts kicked by a bunch of Canadian kids. Participation trophies. I never did get a close enough look to be able to tell for sure.

Seeing these kids, I realized that I could get my own children onto the ice, to make them hockey players. But would that be the same as getting the feel for the ice into them?

Although I've been in L.A. a decade, it still seems funny to be driving home from work on a February afternoon and seeing kids in short-sleeved T-shirts, their skateboards under their arms as they leave school. Growing up in Canada, a kid just never realizes that mid-winter could be anything but snowmobile boots, ski jackets, gloves and a hat, or whatever happens to be in fashion at the moment—and hockey.

In Montréal or Toronto, or almost anywhere in Canada, the ice is everywhere, and the greatest thing to do is grab your skates and stick after school and head down to the corner to play. Then when winter leaves, you just shift the game to other venues—the streets and driveways, your basement, tabletops, your imagination. It surrounds you and invades you, and you love it like nothing else.

That's what I want for my kids. They may never make the NHL. In fact, it would be a huge reversal of genetic propensities if they did. But they can believe that they will, at least while they're young, and they can take that love of the game with them for life—watching hockey on TV, going to games, taking shots at a beat-up net that has lost half its strings—never getting any bigger than the game as it was when they first fell in love with it.

This is what it is to grow up hockey.

Born in Montréal, Brian Kennedy spent much of his hockey-playing youth in Ontario. He went school in the U.S. in 1981 and ended up in L.A. He's been a hockey fan since the age of five and played hockey as a child, retiring three different times.

Brian holds a PhD in English and teaches at Pasadena City College. He is also a freelance sports writer, using his writing to get him everywhere from NHL locker rooms to the race shops of famous drivers of the past and present. He covers the Anaheim Ducks and the L.A. Kings, and in his spare time he rides a racing bike, practices karate and preserves memories. He still has many artifacts from his youth, including the curved, yellow hockey stick featured in chapters in this book. The story of how hockey came with him to L.A. is one of the important subthemes of *Growing Up Hockey*. Brian has a website just for this book—www.growinguphockey.com —and he would be pleased to hear your hockey stories!

LEVIATHAN

LEVIATHAN

Or
The Matter, Forme & Power of a
Common-wealth Ecclesiasticall
and Civill

THOMAS HOBBES OF MALMESBURY

WITH AN ESSAY BY THE LATE
W. G. POGSON SMITH

INTRODUCTION TO THE NEW EDITION
BY JENNIFER J. POPIEL

BARNES & NOBLE
NEW YORK

10

CONTENTS

PART II
OF COMMON-WEALTH